THE FUTURE HAS OTHER PLANS

Planning Holistically to Conserve
Natural and Cultural Heritage

OTHER BOOKS IN FULCRUM'S APPLIED COMMUNICATION SERIES
EDITED BY SAM H. HAM

Interpretation—Making a Difference on Purpose, by Sam H. Ham

Designing Interpretive Signs: Principles in Practice, by Gianna Moscardo, Roy Ballantyne, and Karen Hughes

Conducting Meaningful Interpretation: A Field Guide for Success, by Carolyn Widner Ward and Alan E. Wilkinson

Interpreting the Land Down Under: Australian Heritage Interpretation and Tour Guiding, by Rosemary Black and Betty Weiler

Guide to Global Environmental Issues, by Terry Lawson-Dunn

Effective Slide Presentations: A Practical Guide to More Presentations, by Jon Hooper

The Passionate Fact: Storytelling in Natural History and Cultural Interpretation, by Susan Strauss

Environmental Interpretation—A Practical Guide for People with Big Ideas and Small Budgets, by Sam H. Ham

THE FUTURE HAS OTHER PLANS

Planning Holistically to Conserve Natural and Cultural Heritage

Jonathan M. Kohl and Stephen F. McCool

Sam H. Ham, Editor

Applied Communication Series

FULCRUM

Fulcrum Publishing

The authors would like to thank PUP Global Heritage Consortium for their assistance in the development of this book.

Text © 2016 Jonathan M. Kohl and Stephen F. McCool

Library of Congress Cataloging-in-Publication Data

Names: Kohl, Jonathan M., author. | McCool, Stephen F., author.
Title: The future has other plans : planning holistically to conserve natural
  and cultural heritage / Jonathan M. Kohl and Stephen F. McCool.
Description: Golden, CO : Fulcrum Publishing, 2016.
Identifiers: LCCN 2016040038 | ISBN 9781682750001 (paperback)
Subjects: LCSH: Conservation of natural resources--Planning. | Cultural
  property--Protection--Planning. | BISAC: NATURE / Environmental
  Conservation & Protection. | EDUCATION / Higher.
Classification: LCC S944 .K64 2016 | DDC 363.6/9--dc23
LC record available at https://lccn.loc.gov/2016040038
Printed in the United States of America

0987654321

Cover photo by Jon Kohl. The Church of St. John at Kaneo overlooks Ohrid Lake, which separates Macedonia from Albania in the city of Ohrid, a Mixed World Heritage site. Along with Lake Ohrid, Galicica National Park, in the background, combine as part of the UNESCO designated site.

Fulcrum Publishing
4690 Table Mountain Dr., Ste. 100
Golden, CO 80403
800-992-2908 • 303-277-1623
www.fulcrum-books.com

To all those heritage managers who sensed there was a better way to plan, but weren't sure how to get there.

Contents

Part I: The Conventional Planning Story Is Poorly Adapted to a Changing World

NOTE FROM THE SERIES EDITOR

Jon Kohl and Steve McCool are two of the world's most respected voices in protected area management who, together, bring an uncommon perspective to heritage site planning. Rarely in the scholarly literature related to planning do we find two authors whose ideas have been so nourished by decades of on-the-ground practical experience. It is no surprise that their thinking has impacted how some of the world's most special places are being cared for and preserved today, or that tens of thousands of stewards of natural and cultural heritage on virtually every continent have been the beneficiaries of their work. That's why I am so happy they decided to capture their combined wisdom in this book. The fortunate reader of *The Future Has Other Plans* will be treated not only to a journey of introspection and self-reflection related to their understanding of heritage site planning but also to a stark realization that we have been doing things wrong for much too long.

When Jon and Steve first spoke with me about an early draft of their manuscript, I knew even then that I wanted their book in the Applied Communication series I edit for Fulcrum Publishing. Not only is communication with and among stakeholders a necessary dimension of any successful planning process, it is also the heart and soul of a truly collaborative and Holistic Planning approach of the kind Jon and Steve have brilliantly detailed in these pages.

Long gone is the naive "sponge model" of communication in which things were thought to begin with some sender who transmitted a one-way message to a passive receiver who in turn simply absorbed it and acted on it. Dozens of studies since the 1990s have shown that the communication playing field is far more complex than this model suggests, and that the audience is far from "sponge-like." Indeed, when communication actually occurs, the audience is quite active—processing information as it arrives, agreeing, disagreeing, questioning and wondering, and sometimes counterarguing. Such is the real world we live in, one in which everyone involved in an act of communication unavoidably contributes to co-constructing whatever meanings result.

And according to Jon and Steve, so it is with planning. While conventional observers have viewed planning as nothing more than a one-way technical protocol to arrive at peer-reviewed, polished, and published planning documents, this conventional approach has resulted largely in plans that went unimplemented and doomed to obsolescence even before the ink on them was dry.

However, readers who turn these pages will discover a new and compelling real-world view of planning—a view that treats planning as a continuous, facilitated conversation among heritage area community members. They argue that although a heritage area planning process usually produces a temporary plan to record commitments to carry out actions in both the near and intermediate future, it is founded on an understanding that, because the world changes so rapidly, the plan will never be complete or finished. Rather, in this planning model the temporary action plan produced at the outset merely marks the beginning of a continuous decision-making process that lives on indefinitely—forever. And this is what distinguishes the Kohl-McCool Holistic Planning process from a conventional approach—in their holistic view, the planning conversation never ends. So planning is not simply a time-bound technical-scientific process. It is, at heart, a dynamic n-way communication process applied to heritage communities.

In *The Future Has Other Plans*, planners are no longer seen as people who simply collect information and write plans. Rather they are seen mainly as facilitators of communication between all members of a heritage community, often in the heat of clashing objectives and conflicting ideas about how the future should look. Importantly, holistic planners not only help participants communicate within themselves to understand their own personal visions and needs, they also help participants to communicate with each other by teaching them the communication skills of planning, such as dialogue, conflict resolution, and group facilitation. The planners then work with the community to produce policies, incentives, tools, and institutions necessary for change to take place.

As every reader of this impressive book will see, such an approach to planning depends entirely on communication carried out in a complex, ever-changing environment. And it is precisely why I am so pleased to count *The Future Has Other Plans* as the newest volume in Fulcrum's Applied Communication series. May heritage areas everywhere be better for it.

Sam H. Ham, Series Editor

Moscow, Idaho, United States

FOREWORD

During the 1860s, at the height of Britain's Industrial Revolution, which would profoundly alter the ways of the world, Matthew Arnold wrote a series of now classic essays, published as Culture and Anarchy in 1869. Arnold already lamented the "worship of machinery" and the resultant mechanical way of doing things, instead of "turning a stream of fresh and free thought upon our stock notions and habits" (pp. 5–6). This period, which would later be identified as the beginnings of Modernity, saw also the birth of urban planning as a rational and comprehensive discipline for the management of urban development. It blossomed in the twentieth century, and gained added momentum after World War II, with the aim to guide large-scale urban growth and rehabilitation processes.

Modernism of the 1920s and 1930s, however, planted a bad seed, fracturing the previous relatively unitary approaches to management of the urban environment—since then, specialization and fragmentation, increasingly the norm, have resulted in an ever-more disjointed process to managing the city, both historic and contemporary. Now, at the start of the twenty-first century, the urban planning discipline has not only lost its appeal but also its ability to govern urban growth and development processes (Bandarin 2014); these have largely been replaced by ad hoc urban projects and zoning and strategic planning, among others. Rem Koolhaas has referred to this shift as "the death of urbanism" (Koolhaas and Mau 1995).

Reacting to an increasingly mechanized way of planning with fragmentation and standardization of the built environment, several lines of thought have emerged, both with regard to urban and territorial planning, for example, seeking a more ecological foundation and connection with the human environment[1], and the management of the historic city, in particular seeking an integration of the conservation of urban heritage within the urban development process[2]. This book, *The Future Has Other Plans*, by heritage management experts Jon Kohl and Steve McCool, is the latest in this search for innovation—in particular how a new kind of planning could be envisioned that would integrate the disciplines of planning and conservation, their principles, and their operational realities.

Because our contemporary world is characterized by accelerating change and interconnectivity, their argument goes, planners require an approach that starkly deviates from the reductionist Modernist view of the world and instead encompasses Postmodern values, such as integration of principles and processes; dealing with increasing complexity, including advanced civic engagement and democratization of societies; consensus forming and conflict negotiation; and lots of interdisciplinary context analysis; among others. Anyone working in the current context of heritage management, whether in the developed or in the emerging world—as I do—would wholeheartedly agree. We have clearly come to the end of the road and urgently need a new way of seeing and doing things.

Both authors have an extensive track record in working in heritage places—both natural and cultural—around the globe, and many among them are World Heritage sites. Their working relationship with UNESCO started in 1998 with the establishment of Public Use Planning (PUP), with the assistance of the World Heritage Centre in Paris, and it has subsequently grown into the PUP Global Heritage Consortium (cosponsor of this book).

One key requirement for achieving World Heritage status is the presence or establishment of a "management system" to ensure protection of the site and its values, and the conservation of the site's attributes that convey these values. With the exception of a few traditionally managed sites, that is, through customary law and practices (such as at East Rennell in the Solomon Islands), the overwhelming majority of World Heritage sites have developed or are developing management plans as the foundation of their site management systems. In fact, it would be fair to say that the development of management plans for heritage sites, even more than conservation plans, is a primary business in the heritage field nowadays, occupying local governments and employing scores of consultants everywhere.

This book's key point and purpose—as well as that of the PUP Global Heritage Consortium itself—is based on the assumption that many of these management plans for protected areas and cultural heritage sites end on shelves and remain unimplemented (the problem presented in chapter 1). The authors argue that the root cause of this crisis lies in the way the plan has been established: primarily through a standard Modernist, scientific-technical approach (Arnold's "mechanical way"), which does not work in practice for a variety of reasons, as chapter 3 outlines. By the 1960s, the planning literature had already started to notice this challenge and has been arguing ever since for more participatory, collaborative, empowering, bottom-up approaches that contribute to collective learning processes (as opposed to outsourcing to consultants). This frustration and general failure of the status quo have motivated the authors to start working with Public Use Planning as a methodology and to write this book.

One reality, the authors stress, is that the conventional planning paradigm dominates the global community of heritage management. No matter in which country or culture a site is located, its management plan largely follows the same approach—and thus the same fate of not being (properly) used in practice. This book draws on multiple examples from around the world based on the authors' personal experiences, demonstrating that the global community largely uses the same paradigm. Having worked on all the world's continents, and currently deeply engaged in Asia and the Pacific's heritage management, I fully endorse their views, as well as their strategy—as demonstrated in my own recent book (Reconnecting the City, Bandarin and van Oers 2014).

In chapter 2, the authors discuss their new vision as opposed to prevalent paradigms. They have been inspired by, among others, American philosopher Ken Wilber's remarkable synthesis of the world's spiritual and philosophical frameworks, which took him more than three years to compile. Wilber's Integral Theory (IT) and his Integral Map use the four fundamental perspectives: Interior-Individual (Self), Exterior-Individual (Behavioral), Exterior-Collective (Social), and Interior-Collective (Cultural). Each implies different realms of analysis, research, training, and action (explained in chapter 4). Before arriving at Integral Theory, however, they explore in great depth and breadth the rise and fall of Modernism, the rise and fall of Postmodernism, and then the rise of Holism, or Integralism. After a critique of Technical Rationality across the board, they go on to demonstrate how a new Integral framework is the next step in the evolution of consciousness and societal thought and practice. In short, their book covers a large, holistic context and then gives concrete examples of what this new kind of heritage planning might look like.

An important component of the paradigm change involves training, which, based on my own experience of working for two decades in heritage conservation and management, I fully embrace. Because the authors describe Holistic Planning, the training they advocate is holistic: it refers not only to traditional skills training but also to training to work with oneself, one's values, emotions, and mental discipline. The training works with teams to learn to work with cultures, paradigms, communities, and beliefs of different groups; it is also training that works with institutions, tools, and policies—all realms covered in Wilber's four perspectives, essential to initiate and nurture development in its broadest sense. *The Future Has Other Plans* is truly insightful and innovative in its thinking about the application of new modes of reasoning stemming from key thinkers today, and then translating that to the operational practice of the planning and management of natural and cultural heritage sites.

As a final word of encouragement, I would like to point out that Jon and Steve present some new ideas in their book that might be challenging to some—certainly to those who feel comfortable with the status quo. I sincerely advise people to suspend their assumptions and preconceptions for a while and embrace the journey that this book represents. It will be a rewarding exercise to allow "a stream of fresh and free thought upon your stock notions and habits," which will surely alter the way in which you see things, foremost as regards the proper management of heritage resources—and hopefully also in the way you will subsequently do your stuff.

Ron van Oers, Vice Director

World Heritage Institute of Training and Research in Asia and the Pacific (WHITRAP)
under the auspices of UNESCO, Shanghai, September 2014

We regret that Ron never saw this foreword in book form as he passed away on mission in Tibet on 28 April 2015.

PREFACE

Man plans and God laughs.

—Yiddish proverb

How Each of Us Came to Write This Book

From Jon

I started working with RARE Center for Tropical Conservation in 1997, and although the organization was grassroots and perhaps ahead of many in participatory approaches, we still worked with a strong rational comprehensive bias. When the task of creating a public use planning effort fell upon me, I first studied how other conservation organizations, such as the Wildlife Conservation Society and The Nature Conservancy, conducted planning in protected areas: they used Rational Comprehensive Planning. It would be several years before I met the concept face-to-face; I only knew that the president of RARE had issued a mandate to create a planning process that identified and avoided plan implementation barriers that sent so many plans to the dungeon.

In 2000, with UNESCO funding, our team developed the Public Use Planning (PUP) Program. I had already concluded that outsourcing planning and writing to expert consultants constituted a recipe for plan implementation failure, so our program's focus switched to training on-staff personnel we called "public use coordinators." We trained them in facilitation, planning organization, and writing skills. We taught them to use and modify our basic public use planning modules (public use product development, monitoring, financial planning, etc.), and we offered intensive one-on-one mentoring as well as some financial support. Our fundamental assumption held that if the public use coordinator, with our help, had not achieved the integration of this new do-it-yourself-and-learn approach into the rest of the park's technical staff within three years, there was a good chance the public use coordinator would move on, effectively burning the bridge we had built with the park.

This approach resulted in elaborate multisegmented, training-mentoring interventions. Our first round of training, however, produced far less than we had hoped. Rio Platano Biosphere Reserve in Honduras and Sian Ka'an Biosphere Reserve in Mexico recast some of the modules to fit into their conventional management plan that later were not implemented; Vizcaíno Biosphere Reserve in Mexico decided that it simply did not want to play at all. At our most hopeful location, Tikal National Park in Guatemala, we teamed up with The Nature Conservancy, which had also received simultaneous UNESCO funding, to create a management plan using its Conservation Action Planning (CAP) methodology. We had hoped to create a prototype mini-park within the larger park where staff could experiment and learn about new management techniques that the park could later either discontinue or expand to other locations, depending on their reaction. The Nature Conservancy, however, hoped that we would produce the public use content of the management plan, an aspect that CAP was not designed to handle. In the end, the government terminated our idea for a safe space to practice and innovate, and we produced public use components that then ended in a conventional plan that suffered the expected implementation woes of Rational Comprehensive (management) Planning.

In 2003 in Indonesia, the Public Use Planning Program hired Indonesians to work more closely with public use coordinators and with other local actors, creating more participatory workshops and distributing the work more widely in the constituent community. Despite government pressure to create published, polished, and approved plans in Komodo and Ujung Kulon National Parks, there was no money to help parks implement, and eventually those plans, too, ended on the shelf.

Jump forward to 2009, when we worked completely under UNESCO in Vietnam with two World Heritage sites (My Son and Hoi An) and one biosphere reserve (Cum Lau Cham). In addition to PUP's traditional staff training, we began to integrate Block's techniques for engagement and organizational learning, both to more fully motivate our technical assistance team and lobby the government to avoid some of the traditional barriers. In one informal lunch meeting with the vice chairman for the Department of Sports, Culture, and Tourism, Mr. Hai agreed that publication and approval did present additional barriers to implementation (Kohl 2011).

At the time of this writing, the future version of PUP will include a strong component on strengthening the constituent community through vision workshops, aligning objectives, conflict mediation, and distributing decision-making power, as well as formal negotiations to reduce bureaucratic barriers before planning begins. I now regard planning as a facilitated conversation that both integrates learning throughout the process and focuses on the community culture, not just on the heritage site staff's technical skills (the full definition of Holistic Planning will come in chapter 9). There is a long way to go, but I can now trace this program's development from its largely Modernist origins to its holistic future.

From Steve

My beliefs about natural resource planning, while always taking a skeptical perspective, began to change in the 1980s. For many years I had considered planning to be the application of science to making choices about the future, but it was also informed by my strong beliefs about democracy in action. I had often admonished my students that the responsibility of planners was to recommend the technically best alternative to decision makers. At the same time, I was a strong advocate for public engagement throughout the planning process. It seemed to me that good ethical practice warranted involving those impacted by decisions into the decision-making process.

My attitudes began to change significantly in the 1980s, however, when I helped facilitate a planning process for a large protected area in Montana. That process was modeled on Friedmann's Transactive Planning Theory. Friedmann argued that the dominance of technical expertise in planning had resulted in what he called the "Crisis of Knowing" between planners and the citizens they served. This gap meant that citizens did not understand what planners were doing and why, and planners had become insulated and isolated from their clients and no longer understood their visions, dreams, and needs. The gap could be overcome, Friedmann argued, by undertaking dialogue in small groups involving both planners and citizens. Through this dialogue, social learning (about the problem) would occur, and eventually a consensus about the appropriate future and actions could be constructed.

During this period, the US Forest Service was mandated by Congress to initiate forest-level planning, in response to an emphasis on timber harvesting at the expense of other values. At the time, a strong wave of concern about timber harvesting levels on national forests swept the country, and the agency frequently found itself facing protests, litigation, and civil disobedience. Those forest plans were contentious, each one often receiving dozens of administrative appeals. Quite clearly, the paradigm of Forest Service planning, based solely on a rational comprehensive model was under attack.

In the late 1980s, I began to ask, "Why are all these plans, both Forest Service and other natural resource plans, failing?" My measure was the extreme level of contention and the lack of implementation. And, "Why, in the face of overwhelming evidence of failure do natural resource planners continue to use the same planning process?" It was then, as a result of this questioning, that I began to change the content of my senior-level planning class—moving away from technical aspects to more planning theory. Most of my reading—and consequently most of my students' readings—began to focus on the urban planning literature and away from the visitor and recreation planning literature—the area in which both my research and teaching focused. The urban planning literature was dealing with similar issues and could inform natural resource planning. (The most classic critique of modern urban planning is by Jacobs [1961].)

Eventually, I realized that the cause of planning failure was occurring at a systemic level rather than at the operational level, that issues that were inherently questions of values were being treated as if they were simply matters of technical inconvenience. For example, the debate over permitting snowmobiles in Yellowstone National Park is one that derives from different societal preferences about what a park should be, but it was often posed as a technical question of environmental impact. As a result, the values most important to people (solitude, escape, supremacy of nature) were often marginalized in the planning, frequently because they could not be measured and placed into quantitative computer models.

This turn in my thinking was fundamental—and irreversible. While Rational Comprehensive Planning (RCP) had some good points (such as the search for evidence in assessing consequences of alternatives), the weak points (e.g., marginalization of experience, a desire for all possible information) could not be overcome with improvements in the models. RCP needed something else, and that something else was a fundamental redesign of planning.

ACKNOWLEDGMENTS

To write this journey has been a journey. Along the way, numerous people have contributed ideas, reviewed pieces, and shared comments. Before mentioning them, we would like to thank above all our wives, Marisol Mayorga for Jon and Ann for Steve, who put up with us as we found our way through the dark forest of society's collective mind that has led to widespread nonimplementation.

We would also like to acknowledge contributors including, in alphabetical order, Barrett Brown, Mac Chapin, David Christenson, Jim Collins, Kimberly Comeau, Merrick Hoben, Gail Hochachka, Lizbeth Infante, Emine Kiray (deceased, February 2016), Kerstin Manz, José María Lobo de Carvalho, Jonathan Mariño (our illustrator), Michael Meyer, Sue Moore, César Moran-Cahusac, Alexandra Murphy, Charles Parry, Art Pedersen, Brit Rosso, Michael Simpson, Paul Steinberg, Caroline Stem, Matt Walenski, Ken Wilber, Chris Willis (editor of cover photo), and Francisco Valenzuela.

A thank-you goes out to Ron van Oers who accepted our invitation to write the foreword without previously having heard of us.

We also must acknowledge Sam Ham for accepting and editing our book in his Applied Communication series and for Sam Scinta at Fulcrum Publishing for publishing it. Similarly, the book would not be as good as it is were it not for Fulcrum's editor Alison Auch.

INTRODUCTION

I would not give a fig for the simplicity this side of complexity, but I would give my life for the simplicity on the other side of complexity.

—*Oliver Wendell Holmes, Jr.*

Why Did the *Titanic* Sink?

The call of Frederick Fleet, high up in the crow's nest—"Iceberg, right ahead!"—pierced the frigid, moonless night on 15 April 1912, and warned the *Titanic*'s crew of imminent collision. Thirty-seven seconds later, despite a sharp veer to port, the impact buckled the hull, popped rivets, and flooded the ship with icy North Atlantic seawater. In just a few hours, less than a third of the 2,223 people on board were alive.

For 100 years, authors and artists have retold the story of the *Titanic* in movies, books, documentaries, and other explorations of the ship's fated finish. How could such a ship, built to the highest standards of engineering design, proclaimed "unsinkable," vanish underneath the inky black ocean on its maiden voyage?

While many often attribute the ship's sinking to the iceberg, we must dive deeper to the bottom of another iceberg—a metaphorical one in this case—to understand the circumstances that precipitated this titanic demise.

Decisions that led to *Titanic*'s destruction occurred many years earlier when the ship was still but a blueprint. Naval architects, and even more so the owners, were so confident of its engineering that they boasted that their ship was "unsinkable." They felt that even in the face of the worst possible accident—a direct hit from another ship—the ship would not sink for two to three days, if ever, leaving enough time for a safe and orderly abandonment of the vessel.

When we dive deeper along the metaphorical iceberg, we see the mental model that described the ship as "unsinkable" resulted in White Star Lines' placing only twenty lifeboats on board; fully loaded they would have saved only half the passengers. Because passengers too had been thoroughly convinced of the ship's invincibility, however, they failed to board lifeboats quickly. Many lifeboats, sadly, carried few passengers to safety. Finally, while nearby ships had radioed about the dangers of ice floes, the *Titanic's* radio operators were busy relaying passenger messages.

While the immediate cause of the *Titanic's* sinking may have been the violent crash, it ultimately succumbed to an aura of unsinkability precisely because that aura accompanied not only an extreme overconfidence in the ship's resilience.

So many lives were lost at sea, not from any mechanical or engineering fault but rather from a fault in assumptions about an "impossibly" fast sinking. Like many human-initiated disasters, the causes of the *Titanic's* demise were multiple, but also traceable to fundamental, deeply held assumptions about both human and environmental contexts through which the ship had to sail. The notion of an unsinkable ship has parallels in many areas of human life, including conservation and management of natural and cultural heritage: that armed solely with the best science, managers can plan to prevent the sinking of a protected site's heritage values. Implicit assumptions about the social and political context within which conservation and protected area planning exist often eerily echo planning failures of the *Titanic*.

Why Did the Interior Columbia Basin Ecosystem Management Project Collapse?

Eighty years after the *Titanic's* disastrous collision, the US White House initiated a large-scale conservation planning project to address forest and rangeland health and management of fisheries in the Pacific Northwest. This conservation planning project, titled the Interior Columbia Basin Ecosystem Management Project (ICBEMP, pronounced "ice bump") was based on the application of best available science to conservation problem solving. The science followed the newly developed concept of ecosystem management, itself a replacement for the decades-old notion of multiple-use management. Ecosystem management attempts to emulate naturally occurring ecological processes rather than manage for multiple products such as timber, forage, wildlife, and recreation.

The project followed a similar program for the west slope of the Cascade Mountains of Oregon, Washington, and California, initiated by then President Bill Clinton to resolve controversies enveloping management of old-growth forests and the endangered spotted owl. ICBEMP, however, covered a much larger area: 30 million hectares of eastern Washington and eastern Oregon, Idaho, and western Montana. ICBEMP employed numerous biophysical, social, and economic scientists; two teams devoted to writing large-scale environmental impact statements; and a communications staff charged with managing public meetings and inquiries.

Several teams were established: landscape ecology, aquatic ecology, terrestrial ecology, economics, social science, and geographical information systems. Each team was to provide objective, insightful information about the basin area that would inform two environmental impact statements. For the first several years, the budget flowed essentially unlimited, allowing scientists a free hand to collect all data they felt necessary. Scientists input data into a spatial model to predict vegetation patterns and consequences of various management alternatives.

After seven years of scientific study and drafting environmental statements, the project collapsed as surely as the *Titanic* had sunk. The teams prepared and published the two environmental impact statements as drafts, which collided with universally negative public comment. The public found the scale of the project too large and abstract, the proposed actions were too intrusive, and for many people living in small communities dependent on wood products, the plan simply ignored their plight. Native American tribes also objected to the plan for not going far enough in conserving landscapes and culturally significant plants and animals.

Managers prepared final environmental impact statements, but authorities never signed a formal record of decision to implement them. Eventually, the sheer weight of the scientific process ripped tears in the fabric of the project's assumptions, causing the titanic effort to sink in the dark waters of history.

Some assumptions that did not hold water were technical. For example, scientists assumed that all data needed for the model could be gathered at a 1-square-kilometer pixel size. Other assumptions were social, such as the preexistence of a social agreement that land management should attempt to replicate the "historical" range of variation of the ecosystem prior to the arrival of Euro-American immigrants.

Other assumptions were embedded in the scientific process itself: scientists were uniquely qualified to carry out what they perceived as a wholly technical task for which other participants were not qualified. They could come up with an optimal and comprehensive decision with their abundant data, finances, and time, and the general public would agree with the scientific conclusions.

Icebergs, Plans, and the Search for Understanding

As with the cases of the *Titanic* and ICBEMP, innumerable barriers surface in the course of planning for the protection of natural and cultural heritage. Often, while such planning produces a sleek document, the planning itself begins to fail long before the document reaches the printing press: it fails to muster public support, be funded, offer solutions to complex problems, or demonstrate a path toward implementation. To answer why, this book provides readers with new navigational equipment to dive deeper, to see into the opaque depths of reality, to search for good explanations of plan failure. Good explanations help us understand and, in so doing, design more effective plans and planning processes. To guide our search—to help us see below

the surface of planning events—we follow the elusive contours of a metaphorical iceberg often used by systems thinking authors.

This iceberg suggests that under the surface of easily observable events, like the collision of a ship with an iceberg or the failure of a heritage site management plan to be implemented, layers of explanation lurk. And the deeper we dive, the more those failures' various faces become visible. These layers of understanding involve patterns and trends, structures, and mental models that determine how we construct any kind of activity, whether marriages, jobs, political orientations, or planning processes. The layers and iceberg metaphor in fact descend deeper than mental models, but these we leave to discover later in the book. Once we reach the icy bottom of the iceberg, however, we can then rise up the other side toward the light of a new approach.

Like both ICBEMP and the *Titanic*, the reasons for protected area plan failures almost never lie at the surface where a lookout in a crow's nest can spot them but rather ply deep below the surface, where most of a giant iceberg's dark mass floats suspended in silence. Understanding why planning processes fail is one objective of this book, as we describe in Part I. The North Atlantic of planning proves treacherous with a minefield of icebergs; steaming full ahead and making a sharp turn to port will not prevent a plan from sinking. Successful plan implementation does not merely happen; it must rise from a framework not just technically, but psychologically, culturally, and institutionally appropriate as well.

In Part II, we suggest ways of constructing planning processes more appropriate for the complex, uncertain, and contentious challenges and opportunities of the twenty-first century. We term this approach "Holistic Planning" because it transcends and includes the more partial approaches that have marked the course of heritage planning in the past century. When we come up the other side of the iceberg's complexity, we will find a new integral simplicity, on the side of the iceberg that the *Titanic* never knew.

> *If you want to build a ship, do not drum up people to collect wood and do not assign them tasks and work, but rather teach them to long for the endless immensity of the sea.*

> —*Antoine de Saint-Exupery*

Part I
The Conventional Planning Story Is Poorly Adapted to a Changing World

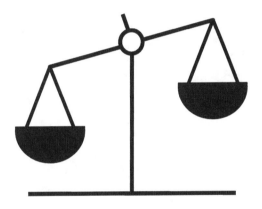

CHAPTER 1

Conventional Site Planning
Shipwrecks on Rocky Assumptions

It has become clear to me and many of my colleagues that protected area managers, community leaders, and policy makers will need to modify their current approaches to planning and management, or be swept away on the quickening currents of global change.

—Kenton Miller

THE OTHER
SIDE OF
COMPLEXITY

EVENTS

PATTERNS

STRUCTURES

Plans Shipwreck on Conventional Assumptions

Eighty-six years after the *Titanic* sank in the icy seas of the North Atlantic, the president of Pico Bonito National Park in Honduras, Fito Steiner, approached Jon Kohl with a question: "We have $5,000 from the Angelica Foundation to make a public use plan for the park. Do you know anyone who could help us do it?"

At the time, Jon was a twenty-eight-year-old conservationist working with a small group called RARE Center for Tropical Conservation, based in Arlington, Virginia. The organization had hired him to train local bilingual nature guides around national parks in Honduras. Jon had known Fito for two years, and such a request hardly seemed out of order.

"I don't, but we can certainly look around," he replied. So Jon and Fito checked contacts, searched the literature, and surfed what existed of the Internet at that time. Through their informal survey, they glimpsed the park planning landscape across Latin America. Instead of finding a consultant or methodology they could recommend, however, they found a landscape strewn with dead and dying protected area plans—partially or totally unimplemented—populating office shelves, under dusty stacks of long-lost documents, and virtually banished to floppy disks and computer hard drives.

Jon summed up his findings: "I'm sorry, Fito, there's nothing out there we can recommend." Since RARE specialized in ecotourism development and facilitated grassroots conservation, he continued: "But maybe we can help Pico Bonito write its public use plan. I'm sure we could come up with a methodology at least as good as anything out there."

When Jon broached the idea to his boss, Brett Jenks, Brett replied, "Fine. But I don't want another plan lying on a shelf. If you're going to do this, we need to figure out what the implementation barriers are and try to avoid them."

Although unknown to them at that time, the first and perhaps most famous national park in the world had been suffering planning shipwrecks of its own. Since 1990, Yellowstone National Park has accumulated seven proposed winter use plans. Aside from enjoying the highest density of large mammals such as bison and elk in the continental United States, Yellowstone had also earned popularity among snowmobilers. The key question for the National Park Service, however, was how much clean air and quiet landscape should snowmobiles be allowed to consume?

The National Park Service produced the first winter use plan for Yellowstone and neighboring Grand Teton National Park in 1990. Because their visitation projections for 2000, which would trigger additional planning, were already exceeded by 1993, the parks quickly needed a new plan. The next one, whose process kicked off in 1994 for the Greater Yellowstone Area (including surrounding national forest lands), used multiple studies and experts to identify how much impact from winter use, including snowmobiling, would be acceptable. The team released an assessment in 1997 followed by a four-month public review period.

The Fund for Animals and other organizations then sued the National Park Service over the winter use plan in Yellowstone and Grand Teton National Parks. They alleged that the Park Service had failed to prepare an environmental impact statement for the effects of winter-road snowmobile use on bison migration, had failed to consult with the US Fish & Wildlife Service about the effects of winter use on threatened and endangered species, and had failed to evaluate the effects of trail grooming on wildlife and park resources.

The court ordered a new plan. After that was released in 1998, the organizations filed another suit accusing the Park Service of not having enough information to make decisions about road closures in Yellowstone, and that it had violated the previous decision by not closing stipulated roads. Filed with different courts, further suits and litigation rained down, leading to sometimes opposing judgments.

The current winter use plan or "rule"—the seventh in this line of conflict—began in the winter of 2014–2015 following a transition season the previous year, in order to allow time for new concession contracts to be implemented for providing snowcoaches, which carry ten to twelve passengers, while snowmobiles transport only one or two people at a time. The new plan is supposed to be a long-term decision to use variable limits on the number of snowmobiles and snowcoaches allowed to enter Yellowstone on a daily basis.

The Yellowstone winter use planning experience demonstrates that planning is about much more than just technical issues associated with snowmobiles (such as emissions and wildlife impacts). It includes more value-laden questions, such as those of natural soundscapes and appropriateness of various visitor experiences. It demonstrates that no matter how much data a plan may offer, managers cannot manage human values with technical and scientific analysis alone. The "culture of technical control" that Yankelovich (1991) so eloquently criticized more than twenty-five years ago simply cannot begin to handle the many contentious issues facing heritage managers in the twenty-first century. Bart (1993) demonstrated that too much formal control in the planning process stifles creativity, an important factor in plan implementation.

Similar anecdotes echo around the world about how politics scuttle plans, lack of resources stop implementation, stakeholders halt progress, or plans simply get lost (e.g., Terborgh 2004).

No one in the protected area world, in our years of asking, seems to have slipped by without being involved in—or at least knowing of—a planning experience that ended in disappointment, if not frustration or outright anger. It has almost been taken for granted that resources and political situations do not allow plans to enjoy their intended fruition.

Ironically, few academics or conservationists have asked why such failures occur so frequently and with such devastating consequences. In the early 2000s, both of us were involved in two of the first studies examining why plans fail in conservation and protected area management. Steve and his student Paul Lachapelle (Lachapelle et al. 2003) examined four cases in Montana, including the Bitterroot Ecosystem Grizzly Bear Recovery Plan (restoration of the grizzly bear population), the Blackfoot River Recreation Management Plan (recreation), the Glacier National Park General Management Plan (park management), and the Upper Clark Fork River Basin Management Plan (focus on water). They found that the principal barriers to implementing plans included lack of agreement on goals, rigidity in process design, procedural obligations and requirements, and a lack of trust. More fundamentally, institutional barriers in the design of natural resource planning processes often lead to more operational level issues. Interestingly, they did not find that lack of data, poor technical capacities, or absence of GIS were reasons for plan failure.

When Jon worked at RARE, he advised Austin Lane, then a graduate student at Duke University, who identified barriers to implementing Honduran management plans (Lane 2003). Lane surveyed managers associated with twelve protected area management plans. Those interviewed indicated the main obstacles to implementation were low levels of manager and staff capacity, political conflicts, inappropriate use of consultants, and low stakeholder participation in the planning and implementation process.

Robles et al. (2007) reinforced these findings at CATIE (a postgraduate natural resources management university in Costa Rica). They studied five national park management plans in Costa Rica, all of which suffered partial implementation due to institutional, technical (poor planning techniques), and conceptual barriers. According to Bernal Herrera, The Nature Conservancy's (TNC) science manager in Costa Rica at the time and the study sponsor, the main conclusion was, "Although the number of barriers we identified was surprising, the problem is much more complex than we thought" (pers. comm., Herrera 2006). They had every reason to believe that these same barriers (especially the institutional ones) combined in complex ways to afflict all protected areas in Costa Rica's national system and likely most every system in Latin America, if not beyond.

In 2014, Gebhardt and Eagles studied municipal parks in Ontario, Canada, identifying numerous factors involved in plan implementation: twenty-six in plan content, ten in human/implementation, and thirteen obstacles to implementation. They concluded that "some of the planning deficiencies found were due to the absence of a coherent provincial policy toward plan development and content. In addition, the research found weakness in the capability of many [parks and recreation] agencies, and especially those of smaller municipalities to undertake and implement strategic planning."

Although global data come only in the form of anecdotes, one indicator of how deep the problem of shipwrecked plans goes is expressed by UNESCO's World Heritage Center, an agency charged with supporting more than 1,000 cultural and natural heritage sites inscribed on the list of World Heritage. While the process of being inscribed requires that sites have management plans or systems, officials at the center know that these plans often go unimplemented.

Art Pedersen, founding director of the center's Sustainable Tourism Programme, notes (pers. comm. 2009) that

> since many World Heritage Sites are iconic [Taj Majal, Great Wall of China, Banks of the River Seine, Kilimanjaro, Acropolis of Athens, Pyramids of Giza, Great Barrier Reef, Statue of Liberty] they often face exceptional pressure from tourists and tourism developers. Very few sites have public use or tourism management plans, or their management plans often only deal superficially with tourism. Many plans do not get implemented, so the planning approach really does need to change.

Places like Sian Ka'an Biosphere Reserve in Mexico find themselves squeezed between a large local population and rapid rates of development, situations that demand careful and sensitive stewardship, continuous interaction with local constituencies, and attention to process in order to implement plans. An implemented plan, especially a tourism-related plan, can both help a site's own management and justify UNESCO's intervention to take on inappropriate developments. UNESCO expressed this possibility in 1998 when it intervened on behalf of the Historic Sanctuary of Machu Picchu in Peru. There, a hotel developer promoted the creation of a cable car that would have lifted tens of thousands of visitors to the top of Machu Picchu's most famous geological face. The government eventually sank the idea thanks to UNESCO recommendations, one of which was the creation of a public use plan for the site.

Many other World Heritage sites have shipwrecked plans, if they have any plans at all. Examples include an environmental education and interpretation plan in Galápagos National Park, a management plan in Lake Malawi National Park, and a public use plan in Ujung Kulon National Park in Indonesia. Of course, if this problem afflicts World Heritage sites, then it runs rampant through other protected areas in many places.

These examples suggest that if we dive deeper to understand why plans fail with such frequency we will come to understand planning weaknesses. Diving deeper resembles following an iceberg into its depths. If we think of a plan's failure as an iceberg, then the failure may be viewed as the visible tip—the 10 percent or so above the surface—or an event. If we dive deeper alongside the iceberg, we will not only find more insightful reasons for why the plan failed but also greater leverage to avoid it. Many of those reasons that lead to failure, as we will discuss later, include deeply flawed assumptions about how the world works that also lay the foundation for conventional planning.

Viewing conservation and protected area plan failures as individual, unrelated events makes the problem even worse by focusing failure on symptoms rather than root causes. The anecdotes above, when viewed through a different lens, demonstrate common underlying patterns and structures that lie deeper in the iceberg: weak institutions, managers poorly equipped to deal with twenty-first-century expectations and demands, a planning culture dependent on specialized consultants; lack of trust in public protected area agencies and ownership in plans, and procedures and processes built upon antiquated beliefs about planning.

Although one can debate the definition of implementation success (Outside the Box 1) or degree of implementation of any particular plan, few, if any, heritage managers would deny that a widespread pandemic afflicts management plans. Many of these fail to meet expectations and have become part of the unfortunate heritage of protected area management. The problem looms not only as potentially gigantic but also astonishingly overlooked. Given the more than 210,000 nationally designated protected areas, the more than 15 percent of the globe's terrestrial surface, the 3.4 percent of oceans (Juffe-Bignoli et al. 2014), and the thousands of organizations associated with protected areas, it confounds us that the problem of nonimplementation is not under the microscope. Perhaps this is because the community does not use a lens that permits it to see the problem in the first place.

Outside the Box 1 | *What Is Implementation Success, Anyway?*

Conventional planners measure plan implementation by the proportion of tasks completed in a plan. In fact, in some countries such as Costa Rica, park services evaluate their units' success based on this criterion. Some academics call this "conformance," the degree to which actions conform to plan objectives. But the world is so uncertain and messy, always throwing curveballs, making it nearly impossible to implement an action plan task-for-task as written. As soon as we plan tasks, the situation changes and throws them out of date.

An alternative measures plan "performance." This way, we measure plan success not just by tasks completed, but also plan quality (see Eagles et al. 2014 and Dvir and Lechler 2004), strategy quality, planned achievements, influence on the planning field, stakeholder use of the plan as they plan even if they do not formally implement listed actions, and unplanned benefits that result from planning and implementing: additional research, formation of new community organizations, new proposals and policies that emerge simply from conversations, and networking. This book refers to performance when talking about plan success, implementation, and shipwrecks.

It is also worth mentioning that planning scholars have been addressing plan implementation for quite some time, sometimes measuring conformance and other times performance. The following references outline this research: Alexander and Faludi (1989); Berk et al. (2006); Brody and Highfield (2005); Kohl (2006); Kohl (2005); Laurian et al. (2004); Lundquist et al. (2002); Mastop and Faludi (1997); Talen (1997); Talen (1996a, b). In addition, Pinto (2013) considers project plan failure to include failure to deliver critical specifications with cost and time overruns, and poor return on investment, among other quality indicators.

Conventional Planning Wreaks Havoc on Heritage

Shipwrecked plans themselves exact a countless toll on the conservation of natural and cultural heritage, when money, human effort, and credibility that could have otherwise been directed to promote conservation are lost overboard as the public shakes its collective head in wonder when plans end up on shelves.

Bernal Herrera, the sponsor of the CATIE study, had invested significant cash in a project that produced seven management plans in the Osa Peninsula of southern Costa Rica (Arguedas

2007). During the project, as implementation barriers became increasingly evident (such as the rangers' lack of capacity to implement management plan monitoring), the question of return on investment reemerged in Herrera's mind. He noted, "I started thinking about implementation three to four years before the CATIE study." With each management plan in 2006 (pers. comm.) costing on average $30,000 and the government desiring that all national parks have such plans, someone would have to produce a million-dollar purse to produce plans for all the parks.

TNC, moreover, has been party to the generation of many park plans around the world, thanks in part to its heavily used Conservation Action Planning (CAP) process, which takes local planners through a series of steps to identify threats and strategies to mitigate them. While CAP easily generates plans, they still need to be implemented. "Many of our [conservation] organizations are much more worried about planning and not paying attention to the implementation phase," Herrera (pers. comm. 2006) admitted.

While funding is important, other factors influence planning success and failure. Sites often take extraordinary amounts of time to plan whether Yellowstone or Panama's Coiba National Park—begun in 2006, management plan published in 2009—or Copan Archaeological Park in Honduras—two years to plan, four years to publish. The gap between planning and publishing may result from extended site research, lengthy public comment and review period, or a slow approval process.

The high costs of conventional planning also create great expectations for implementation. When plans end up shelved after stakeholders have contributed so much time and thought to their creation, expectations decay into a loss of faith in the planning process, a loss of trust in the heritage management agency, and a loss of credibility in the government. These consequences may carry over into subsequent planning processes, resulting in a jaded, unenthusiastic public.

For example, in 2000, archaeologist Richard Hansen and the Global Heritage Fund proposed the Mirador Basin Special Protected Area, which would have covered 210,000 hectares in northern Guatemala, consisting of El Mirador, the Mayan site with perhaps the largest temple in the world as well as many Preclassic Mayan sites. Jeff Morgan, executive director of the Global Heritage Fund, stated, "What we have is a once in a lifetime opportunity, like Yellowstone, to establish a 243,000-hectare roadless wilderness and archaeological preserve that will rival any park in the world" (Hubbard n. d.). Ten million dollars would have come with this declaration as well as a stamp of approval by Guatemalan president Alfonso Portillo. Guatemala's Congress quickly passed the decree in 2002.

Uproar immediately followed. The proposal had irked both industrial loggers who feared losing their forest concession contracts and conservationists who dreaded the potential of opening protected area laws to interest group manipulation. A battle ensued, Congress rescinded the decree, and bitterness turned to taboo. Planners could not talk about the proposal; community groups could not stomach it.

Finally, an Inter-American Development Bank loan for regional development broke through the inertia, and the government hired consulting firms to prepare plans—plans that still met strong local resistance despite attempts at stakeholder involvement. Locals claimed that the participation was little more than a government ploy to alleviate conflicts without ceding any power. The Association of Forest Communities even video recorded meetings in order to have legal evidence for future litigation. Rather than assuaging tensions and creating a shared vision, this top-down process exacerbated the conflict (Radachowsky et al. n. d.).

While shipwrecked conventional plans cost millions of dollars and uncountable hours of site community time every year to produce, the largest cost heritage sites must themselves bear is the degradation their natural and cultural qualities suffer while waiting for their managers to get organized.

Not just natural heritage is threatened by planning gone bad. Cultural heritage as well: Languages are one manifestation of culture. UNESCO's *Atlas of World's Languages in Danger* lists 2,500 endangered languages (230 have gone extinct since 1950), and while most do not have a corresponding protected area and policies to promote their use and protection, some in fact do (UNESCO 2010). For example, Aboriginal owners and Parks Australia co-manage Kakadu National Park (World Heritage Site); half of these lands are owned by Aboriginals, with much of the remaining subject to Aboriginal claims (Nettle and Romaine 2000). The park area covers a significant portion of certain aboriginal languages. Thus, conservation priorities include protecting both natural and cultural values, which are often as intertwined as strands of a rope. Aboriginal managers use native languages in meetings to emphasize the need for protection of both landscape and language, something conventional planning would be challenged to achieve.

Conventional planning, given its relatively poor record in the immediate past of effectively protecting biodiversity, may not be equipped to meet this challenge. In one of the few global level studies of protection effectiveness, Leverington et al. (2010) indicated that at most only one-third of the world's natural protected areas are managed effectively; that is, achieving the objectives for which they were established. Masica et al. (2014) found that more than 500 protected areas around the world had been downsized, downgraded, or degazetted due to industrial-scale natural resource extraction, local land claim disputes, and inadequate conservation planning.

Planners Must First See That Planning Itself May Be Failing

Although planners are, as John Forester (1989) says, "selective organizers of attention to real possibilities of action," they often do not pay attention to causes of conventional shipwrecks. This inattention results in churning out plan after plan, cast from the same mold, destined to failure, all the while never questioning that mold and its underlying assumptions, despite overwhelming anecdotal evidence. We have almost no systematic evidence of why plans fail, moreover, because almost no one has put the anecdotes together.

We don't want to be overly hard on the protected area community—after all, blind spots in our vision occur wherever human minds wander. The Chinese ignored pleas by human right activists, environmentalists, geologists, public health specialists, and many others when they built the $24 billion Three Gorges Dam on the Yangtze River between 1994 and 2012. In effect, their policy was simply, "Dam(n) the environment." Now, however, they see the social, environmental, and economic costs quickly piling up into a mountain of problems for their country, and they admit, as Weng Xiaofeng, overseer of the project for the State Council, says, "We simply cannot sacrifice the environment in exchange for temporary economic gain" (Hvistendahl 2008). Why could they not see this before they built it?

Jared Diamond, author of *Collapse*, comments on Mayan cities and the environmental and social problems—deforestation, hillside erosion, increased fighting, drought—that led to their abandonment (2005, p. 177):

> We have to wonder why the kings and nobles failed to recognize and solve these seemingly obvious problems undermining their society. Their attention was evidently focused on their short-term concerns of enriching themselves, waging wars, erecting monuments, competing with each other, and extracting enough food from the peasants to support all those activities. Like most leaders through human history, the Maya kings and nobles did not heed long-term problems, insofar as they perceived them.

If our community does not manage change soon, we may go down with the *Pequod*-like Ahab pursuing Moby Dick, or Captain Edward John Smith of the *Titanic* pursuing a world record in crossing the Atlantic. Whether white whale or White Star Line, both led to the bottom of the sea. Both focused more on the plan than on its implementation.

> ## Toolbox 1 | *The Park Guard: Figuring Out Where the Intruders Are*
>
> Centuries ago, kings posted guards with swords and bows to protect royal forests and game from marauding hunters. Centuries later, the English deployed armed guards around African game reserves to make sure that natives stayed out of their former territory. More recently, park guards continued their long and storied tradition facing off poachers, tomb raiders, militia groups, and drug traffickers. But over time, the notions of park borders has blurred, whether through integration with transboundary parks or with protected areas in other categories or through threats that originate beyond traditional physical borders such as budget cuts, international black markets in heritage artifacts, laws that pit conflicting land tenants against each other, upstream water pollution, forest fires from neighboring forests, pine bark beetle invasions, and civil wars that exile waves of refugees in desperate search of shelter.
>
> So parks now often turn their tool inward, assigning guards to guard against visitors, sometimes replacing guns for interpretive talks, bathroom checks, bird checklists, and nonlethal citations. The evolution of this age-old tool has far from ended; eventually the very concept of the park guard may share little with the paramilitary image parks have cultivated over centuries.

Modern Heritage Site Planning Steams toward an Iceberg

As plans pile up, governments and donors allocate more money to conventional plans, non-profit and academic institutions invest more labor in devising new conventional planning tools, sites continue to ask the same old conventional questions and use the same conventional formats and recipes, all pedaling faster and faster to try to outpace problems bearing down. We cannot solve these problems by pedaling faster, developing better technology, or injecting more money, time, data, and people into the system but rather by putting on new lenses that let us see things that we cannot now and then responding appropriately.

And that is what this book proposes: the problem of conventional planning is not so much a technical problem. The problem is rather conceptual, and requires a new concept—one that we call "Holistic Planning."

Like the iceberg that sank the *Titanic*, the explanation for why site plans fail goes deep below the choppy surface. Unfortunately, planners are equipped to see only events (plan failures, budget crises, species extinctions) and patterns (series of plan failures, multiple species going extinct, revenue shortfalls over several years). That way of seeing, however, cannot penetrate far underwater—that way of seeing reacts to events (called single-loop learning, Fire Box 1), but it doesn't prevent their occurrence.

Inside the Box 1 | *Choosing Science and Technology at the Cost of Wisdom*

Western society hides a common shadow that encourages its people to replace the benefits of integrated growth (emotional, mental, physical, spiritual) and wisdom for technological convenience. As Senge et al. write in *Presence* (2008, p. 214),

> We use hand calculators and forget arithmetic.... We buy a larger car in order to feel more secure instead of learning how to understand one another and create personal security for one another.... After a while, power through our technology is all we know.... The growing gap between technological power and wisdom arises not from technological progress alone but from the way it interacts with more integrative human development. After a while, the very need for such development is all but forgotten. Today we define progress by new developments in technology rather than by any broader notion of advance in well-being. Thus, the ever-widening gap between our wisdom and our power is not accidental or due to bad luck. It arises from a basic structure we enact in modern society. It will continue to get worse until we see this structure.

This is true in heritage management as well. The entire planning process has shifted the burden to consultants and high-tech planning, atrophying our capacity to think, converse, make decisions together, clarify values, and act. When carrying capacity becomes the golden hammer of our management toolbox, our own development as managers becomes the black hole. There is nothing for the human soul in carrying capacity.

Rather than cruise the surface, this book dives like a submarine, with each passing chapter, deeper and deeper alongside the iceberg. When we reach the bottom of the ice, where waters diffuse and refract light, we will see planning and managing entirely differently. With this new view, unimagined solutions hover and spurt in inky depths. We will see that moving ahead requires jettisoning conventional planning and thinking behind.

Chapters 1 through 4 guide us slowly down the iceberg, providing time enough for our eyes and more importantly our minds to adjust to the darkness. At the beginning of most chapters, we identify an increasingly lower level on the iceberg; in several chapters as well we talk about increasingly deep learning loops (Fire Boxes 1–4) and how the deeper into a system (starting at events and patterns) we peer, the more leverage we wield to change the system.

We continue the discussion with a whole new lens that describes Integral Theory's (the basis for Holistic Planning) four universal perspectives for all phenomena. We learn that if we ignore any one perspective, our understanding of reality suffers greatly as does our plan implementation.

Chapter 5 looks at how managers' minds—their beliefs, motivations, values, consciousness, and mental health—affect deeply the plans they write (the first perspective).

Chapter 6 observes how individuals' skills, abilities, behaviors, and physical well-being strongly influence plan implementation (the second perspective).

Chapter 7 reveals how organizational collective culture and communication, its beliefs, worldviews, shared visions and goals, stories, and myths alter everything to do with plan implementation (the third perspective).

Chapter 8 details how the systems and institutions we build affect not only plan implementation but the very protected areas we hope to conserve (the fourth perspective).

Finally, chapter 9 concludes that we really are not talking about planning implementation at all; that by integrating all four perspectives, we also integrate planning and implementation, thinking and doing, and learning and acting, and that what we are really talking about is something much more relevant to our daily mission: the reconceptualization of *management* itself. To do this, we must come up the other side of the iceberg, a side the *Titanic* never knew.

Fire Box 1 | *Single-Loop Learning: Total Fire Suppression*

React

Single-loop learning

Modify techniques

Propose remedies

PROBLEM

React to events and patterns. All modifications or proposed remedies occur within a single frame of reference or mental model.

Single-loop learners thrive within boxes cut from their own assumptions. Since about 1910, American forest policy was simple: suppress all fires immediately by ten o'clock the morning after they were detected. Thus, the US Forest Service, National Park Service, and other agencies purchased more shovels, trained more smokejumpers, dug more firebreaks, developed better forecasting models, and enlisted Smokey Bear to convince people to snuff out campfires before leaving campsites. While suppression can be highly effective in the short term, eventually the buildup of woody fuel in some forest types leads to larger, hotter, and more dangerous fires, often carbonizing the oldest and largest trees that previously had survived fires. This buildup and its consequent conflagrations reduce forests' resistance to future fires.

For double-loop learning, see chapter 2.

Your paradigm is so intrinsic to your mental process that you are hardly aware of its existence, until you try to communicate with someone with a different paradigm.

—*Donella Meadows*

Rational Comprehensive Planning Floats in a PLUS World

All major cultural realignments and shifts in worldview carry great confusion, lack of personal integration, and the usual fringe elements. This was true with the Reformation and the Enlightenment, and it is true with our current cultural crises.

—*Mark B. Woodhouse*

THE OTHER
SIDE OF
COMPLEXITY

EVENTS

PATTERNS

STRUCTURES

MENTAL MODELS

It Is the Eyes More Than the Evidence

If the human mind were as objective as we often assume, then the abundant anecdotes of plan failures should have set off a panic a long time ago among heritage professionals. The mind, however, rarely achieves objectivity; as philosopher Henri Bergson said, "The eyes see only what the mind is prepared to comprehend." Psychologists have amassed evidence (Kahneman 2011) that our minds filter out evidence according to built-in patterns, categories, preconceived notions, paradigms, cognitive schema, or mental models. This mass of psychological evidence, like that of plan failures, has also failed to alarm those who believe humans to be scientifically objective.

We create mental models, which are simplistic representations of the real world, to deal with overwhelming complexities that surround us. We build mental models from our everyday experience in order to help get through the day by indicating which things to attend to and which to ignore. Our mental models determine how we characterize situations, such as a planning task. They are internal representations of the external world that then influence our behavior; what we see and how we act are influenced by our mental models (Jones et al. 2011). These serve another important function: they simplify our perceptions of how real world systems behave, making it possible for humans to operate in a complex and uncertain world by filtering out unneeded information. Focusing on what is important helps build our situational awareness so we can better make sense of it (McCool et al. 2013).

Barker (1992) notes how paradigms and mental models affect all our senses, not just sight, to the point where "you are quite literally unable to perceive data right before your eyes." He provides many examples of not seeing things in plain sight, such as the Chernobyl nuclear disaster in 1986 during which scientists were so sure that a meltdown was impossible, that even when they saw black chunks on the reactor vessel floor and in the turbine room, it never occurred to them that graphite, used to control nuclear fission, had been blown from the reactor core. The engineers looked straight at the proof of reactor explosion and saw no proof at all.

In addition, our paradigms can create things that are *not* there, such as oasis mirages or ghosts. How about planning? Can paradigms affect our plans as well? Examples abound.

Over the years, conservation has experienced the comings and goings of various underlying paradigms, including the idea called "fortress conservation." Brockington (2002) defines it as "an approach that seeks to preserve wildlife and their habitat through forceful exclusion of local people who have traditionally relied on the environment in question for their livelihoods."

Integrated Conservation and Development Programs (ICDPs), similarly, represent another paradigm involved in protected area planning, developed in response to failures of fortress conservation. The basic assumption behind ICDPs states that in order for conservation to work effectively, local people have to be involved so they can embrace economic alternatives to hunting and extracting natural resources. The big international nongovernmental and aid organizations launched numerous projects around the world to do precisely this.

In Africa, one of them emerged around Cameroon's Korup National Park and was slated to reduce poverty of seven indigenous villages inside the park and dozens more just outside. The World Wildlife Fund (WWF) ran this ICDP that, like so many others, never met expectations. The principal project evaluator (Schmidt-Soltau 2004) writes, "What seems clear is that the Korup Project did not reduce poverty. *It caused additional impoverishment* [italics from cited source]. While ICDPs were put forward as a win-win concept, the reality has turned out differently."

In 2004, Chapin published a controversial article in *WorldWatch* about the failure of conservation and development organizations to include indigenous peoples in their conservation plans and how they absorbed so much conservation money in the process. The ICDP paradigm also assumed that big, outside conservation organizations could decide what economic opportunities local people needed without significant participation by the same local people. Chapin said, "On the ground, ICDPs were generally paternalistic, lacking in expertise, and one-sided—driven largely by the agendas of the conservationists, with little indigenous input."

Paradigms Filter the Universe

These examples and many others exhibit the power that paradigms have in determining our perceptions and actions. Many authors have worked in this area, but the true master must certainly be science historian Thomas Kuhn who in 1962 published his classic, *The Structure of Scientific Revolutions*. Kuhn says that, in the context of science, the term *paradigm* most directly describes "accepted examples of actual scientific practice, examples which include law, theory, application and instrumentation together—[that] provide models from which spring particular coherent traditions of scientific research." Those who share the same paradigm, share the same rules and standards of practice, filter their observations in similar ways, and respond to stimuli in like fashion.

Paradigms tell us about many things, including the universe, existence, and of course protected areas. We often see conflicting paradigms, such as the following examples from Barborak (2010):

- All creation occurred at once vs. creation evolves

- Humanity is part of nature vs. humanity is separate from nature

- Economic growth can expand forever vs. economy has limits to growth

- Society must protect small islands of wild habitat with distinct boundaries vs. society must integrate networks of protected area ecosystems into human systems with no distinct boundaries

- Fortress (fences and fines) conservation vs. community-based conservation

- Protected area management must be described in a management plan vs. management must be ongoing experimental, learning with no overarching management plan

- Biodiversity protection vs. ecological services provision

- Co-management vs. top-down central government management

- Identifying visitor carrying capacity vs. identifying acceptable conditions

- Focused on site and species vs. region and systems

- Managed by scientists and technicians vs. managed by people with a diversity of experiences and skills

- Knowledge is fixed vs. knowledge is tentative

For conservation and heritage planning, we are beginning to understand that worldviews (which have their own set of assumptions) permeate our paradigms of planning and management. With that understanding we possess power to change those mental models (Fire Box 2), to build models of planning more effective than the current dominant model of planning. Many planners, often unknowingly, defend this model, even though the world of the future is different from the world in which it was constructed.

Paradigm Pioneers Often Face Resistance

People can however transcend dominant paradigms. Barker calls those who lead paradigm change, "paradigm pioneers." Kuhn (1972) says that paradigm forerunners usually hold little hard evidence that points to a new paradigm waiting to spring forth and overthrow normal science. IBM could not know that the personal computer would ultimately usher in a new way of modern life. Alfred Wegener could not convince the world of continental drift until new evidence appeared after his death. Copernicus's calculations scarcely improved on Ptolemy's predictions until Kepler advanced them beyond dispute.

Barker (p. 74) says that "the essence of the pioneering decision is: Those who choose to change their paradigms early do it not as an act of the head but as an act of the heart." To propose a new paradigm, pioneers usually detect some anomaly that current theory cannot adequately explain and that might indicate a better explanation or paradigm around the corner. For example, astrophysicists have noted that the motion and distribution of galaxies do not match up with known laws of gravitation. This anomaly has led to the theory of dark matter which still has not yet been proven.

Anomalies erupt from different amounts of evidence; some are minute, while others sport cracks large enough to sail a cruise ship through. Where then does that leave the abundance of failed plans all around the world? Is this an anomaly and if so, how big? Why aren't more people in the protected areas community alarmed by this? Could there be a new paradigm in planning just waiting for the right paradigm pioneers to rub the genie's bottle?

The Paradigm of Conventional Heritage Site Planning

Although Kuhn designed his theory of paradigm change based on revolutions in physical science, many social scientists have eagerly embraced his theory and adapted some of their own paradigm change models (for example, Mungazi 1989). Some criticize this adoption, as open social systems never work as cleanly as closed physical science ones do, yet his elegant and internally consistent theory appeals to intuition. Accepting that caveat and realizing that paradigms do exist outside the physical sciences, the notion of anomaly seems to apply only too well to planning.

To restate the crack in the hull of conventional planning: plans continue to end unimplemented in large numbers, and yet no one has been able to solve the problem, not with new tools, not by injecting more money, not by making them more scientific, not by making them more participatory, not by anything so far. Plan failure is an anomaly, as it goes against the paradigm of scientifically based, expert-driven models of change. Only a few have recognized this crack, and fewer are working today to weld it shut. As of this writing, we know only of the studies mentioned in chapter 1, a small handful of practitioners, this book, and the PUP Global Heritage Consortium.

The question then surfaces: Will the crack lead to a revolution in heritage site planning or will it eventually sink the entire enterprise? Water now rushes into the hull of site planning, drowning efforts to better manage protected areas. The *Exxon Valdez* shipwrecked before the paradigm changed from single to double hulls. The *Titanic* sank before new rules about ship safety could be devised.

The lack of apparent investigation into this problem, the tendency to blame a paucity of money/time/people/information/political will (the Big Five excuses for nonimplementation), and the general habit of focusing on events and patterns rather than deeper system elements such as mental models and beyond indicate that people are not really sure where the problem lies. Lynton Caldwell (1992), a principal author of the US National Environmental Policy Act, which requires US federal agencies to consider the environmental effects of their actions, argues that people can attribute the cause of a problem to one of various levels, which include operational (e.g., not enough public meetings or insufficient budget) and systemic (e.g., the entire planning process is fatally flawed). The level one chooses influences the solution one chooses. An operational problem receives an operational solution (more money/time/people/data/political will). Caldwell notes that environmental challenges are usually systemic, but when people apply operational solutions, they inevitably fail.

For some of our readers, especially those heavily invested in the conventional planning paradigm, what follows may be difficult to accept. Indeed, the book took us seven years to write as we grappled with the same issues. We strongly encourage you to proceed, nevertheless, for as French writer Marcel Proust wrote, "The real act of discovery consists not in finding new lands but in seeing with new eyes."

Conventional Planning Paradigm Has Deep Roots

Some of the greatest scientific minds—Galileo, Descartes, Newton, Bacon, Hobbes—emerged from the Enlightenment and energized science with a new sense of optimism that, by the turn of the nineteenth century, had turned into a doctrine known as Positivism. The Positivists believed that people could only construct authentic, valid knowledge through experiences based on their senses. If you can measure it, it exists. If you cannot, it does not. Frenchman and first modern sociologist August Comte gave Positivism its founding principles:

1. Empirical science was not just a form of knowledge but the only source of positive knowledge of the world.

2. It was necessary to cleanse people's minds of mysticism, superstition, and other forms of pseudo-knowledge.

3. Scientific knowledge and technical control had to rein in human society, to make technology, as Comte said, "no longer exclusively geometrical, mechanical, or chemical, but also and primarily political and moral."

Positivism's popularity deeply entrenched itself in Western universities in the late nineteenth century, and from there took over the professions in the early twentieth century. At that point, Positivism morphed into Technical Rationality.

Technical Rationalists held that professionals could perfect society through science and would be the vehicles to channel scientific knowledge from universities to the field. That is, professionals identified problems, the scientists and experts developed solutions to those problems, and professionals then tested their solutions and put them to practice. This technical precision works well for building bridges or running an emergency room at a hospital. But a big problem emerged when social scientists such as planning professionals discovered that many problems are not technical but involve conflicts in values.

Planners desired the same level of control, the same quantitative, mathematical, objective, and clearly definable practices that their colleagues in medicine and engineering seemed to enjoy. The problem for social scientists and conventional planners in particular was that their problems were not easily defined and were much more complex and messy than natural science laboratories, engineer workshops, or even hospital operating rooms. That did not matter, at first, because Technical Rationality declares, according to Schön (1983, p.145), "that practice should be based on scientific theory achievable only through controlled experiment, which cannot be conducted rigorously in practice. So to researchers and the research setting falls the development of basic and applied science, while to practitioners and the practice setting falls the use of scientific theories to achieve the instrumental goals of practice."

Because planners, both practitioners and academics, can never simulate their planning situations in the lab as controlled experiments, they had to carry out their studies in the field, live with real people behaving in diverse and often mystifying ways. Thus with this study-in-the-field approach to planning emerged the newest form of planning based on Technical Rationality—what we call "conventional planning"—which we now know as Rational Comprehensive Planning (RCP).

To be fair, other approaches to planning have emerged since the 1960s in response to the problems with RCP. They include incremental (making decisions that are "possible" rather than those that derive from comprehensive assessment of alternatives), transactive (planning that works with constituencies to build learning and consensus), advocacy (planning that defends interests of weak, poor, and disenfranchised), and radical (planning that views problems as a result of structural deficiencies in political systems). For a comparison of these theories, see Hudson (1979); see also Friedmann (1993, 1973). The latter is one of the earliest formal and well-thought-out statements in response to the failures of Rational Comprehensive Planning.

Rational Comprehensive Planning Takes Over Protected Areas

Professional planners throughout society developed RCP as a scientifically based approach to planning for highways, urban housing, national defense, new cities, subdivisions, and parks and heritage areas. They raised RCP on a number of assumptions and ideal conditions, often implicit and frequently difficult to achieve:

1. Complete understanding of the cause-and-effect relationships of a system

2. Agreement on objectives or consensus about what the public interest is

3. A well-defined problem

4. A full array of alternatives to consider

5. Full baseline information

6. Complete information about consequences of each alternative

7. Full information about the values and preferences of citizens

8. Sufficient time, skill, and resources to carry out planning

9. Plan implementation upon completion

Their planning process, once funding was secured, proceeded in a fairly linear way step by step, completing one before moving on to the next. While there are differences from one organization to the other, the hallmarks include the following:

1. Frame the problem.

2. Identify objectives and goals.

3. Imagine a desirable future based on application of technical interventions.

4. Design study methodology using best available technical tools and protocols.

5. Describe baseline conditions generating best scientific data given available resources; may include site and threat analysis for protected area planning.

6. Identify alternative strategies and actions to reach that possible future.

7. Describe constraints to be mitigated or removed (often lack of money, personnel, time, data, political will).

8. Predict consequences of actions and strategies.

9. Create action and monitoring plans.

10. Write document.

11. Submit to public and other agencies for review.

12. Revise draft plan in response to comments.

13. Submit for approval.

14. Publish.

15. Hope for and seek additional funds to implement plan.

One can see how closely the planning process follows the scientific process of conceiving, designing, planning, developing, executing, writing up, peer reviewing, and publishing a scientific study. Since most planners hold similar assumptions about planning as scientists do about research, no wonder resulting plans are very similar throughout the world. Table 2.1 shows how Kuhn's criteria to define a scientific paradigm can also characterize the global conventional planning paradigm.

Table 2.1	*Natural Heritage Conservation Paradigm*	
Kuhn Criterion	**Conservation and Natural Protected Area Examples**
Textbooks	*Measures of Success* (Margoluis & Salafsky 1998); IUCN best practice guides (e.g., Thomas & Middleton 2003); *Planning National Parks for Ecodevelopment* (Kenton Miller 1978); *Protected Area Governance and Management* (Worboys et al. 2015)
Archetypical examples	Galapagos, Yellowstone, Monteverde Cloud Forest, Kruger
Language	Natural resources; we must save biodiversity; stakeholder participation is essential; protected area management; connectivity; ecological integrity; land-use planning; threat mitigation; conservation strategies; management effectiveness—mostly objective, scientific, concrete, material language
Symbols and metaphors	Protected area islands; biological corridors; John Muir; Aldo Leopold; WWF panda
Frameworks	LAC, ROS, VIM, VAMP, TOMM, VERP, Open Standards for the Practice of Conservation (CAP)
Planning leaders	Kenton Miller, Steve McCool, George Wallace, Paul Eagles, Jeff McNeely, George Stankey, Miguel Cifuentes
Planning procedures and instrumentation	Management plan, monitoring and evaluation, indicators, rapid appraisals, zoning, carrying capacity, GIS, logframes, IUCN protected area categories
Problem definition	How to protect natural and cultural resources from economic and illegal activities
Rules	The paradigm of conventional planning dictates how sites create and use their plans. Some rules include: • Look for extraordinary funding to finance the planning process and plan itself. • Find best brains and data managers to buy given available budget and time. • Conduct a baseline study of area and compile existing studies (management plan).

- Invite stakeholders to speak their minds, but retain power to decide what makes it into the final plan based on scientific quality and political expediency.
- Identify conservation threats and mitigation strategies (management plan).
- Identify vision, mission, goals, objectives, strategies, activities, and indicators of success in a logical and hierarchically linked fashion.
- Verify that all recommendations and conclusions are backed by objective, scientific reasoning.
- Choose more tasks than the site can afford to do in the hopes that larger numbers will attract larger donations.
- Put expiration date on plan because it will go out of date and will need to be redone.
- Publish it to increase respectability, authority, and finality.
- Wait while plan is approved by state.
- Regard the annual operating plan as the principal means of implementing the plan.

Note: This table describes the natural heritage conservation paradigm with criteria that Kuhn used to define a paradigm in science.

For professionals to operate under Technical Rationality, they require certain attitudes as well toward their own technical expertise. According to Schön, professionals think the following (p. 297):

- "I am presumed to know, and must claim to do so, regardless of my own uncertainty."

- "Keep my distance from the client, and hold onto the expert's role. Give the client a sense of my expertise, but convey a feeling of warmth and sympathy as a 'sweetener.'"

- "Look for deference and status in the client's response to my professional persona."

Overall, the professional planner or engineer believes that power in general derives from technical knowledge. The planner knows where to find data, which questions to ask, how to perform analyses, how to speak jargon, whom to contact, how to navigate bureaucratic and regulatory protocols, and even how to find money. This information places the planner in an elite position because in this style of planning, technical knowledge and expertise are highly valued. Because power emanates from technical knowledge, planners thus believe they avoid political, social, and subjective interests; biases; and personal conflicts. These only confuse and interfere with the technical process of generating optimal, technical solutions. Although ignoring stakeholder concerns may reduce the apparent complexity of planning (Caron 2014), it can contribute to plan non-implementation down the line.

Conventional planners see their task as technical problem solving (see for example Mallari et al. 2013). The question "Given a set of goals, what is the most efficient way to achieve them?" drives their thoughts, and this logical approach to planning has tremendous appeal. After all, don't we need to know where we are going before figuring how to get there? And, once we know our destination, is it not simply a matter of choosing the most efficient means to get there? Do not most people understand and agree with logical conclusions, anyway?

Yet focusing on gathering data, modeling alternatives, and estimating consequences leads planners' attention astray. Weick and Sutcliffe (2007, p. 26) observe that fixating on the conventional planning process often leads to "mindlessness," reinforcing the conclusion of Lachapelle et al. (2003) that planning procedures themselves are a major barrier to planning: people seek confirmation that their plans, like their expectations, are correct. This behavior grows particularly strong when technical methodologies rather than the broader social goals and values that underlie heritage conservation capture attention. Forester (1989, p. 31) notes, "The technician is not wrong so much as intentionally neglectful. Politics is thought to 'get in the way' of rigorous work." Senge (1990, p. 131) concludes: "We often spend so much time coping with problems along our path that we forget why we are on that path in the first place. The result is that we only have a dim, or even inaccurate, view of what's really important to us."

Conventional planning's focus on technical expertise and rigor allows structures to dominate planning—rules, procedures, and professional conventions permeate a planning bureaucracy, thus constraining reflection, learning, and innovation, factors necessary to deal with the complexity, uncertainty, and even sloppiness (Peters 1988) that haunt our world. When a plan runs head-first into obstacles, planners look to their tried-and-tested explanations: not enough data, too few public meetings, insufficient time or money, incorrect coefficients in models, politicians not caring.

Rational Comprehensive Planning Generates Barriers

Readers may have likely already rubbed their chins and considered some barriers that RCP generates[3]. In fact, ask any group of people involved in planning, and you will get a long list of barriers. For example, Robles et al. (2007) identify 135 different barriers through interviews with a number of planning participants. Obviously many overlap and use different terms for the same barriers, so the researchers distilled those barriers into fourteen general categories covering a wide range of responses:

1. The National Conservation Area System itself (agency in charge of Costa Rican protected areas)

2. Document problems

3. Lack of personnel

4. Lack of training

5. Lack of feeling ownership in plan by protected area staff

6. Economic reasons

7. Planning problems

8. Actor involvement

9. Lack of political will

10. Disempowered protected area director

11. Mental barriers

12. Unapproved plans

13. Donor interests

14. Lack of protected area priorities

After reviewing the literature, they then synthesized their results and developed the model shown in Figure 2.1, which contains three major barrier categories.

Figure 2.1| *Plan Implementation Barriers*

Shadow plan
Exists in managers' minds, not on paper

Plan Implementation

Implementation Gap

Protecting the Optimal Answer

Similarities to Scientific Studies

Extraordinary funding

Collect background data

Analyze data & variables

Draw conclusions

Make recommendations

Submit to peer review

Publish & distribute

Focus attention elsewhere

Lack of staff training due to reliance on outside experts

Discourages errors, uncertainty, and experimentation because have just one shot to get plan right

Low stakeholder involvement due to premium on expert, objective knowledge, not local or subjective experience or other forms of knowing not scientific

Budget dedicated to consultants and their needs not those of stakeholders and implementation

Due to reliance on experts, directors participate minimally

Due to incentives to produce document, implementation is low priority with little or no budget Science is a controlled process; best answer requires centralized decision-making and planning control, usually state is control agent which initiates, finances, designs, facilitates, organizes process; invites participants, hires consultants, decides content, chooses where; sets agenda, influences felt needs, reaps prestige

People are tired
No money for implementation
Nearly untouchable document
Annual operating plan not linked to management plan
Unfulfilled expectations and consultants blamed
Ownership of immutable plan drops as staff changes
"Weapons of the weak" sabotage plan

Intentional Barriers
Approval of plan by state agent
Celebration and public commitment
Bureaucratic update procedures
Prestige Plan considered law
Language of "finality" *

Document format: technical, codified, literal language/format, scientific, published, polished; hard to update and inaccessible to some stakeholders

Protected area does not develop capacity to facilitate, implement, or deeply discuss issues surrounding plan, lack of manager empowerment to implement, use of consultants results in lack of ownership by PA staff

Avoids political conflicts, issues since they are subjective, non-technical variables

Participants contribute needs and problems but do co-create and thus build no commitment, choose no responsibility

One-time event, not continuous, not on-going learning, no experimentation

Low stakeholder involvement means low power sharing and thus low feeling of stakeholder ownership

Planning Process

Time
Money
Staff work
Institutional effort
Stakeholders
Political attention
Expert consultants
Scientific data
Actor expectations
Mental models

Diagnose-recruit-solve-set goals-publish

* "Final," "publish," "finish," "validate"

Rational Comprehensive Planning

Technical Rationality
Reductionism   DesCartes
Materialism   Newton
Rationalism   Bacon
Positivism   Comte

Non-RCP Planning Practice Barriers
Poor stakeholder communication
Participant compensation
Missing components
Confused objectives
Lack of readiness
Shallow reflection
Poor facilitation
Sterile vision

Non-RCP Institutional Barriers
High staff rotation between PAs
Incentives short-term thinking
Low institutional morale
Tech staff stays in central office with best salaries
Poor communication in hierarchy
Misinformation
Lack of staff
Underfunded

This depiction brings some order to the many barriers that RCP constructs. As such, the left-hand column shows the initial conditions established by RCP. Then as planning proceeds, it requires numerous inputs and eventually generates the many barriers in the right-hand column. The Robles team observed that some barriers apparently have no connection to RCP and thus created two additional barrier categories: (1) barriers related to poor planning practice (lower left) and (2) institutional barriers (lower right). Later authors also mention a possible fourth category, those barriers related to greater external circumstances such as earthquakes, coups, political turmoil, financial crises, and computer meltdowns.

They finally suggest that even these two categories, apparently unrelated to RCP, may in fact relate to RCP. Rather than locate the fault with outside organizations, events, and people, RCP generates its own challenges, and when we dive deeper along our own iceberg, as we see later, we need to look inward at what we do as planners and how those actions generate barriers. Try to guess why this might be so; if you want our possible explanations, see this endnote[4].

Other elements in the diagram include the idea of an implementation gap where the plan takes the protected area to one edge of the gap. Crossing that gap and putting the plan into real practice proves challenging, often overwhelmingly so. This gap expands out of the fundamental premise of planning that planners only make recommendations, while others make decisions and implement. When others decide, then implementation is viewed as external to planning.

Finally, the study outlined the imposition of measures designed to make plan revision difficult. Robles and colleagues reason that planners must invest significant resources of many kinds into the production of a plan, a process that only occurs once every five to ten years. These long-term planning horizons assume conditions will not change much, a necessary condition for RCP. For example, in the United Kingdom, Areas of Outstanding Natural Beauty have twenty-year management plans with five-year-review intervals. France's Parcs Naturales Régionaux have twelve-year plans, and natural heritage areas in the United States, such as national forests and parks, have ten-to-fifteen-year plans. For a comparison of the three models, see Barrett and Taylor (2007).

Such time periods may be necessary not only to implement planned actions but also to test assumptions, both implicit and explicit, embedded within the plan. Often planners view plans as a kind of social contract, an agreement between civil society and the agency and thus should be difficult to modify. So they intentionally build this difficulty (e.g., rigorous update protocols or revision of environmental statements) into such plans to free plan implementation from whims and desires of administrators and various constituencies. A plan contains a set of intentions developed under assumptions about the future. When that future arises differently or intended actions contain surprises, the plan will need amending. A significant barrier arises when the process of modification becomes so bureaucratically cumbersome that changes to the plan needed when new information arise or invalid assumptions are exposed never take place.

We will not discuss each listed barrier now because many are self-explanatory, but we will go into more detail in the second half of the book where we discuss solutions to barriers and the RCP mindset in general. To see RCP in the act of generating barriers, see Inside the Box 2.1.

Inside the Box 2 | *Kuna Management Plan: Barriers, Barriers, Everywhere*

A Conservationist Dream That Does Not Come True

Historically Kuna Indians inhabited much of present-day Panama, until the Spaniards arrived and drove them from the mainland to the San Blas Islands. In 1938, the government approved the Comarca de San Blas, which covers a roughly 20-kilometer-wide band of forest from the ridge of the Continental Divide down to the Atlantic Coast and seaward 1 kilometer to include more than 300 small coral islands. The Kuna live on more than forty islands and twelve mainland villages.

Despite assaults by the *conquistadores* and modern civilization, the Kuna not only survived but preserved their culture with a political astuteness and social organization that served their defenses well. By the early 1970s, nevertheless, squatters began encroaching on their land. And the Kuna reacted. So in 1983, a small group of Kuna leaders and technicians began a project to protect their southern border against colonial invasion.

For conservationists, the Kunas' effort was love at first sight. Here for the first time in Latin America, an indigenous group had called itself to arms to create a protected area, set up a management system, and run a program that safeguarded both cultural and biological diversity. But before the group had taken even a few steps, recalls Mac Chapin, an anthropologist who worked with the Kuna and whose experience provides the background for this case study (1997),

> It found itself enshrined in the pantheon of quasi-mythological success stories. People everywhere were desperately searching for successes as a counter-balance to the deforestation and general environmental pillage taking place throughout the tropics. [The management plan project] fit the bill perfectly. It contained all the right elements—an alliance between indigenous peoples and conservationists, indigenous

defense of its ancestral homeland, a biosphere reserve run by Noble Savages, a botanical park and wildlife refuge, scientific tourism—and the word spread widely and fast.

Instant fame immediately lured funding and the assistance of CATIE (the Tropical Agronomic Center for Research and Education based in Costa Rica), USAID, and other donors. At the time, CATIE represented the very best in protected area planning that money could buy. And because the Kuna had no idea about modern park management, let alone Western science, they readily deferred to the experts.

Because the Comarca had been tapped for UNESCO biosphere reserve designation, CATIE immediately directed the Kuna to write the requisite management plan, and they invoked verses from their bible to do it: Kenton Miller's 1978 classic, *Planning National Parks for Ecodevelopment*. Despite their reliance on the conventional park management plan paradigm, they hoped that somehow, in some way they might fuse Western science and traditional knowledge in this campaign.

But before long, the possibility of balance between these two knowledge systems quickly seesawed toward science. Initially the management plan aimed to cover the proposed 60,000-hectare park, but soon CATIE expanded its scope to include the entire Comarca, including marine sectors. Protected area staff projections shot up to more than thirty, and the advisors, unrestricted by budget, created a wish list of sixteen programs and subprograms in a very un-Kuna-like hierarchy.

They assured the Kuna that as soon as they circulated the management plan, donors would arrive like flocks of hungry seagulls.

During the first stage, scientists launched a series of baseline studies: inventories of flora and fauna, land use capability mapping, forestry inventories, and individual research projects. These fed the planning and helped to justify the creation of the protected area.

Rational Comprehensive Planning Barriers Overcome the Plan

If there were a poster child for Rational Comprehensive Planning, the Kuna Management Plan would be it. Chapin says that "development of the plan was essentially a research project in which they gathered information on the physical features of the region, worked with scientists on floral and faunal inventories, and systematized what was known of the ecosystems of Kuna Yala as well as all of eastern Panama. They read large numbers of articles, reports, and books. They received training courses at CATIE and benefited from the visits of scientists."

The goal of fusing science and local knowledge had disintegrated. The management plan evolved into a creature increasingly inappropriate and eventually irrelevant for the indigenous Kuna. Not only did the plan and the entire situation use language, concepts, and formats completely foreign, it imported tools from distant contexts such as environmental education teaching modules from urban schools in Costa Rica. The plan also tried to implant the capital-intensive Costa Rican ecotourism model that did not include having to manage the repressive attention of Noriega's National Guard. The science agenda, furthermore, did not suggest studies that would produce practical results for the Kuna.

And the most important motivation for the Kuna, the reason they launched the entire effort in the first place, was to protect the Comarca's southern border from incursion. So above all, patrolling, demarcating, and protecting their territory most interested the Kuna. Yet plan advisors relegated the task to a subprogram within the Environmental Management Program. Worse for the plan's relevance, the Kuna, independent of the management planning process, had worked out political solutions to manage squatters, thus sapping the management plan's utility even further. One final kick to the project involved the military government's poor relations with the Kuna that resulted in UNESCO never declaring the biosphere reserve, and thus never actually requiring a management plan.

Alas, because the plan focused so wholeheartedly on science, the junta of advisors did not include anyone who knew anything about organizational development. In fact, the advisors had assumed from the outset that the Kuna would somehow manage the program and plan implementation when finished, even though all planning team members were under contract for partial spans during the plan's development, and no donor had dedicated resources to developing an organization that could actually implement.

So within a few years, the entire program of which the management plan constituted a large component, ran out of money without any hungry seagulls, generated internal discord, could not follow up on commitments, could not define if the effort had been a temporary project or a permanent program or organization, did not systematize its internal decision making, could not straighten out lines of communication, became overly dependent on external advisors for the entire process, including international contacts and donors, which left with the advisors. "And most of the outsiders who surveyed the institutional ruins of [the program] concluded that it had lost its status as a 'success' and had become, for reasons that weren't entirely clear, a 'failure,'" laments Chapin.

In the end, the Kuna not only never implemented the management plan, but never even completed it. By that point, the Kuna probably did not care anyway.

If we dive just a bit deeper and reflect on what causes these obstacles, we begin to see how RCP generates other barriers as well. These barriers deal with the human relationships necessary not just to complete a plan but indispensable for implementation as well. They deal with trust, ownership, and social capital, such as working relationships. All three are fundamental not only to conducting planning—particularly when constituencies distrust conservation organizations—but also when implementing plans over long-time horizons that protected area plans usually require (Lachapelle and McCool 2005, 2011; Nkhata et al. 2008).

When the Thinking Stops

We expect RCP to function effectively in a world of diversifying expectations on protected areas; several of us (McCool et al. 2013) wrote that society now expects protected areas to be all things to all people, ranging from protecting attractive landscapes to becoming engines of economic development to reversing the loss of heritage. At the same time, these goals occur within a world of change, uncertainty, and frequent contention. Planning in this context requires mental models that not only simplify it so we can work effectively but also provide useful insights and encourage us to learn. In a sense, we need mental models, paradigms, and assumptions that empower planners to think and act creatively (Toolbox 2).

Ironically, Technical Rationality's very emphasis on individual capacity and rationality can disempower technicians in a planning process. Because technical staff come to rely so heavily on professional expertise and standard practices, they may stop thinking about what they are doing and instead depend not only on direct expert intervention but also on those protocols, templates, formulas, blueprints, and recipes that experts have kindly provided for the rest of us[5].

Even the experts may stop reflecting and fall into habits where learning winds to a halt. Schön notes (p. 69),

> Many practitioners, locked in a view of themselves as technical experts, find nothing in the world of practice to occasion reflection. They have become too skillful at techniques of selective inattention, junk categories, and situational control, techniques which they use to preserve the constancy of their knowledge-in-practice. For them, uncertainty is a threat; its admission is a sign of weakness. Others, more inclined toward and adept at reflection-in-action, nevertheless feel profoundly uneasy because they cannot say what they know how to do, cannot justify its quality or rigor.

Stanley Arguedas (pers. comm. 2009), technical coordinator for the Latin American School for Protected Areas in Costa Rica, recounts a vivid example. When he was in Brazil organizing a network of protected area planners, he shared with them his experience facilitating management plans in five protected areas mentioned earlier in the Osa Peninsula of southern Costa Rica. The Brazilians asked him how long on average it took him and stakeholders in Osa to create their management plans. Stanley answered six months and added that that length of time depended on those particular conditions. Later Stanley discovered that the Brazilian planners had actually chopped out part of their projected planning process so that the duration would fall in line with Stanley's "expert time prescription." Stanley was shocked at how deep their need for expert recipes had sunk.

The thirst for recipes among time-challenged and overloaded protected area managers is never quenched. Manuals—which this book is not—provide easy-to-follow step-by-step instructions rather than emphasize critical thinking, learning, and understanding. Managers want the "magic number" they assume, for example, that carrying capacity provides. "Just give me a number," they request. Stand-alone manuals are the ultimate reductionist tool, and heritage management agencies from North America to the southern seas continue to publish them.

Dig at the roots of bureaucracy and you will find Technical Rationality, too. Bureaucracies are hives of interlocking professional niches where one technocrat passes data and results to others for further processing. Each person along the chain of protocol expects data to arrive in a predictable format and at a predictable moment, so he or she can process that information and then pass it on to the next stop.

Toolbox 2 | *Mind Mapping—Uncovering Our Mental Models*

We know we have mental models that help us function with all aspects of human life, including managing protected areas. But much of the time they remain hidden in the psyche, invisible to us and especially to others. These mental models, though, embody critical assumptions about how things work, but they may be wrong and inaccurate. So how do we reveal and describe our mental models so that we can make them both public and better? One tool that uncovers the hidden ideas is mind mapping.

Buzan (1993) describes a mind map as a visual representation of how an individual or group relates different concepts or variables to a central concept or idea. Users create a mind map by first identifying a central concept and then the ideas that radiate outwards from this central concept. Eventually, the mind map demonstrates how an individual or group perceives a particular concept, the important ideas influencing that concept, and the relationships between them.

Users can create mind maps simply with paper and pen, or with specially designed software that depicts how concepts relate to each other in ways that trace the outlines of mental models. An example is provided by Mosimane et al. (2013) who used mind-mapping exercises to characterize underlying mental models of human-wildlife conflict in Namibia. An abbreviated version of one such mind map is shown in Figure 2.1. The mind map depicts a mental model of human wildlife conflict that is quite sophisticated, showing that many variables affect the presence, and therefore, management of conflict.

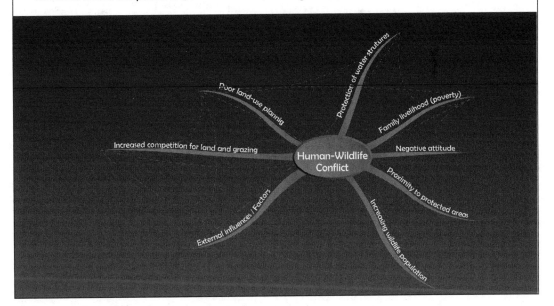

Figure 2.1 | *Simplified Version Of A Mind Map*

The PLUS World Underpins Rational Comprehensive Planning

The grand architect of science, Francis Bacon, knew that with the power of the mind, we could eventually unlock nature's secrets. His fellow Enlightenment thinkers rallied around the idea that science could tame nature and carry humanity up, up, and away. For science to have such potential to overcome nature and overcome society's social and environmental problems, Enlightenment thinkers' RCP descendants must make certain assumptions in their mental model of how the world works. In this world, planners must believe that the world yields its secrets to the prying rational mind; the world behaves courteously while planners conduct their scientific experiments; the world waits patiently while planners deliberate the best way forward; the world pitches balls over the plate every time with no curves, sinkers, or off-speed throws; and the world kindly respects conclusions that planners draw.

This unlikely world we call the PLUS World, our acronym for the assumptions made by conventional planning.

This World Is **P**redictable—Characterized by the Potential to Be Forecast or Foreseen

Isaac Newton, perhaps the Enlightenment's most famous name, demonstrated that if we have enough information about a bouncing ball—its material composition, its angle of approach, its velocity, its mass—we can calculate exactly where and when the ball will bounce. Newton's three Laws of Motion provided the basis for classical mechanics. Predictability is enhanced when we function within tightly coupled systems—where A always causes B, and the only cause of B is A. And the time between cause and effect is relatively short. Thus, light emanating from the Sun takes only eight minutes to arrive at the Earth's surface. Because of that knowledge we know that any solar storm sending out rays of whatever type may disrupt earthly communications in the same eight minutes.

In short, the more we know, the better we can predict. Since management and master plans often last five, ten, or even twenty years, planners must predict toward those time horizons. When there is some understanding of the complicated character of a heritage site, planners will want even more data to develop baselines from which they can craft their predictions. No wonder planners spend so much time and money collecting data before they start creating alternative pathways to the future.

Consider the 2009 management plan (Young et al. 2009) for England's Stonehenge World Heritage Site. It contains 202 pages. Of those, half is background information while only 22 percent contains actual prescriptions. The ratio of background data to actual planning leans heavily toward data.

Predictability also manifests as step-by-step cause-and-effect processes. A leads to B leads to C. I drink water, I feel the urge to go to the bathroom, I go. Easy; straightforward like a line. In reality, however, effects often go back and affect causes, making systems less predictable than they might at first appear. If for example I feel an oncoming urge to go (B), I may cut back on how much I drink (A), changing when I would have gone (C). This is a feedback. And usually multiple causes generate any effect. The kind of beverage (D) affects how much I drink (A) and the kind of beverage such as beer (D) can also affect how much I go to the bathroom (C).

This World Is Linear—Characterized by the Effect/Output Being Directly Proportional to the Cause

Euclid said, "Let it be demanded that from every point to every point a straight line be drawn." He had no idea, though, of the path down which his linearity would take civilization. Today we understand linearity as a given amount of cause generating a given amount of effect. You kick your toe against a wall and it hurts. If you double the force that you kick your toe, expect the pain to double, too. A little bit of global warming will increase the temperature (sea rise, hurricane intensity, crop losses, etc.) a little bit. A little more global warming will increase those things a little more.

Of course toe smashing and global warming do not work that way. Global warming thresholds work more like bending a stick. You add a little force and the stick bends a little; add a little more force and the stick bends a little more; add a little more force, and suddenly the stick snaps with a completely new behavior and ends in a completely new state disproportional to the little bit of extra force you last added. This is the breaking point, tipping point, point of no return, the threshold at which something very nonlinear occurs, beyond which normally there is no going back. In fact, true linear relationships in nature are very rare.

Forecasts can be made in different ways. One way looks at historical trends about each use. For example, if sand and gravel mining has expanded an average 2 percent each year for the past ten years (= historical trend), your projection for the next fifteen (= time frame for planning) can be that sand and gravel mining is likely to expand at the same rate of 2 percent each year (= projection) (Ehler and Douvere 2009).[6]

RCP also tends to use linear tools and reasoning to solve problems. Tourism carrying capacity, for example, is a very popular linear tool. It assumes that with each additional person who enters a site, a fixed, incremental amount of impact (trail erosion, graffiti, noise, visitor dissatisfaction, etc.) results. Two people create twice as much impact as one. Scientists thus can calculate the number of people-impacts allowed—the site's capacity—before the resource degrades.

An example of using carrying capacity is the Sabarimala Temple in India, the second largest pilgrimage destination in the world, attracting more than 50 million Hindus every year. Because it suffers high levels of congestion, India's Center for Earth Science Studies proposed to estimate visitor carrying capacity in its master plan (Sasidharan 2002).

The mathematics of linearity, step-by-step protocols, and proportional relationships between simple cause and effect are so much easier to deal with and much more well behaved for a management plan that will not be updated for several years. Or so we would like to believe.

This World Is Understandable—Characterized by Being Discernible or Comprehensible

Again, we owe gratitude to another of the Enlightenment's greatest thinkers, René Descartes. In his *Discourse on the Method*, he introduced the notion of reductionism. If we take a complex problem—say, how to decrease deforestation—all we have to do is break the problem down into its component physical parts, study and understand these parts, and then put them back together to understand the whole. This has worked well for machines and technology.

In the PLUS World, then, everything is ultimately understandable, and our only limitations to understanding the world are resources: time, money, personnel, and data. Again, as Bacon reminds, if we think hard enough and apply quality science, eventually we can decipher all of nature's secrets. In the case of Sabarimala, the researcher broke down visitor impact into its component parts in order to understand and calculate carrying capacity. The study says,

> The master plan includes aspects related to pilgrim management, development of base camps and transit facilities and the land use–transportation linkages and incorporates latest technological and economically feasible solutions wherever possible. It also analyses the infrastructure requirements, physical and social amenities and services required to support the pilgrimage, land/development

management strategies at Pampa and Sannidhanam, development models for built spaces, implementation and monitoring plan and options on phasing, resource mobilization, disaster management and institutional mechanism to oversee regional development.

Does all this really identify and help understand what it is that a pilgrimage to Sabarimala is all about? And, how do we protect that experience?

This World Is Stable—Characterized by Being Able or Likely to Continue

In a stable world, conditions do change, but seemingly slowly. For planning that means we can assume that conditions under which we plan today will still exist when plans expire. Alternately, because the world is predictable and linear we can easily project those conditions into the future. Some plans take full advantage of this optimistic stability, such as Indonesia's Komodo National Park, which has a twenty-five-year management plan to be implemented in five-year segments. The master plan for Sabarimala, approved in 2007, also has a near-term phase until 2015 and a long-term phase that ends in 2050.

Stability also allows us to plan on "balances." We depend on a balance of nature, balance of local and national interests, and a balance between development and preservation. In a stable world, our plans can help establish these balances, but the notion of balance also assumes some opposition or conflict that can be easily addressed, through win-win solutions.

A stable world, one that behaves nicely, means we do not have to worry about surprises, unanticipated consequences, unforeseen side effects. In a stable world, learning can take its time because change and uncertainty are concepts of little concern. As stability has been correlated with plan success (Bryson and Bromiley 1993), little wonder the PLUS view holds strong appeal.

Ironically, the PLUS World planning process has not as yet served well the pilgrims to Sabarimala. Devotees still must wait for many hours to move through the site, which does not provide proper facilities. The ombudsman for the implementing boards has testified before a court that the master plan needs to create a monitoring committee "because the implementation of the master plan for Sabarimala was at a snail's pace."

The PLUS Paradigm Dominates How We Think

The reader should not assume that PLUS only applies to planning, as most people today still live in the PLUS World. To their credit, the world was once more PLUS—before globalization, rapid advances in technology, and the modern age. Our forebears for a very long time expected only that their kids' future resemble their own present experience. Those times had fewer social connections, simpler systems, and greater stability.

Today, people still behave in a PLUS manner with great frequency. We blame single actors in the system when something goes wrong: Who is responsible for the economic recession of 2008? Which countries are most responsible for climate change? Who created ISIS? Site managers and conservationists too frequently blame single persons or institutions such as local hunters, farmers, and looters, often ignoring cultural norms and the larger socio-economic systems and their structures which influence their behavior.

We build hierarchical and subdivided organizations with the hope that a well-behaved world allows all technocrats to coordinate like clockwork, and then we are surprised when governments cannot seem to solve even small problems. Our schools teach subjects with fragmented curricula, and we still debate whether environmental education should be its own topic or integrated with every topic. We teach our kids to think linearly in school, diminishing their natural systems thinking potential (Sterman 2000).

PLUS-based Technical Rationality fills our cabinets, computers, and heads with formulas, recipes, procedures, templates, and forms to fill out. We tend to offer simple solutions to complex problems or only treat symptoms of deeper problems, such as using aspirin to treat headaches we contract the morning after; we estimate a visitor carrying capacity by considering square meters of space per visitor; forest fires can be suppressed; we can use the past ten years of budgets to predict what money will be available for plan implementation in the future.

However, under very rare conditions, some problems do fit the PLUS World. Forester (1989) tells us which conditions we need for "comprehensive unbounded rationality" (essentially PLUS) to work: we need a rational actor in a room that represents the entire system, working on a well-defined problem, who has perfect information, infinite time, and a practical strategy to optimize or solve an algorithm or develop a technique. He goes on to say (p. 28), "Even technical problems that can be solved with standard methods exist amid conflicting interpretations and interest, established power, and excluded segments of the population—all of which inevitably limit the efficacy of purely technical solutions."

A New Paradigm Is Brewing

The costs of plan failure are not simply measured in damage to a protected area's heritage. Costs accrue to the people impacted by the area—whether counted in loss of potential jobs, or in services and materials an ecosystem may provide—and to the managing agency as well, not just in terms of loss of money poorly spent, but in terms of political credibility and legitimacy. These costs add up to increasingly jaded publics, suspicious constituencies, and politicians increasingly reluctant to find funding for plans. So, failures provide one crack in the hull, but the costs equate to breached bulkheads.

Meanwhile, another world paradigm brews like a storm. Growing waves wash some people overboard, some abandon ship, while others will go down with the ship. The PLUS ship, however, will not sink because of waves; it will sink because of a growing crack in its hull. Evidence of the new paradigm pours in through this crack. All sectors of society now find themselves in a value war between those who prefer the world to be structured, ordered, rational, and well-behaved (for the original formulation of rational planning, see Simon 1945), and those who see a different world emerging.

Physics

The PLUS stalwarts assume the world to be well-behaved and simple in order to maintain their professional status and privilege. They do this despite theories of relativity, chaos, complexity, quantum mechanics, and systems dynamics—none of which hold any allegiance to the PLUS World. The new paradigm envisions a universe in constant change, too complex and subtle to ever be completely understood by mere mortals.

Medicine

PLUS doctors prefer to cut the body into component parts and then treat those parts—that is, symptoms rather than root causes. We take medicine to suppress high blood pressure, even though the medicine only expands blood vessels rather than attends the root cause of the problem. Then we take other medicines to treat the side effects of the high blood pressure medicine. PLUS or allopathic doctors also prefer to fix the body-machine after it is broken (Culbert 1997). The new paradigm, however, welcomes alternative medicine, preventive medicine, and treatment of the entire body as a system—mind and body—rather than as a material machine without spirit.

Spirituality

PLUS advocates prefer a world without spirituality. Their explanations tend to be simple and materialistic, based on the power of the rational mind. The new paradigm, however, sees a world that goes beyond the material and includes much that humans cannot see, touch, and, at times, comprehend. It includes invisible forces, other planes of existence, and an interior dimension that interacts with the material world It also includes a whole new way of seeing (Outside the Box 2.1).

Environment

PLUS planners see a world that can be controlled with human knowledge and rationality. They hope to bioengineer their way out of environmental problems. In the new paradigm, heritage managers recognize they cannot fully know the world. Its behavior is beyond their ability to control, and at best it is only partially manageable. That balance of nature, if it ever existed, has given way to nonequilibrium ecosystem behavior, complex social-ecological systems, nonlinear dynamics, and accelerating climate change.

Ethics

In the simpler world, the strong, intelligent, rational, competitive, and initiative takers thrived. Those who did not enjoy these capacities or did not use them justifiably lost in the PLUS World. In the new paradigm, though, everyone—even the dispossessed, infirm, and lazy—have rights.

Leadership

In a PLUS world, leaders command from atop the hierarchy. They are worth more because they know more and do more. They send instructions down the chain of command. In the new paradigm, leaders facilitate communication, promote people's performance, and enhance an organization's learning and innovation. Those on the front line have different but equally important roles to play, as do executives.

Protected Areas

PLUS managers see protected areas as means to protect biological and cultural resources from the ravages of surrounding populations. The new paradigm broadens those functions to include gene banks, cauldrons of evolutionary development, models of democratic governance, engines of economic development, strategies to alleviate poverty, places to inspire, places to create spiritual meaning, incubators of managerial innovation, and stores to provide ecosystem services.

Schön comments on the limits of Technical Rationality (1983, p. 40): "Increasingly we have become aware of the importance to actual practice of phenomena—complexity, uncertainty, instability, uniqueness, and value-conflict—which do not fit the model of Technical Rationality. Now, in the light of the Positivist origins of Technical Rationality, we can more readily see why these phenomena are so troublesome."

The crack in the hull means we must discard a world that is predictable, linear, understandable, and stable: PLUS. It does not apply anymore, if in fact it ever did. Technological change grows exponentially, not linearly. In the twenty-first century, we will not experience a hundred years of progress as Kurzweil (2004) describes:

> It will be more like 20,000 years of progress (at today's rate). The "returns," such as chip speed and cost-effectiveness, also increase exponentially. There's even exponential growth in the rate of exponential growth. Within a few decades, machine intelligence will surpass human intelligence, leading to The Singularity—technological change so rapid and profound it represents a rupture in the fabric of human history. The implications include the merger of biological and non-biological intelligence, immortal software-based humans, and ultra-high levels of intelligence that expand outward in the universe at the speed of light.

Outside the Box 2 | *The Power to Transcend Paradigms*

The late systems scientist Donella Meadows identified a number of places where one could find leverage in a system in a paper entitled (1999), "Leverage Points: Places to Intervene in the System." In this paper she outlines, from a systems perspective, how the deeper you go in a system, the more leverage you will muster to change that system. Of her twelve points, she writes that the deepest of all is the power to transcend paradigms altogether. The following passage comes from that paper.

There is yet one leverage point that is even higher than changing a paradigm. That is to keep oneself unattached in the arena of paradigms, to stay flexible, to realize that no paradigm is "true," that everyone, including the one that sweetly shapes your own worldview, is a tremendously limited understanding of an immense and amazing universe that is far beyond human comprehension. It is to "get" at a gut level the paradigm that there are paradigms, and to see that that itself is a paradigm, and to regard that whole realization as devastatingly funny. It is to let go into Not Knowing, into what Buddhists call enlightenment.

But, in fact, everyone who has managed to entertain that idea, for a moment or for a lifetime, has found it to be the basis for radical empowerment. If no paradigm is right, you can choose whatever one will help to achieve your purpose. If you have no idea where to get a purpose, you can listen to the universe (or put in the name of your favorite deity here) and do his, her, its will, which is probably a lot better informed than your will.

It is in this space of mastery over paradigms that people throw off addictions, live in constant joy, bring down empires, found religions, get locked up or "disappeared" or shot, and have impacts that last for millennia.

As the PLUS World Shakes, Rational Comprehensive Planning Shifts

By the mid-1960s, some of RCP's fundamental assumptions had already begun to erode. Many advocates had long believed, perhaps correctly for a time, that planners could find a consensus on the national interest. Certainly, during World War II, the national interest was laid bare for all to see as American battleships such as the *USS Arizona* burned and sank in Pearl Harbor. The 1960s, though, brought the baby boomers and age of flower power and peace rallies and environmental sit-ins and free love. Anything that might have resembled a national consensus on the public interest now crumbled into many special interest groups focused on justice, health, and environment.

Academics, too, turned on RCP to argue that in an increasingly uncertain world, a scientifically based, expert-driven planning approach simply did not seem to get plans implemented. Consequently, various branches of planning made conscious decisions, at least academically, to move away from central planning toward greater local participation, discussed later in this book (see Part II). The protected area community, however, remained quite comfortable with RCP, as it has to this day.

So are protected area planners really any different from other kinds of planners? Did they simply not read what planning academics were writing? Were their results superior to those of the urban, regional, and industrial planners? It could be argued that the protected areas field has suffered delays in transitioning to a new paradigm because of its traditional dominance by natural resource managers, such as biologists, ecologists, agronomists, and foresters, or by technical social scientists, such as archaeologists, architects, and art conservators. Applied biologists learn in college how to measure and study populations of nonhuman organisms. They learn to calculate carrying capacities for habitat, take censuses, control invasive species, manage nutrient loading, classify ecological zones, and increase forest basal area. The cultural technicians also employ high-tech analyses to measure monument degradation, calculate ancient human populations, and stabilize historical buildings. Perhaps now that protected areas count among their ranks increasing numbers of businesspeople, sociologists, educators, and multidisciplinary folks, RCP's loyal following will erode as well.

Despite academic warnings, RCP in practice remains the planning option of choice in many fields, heritage sites or otherwise. Professionals and technocrats of all stripes still run modern society with the allure of esoteric and privileged technical knowledge.

Even recently, RCP scuttled major planning endeavors. Only a few years back, China, in response to a crescendo of criticism against its environmental practices, declared that it would construct eco-cities, sustainable in almost every way. It would thus not only demonstrate its leadership in the new green economy but also create living space for its growing population, while reducing what have become plentiful and naked environmental disasters around its vast territory.

So the government proceeded to hire the best minds money could buy. In a 2009 article in *Yale Environment 360*, Christina Larson writes, "Mostly conceived by international architects, China's eco-cities were intended to be models of green urban design. But the planning was done with little awareness of how local people lived, and the much-touted projects have largely been scrapped."

Old paradigms die hard when deeply rooted; Rational Comprehensive Planning, Technical Rationality, and Positivism all draw sustenance through roots that penetrate much deeper even than any assumptions thus far discussed. They grow not just from assumptions about experts and their role in society but also from assumptions about the very nature of how the world—and the universe—works.

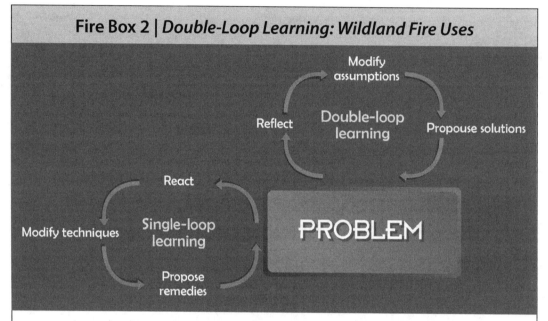

Fire Box 2 | *Double-Loop Learning: Wildland Fire Uses*

Reflect on mental models, beliefs, and assumptions and can subsequently change them.

Double-loop learners stop and reflect on their assumptions, beliefs, and underlying mental models, and thereby come to see the box they have built around themselves. They step outside of their reactive, single-loop routines to ask, "What are my assumptions here, anyway?" Their reflection can result in modifying their mental models (the assumptions about how something works) and thus see problem in a new light, opening up new possibilities and solutions.

Within the US land management community, small experiments and incendiary ideas about, perhaps, not smothering all fires appeared intermittently for decades, almost from the moment the suppression policy began. In the 1960s with the emergence of the ecosystem management paradigm—managing the entire ecological system rather than just parts, such as forest stands—the National Park Service launched official experiments. In 1968, the Park Service loosened its suppression policy, followed ten years later by the US Forest Service, after its first official experiment in 1972 at Bad Luck Creek in the Bitterroot wilderness in Montana. It was only a four-day, quarter-acre burn. But the policy's real test came that same season at Fitz Creek where the fire burned 1,600 acres over forty-three days. The Forest Service took a lot of heat from the public, but since no significant damage occurred, the policy stood like a tree, charred but not incinerated.

Perhaps the most dramatic incident in the evolving policy of fire management took place in 1988 when the National Park Service, based on a 1972 management plan, decided to allow several fires to burn in a remote corner of Yellowstone National Park. Dry conditions and high winds combined with multiple fire starters whipped up a conflagration that burned 1.4 million acres. Though the Park Service had to weather a firestorm of public attention, the landscape later showed vibrant regrowth, reconfirming the ecological benefits of fire.

American land agencies now recognize that fire offers a variety of benefits in ecosystems that naturally require fire, both in controlling costs to fight them and in developing forest resilience. When combined with prevention (fire-safe communities), preparation (evacuation plans, hazard fuel reduction, etc.), and suppression, fire managers are more prepared to use fire effectively. Each day, furthermore, research helps them to better understand how to manage fires both for today and the future.

In science, our assumptions or paradigm or worldview shape our questions.
Our questions shape our methods. Our methods then shape our answers
and our answers shape our theory.

—*Marilyn Schlitz*

CHAPTER 3

Changing Seas Threaten
the PLUS World

Some things cannot be spoken or discovered until we have been stuck, incapacitated, or blown off course for a while. Plain sailing is pleasant, but you are not going to explore many unknown realms that way.

—*David Whyte*

THE OTHER
SIDE OF
COMPLEXITY

EVENTS

PATTERNS

STRUCTURES

MENTAL MODELS

Beyond PLUS Lies a World That Was Always There

While many sites remain stubbornly mired in conventional assumptions about the world, some scholars and planners have boldly, and with little support, set sail toward new assumptions about a fresh world that looms just beyond park gates.

Schön (1983, p. 42) describes what we call in this book the PLUS World, as if it were highlands:

> There is a high, hard ground where practitioners can make effective use of research-based theory and technique, and there is a swampy lowland where situations are confusing "messes" incapable of technical solution. The difficulty is that the problems of the high ground, however great their technical interest, are often relatively unimportant to clients or to the larger society, while in the swamp are the problems of greater human concern. Shall the practitioner stay on the high, hard ground where he can practice rigorously, as he understands rigor, but where he is constrained to deal with problems of relatively little social importance? Or shall he descend to the swamp where he can engage the most important and challenging problems if he is willing to forsake technical rigor?

Certainly, the highlands, the PLUS World, offer us familiarity and an illusory sanctuary from the swampy and uncertain lowlands, where just deciphering a problem can daunt managers as much as trying to solve it. One of those swampy areas in planning is poverty, explored by Rittel and Webber (1973) to exemplify the "wickedness" of today's social problems. To conventional planners who prefer boundaries to be fixed, clear, and impermeable, poverty is of little concern, but to an increasing number of site managers it bangs on their front doors as they realize that the social welfare of inhabitants and neighbors can influence the success of a protected area. To "solve" poverty, though, first we must figure out what the heck the poverty problem is.

Does poverty mean low income? If so, what determines low income? Does poverty result from national and regional economic problems or cognitive and occupational skill deficiencies of those impoverished? If so, then the problem "solution" must include education. So wherein the educational system does the real problem lie? What does it mean to improve the system? Or, is poverty more a result of deficient physical and mental health? If so, we must search the health services field for a possible cause to poverty. Maybe we want to investigate geospatial, political, cultural, and social deficiencies instead? We can continue searching other areas for as long as we like. If we could actually define the problem by tracing it to some kind of cause—such that we can say, "Aha! That's the source of the difficulty," then we have also identified the solution. To find the problem is thus to find the solution.

According to Rittel and Webber, problems then in the swampy lowlands are actually "wicked problems," as opposed to "tame"—problems that can be clearly defined and solved like a mathematical equation and where everyone agrees what the problem is and what the goals should be. At best, Rittel and Webber note, we can only re-solve problems (coming to an agreement rather than an "answer") over and over again, not only because of their "ill-defined" character—lacking a consensus on how they are framed—but also because their context constantly changes, often in unpredictable ways.

In the highlands, we define and solve problems with discrete answers, whether landing on the moon, designing that bridge over the river, or balancing a museum budget. Innes and Booher (2010, p. 5) observe that "traditional linear methods relying primarily on formal expertise are being replaced by nonlinear socially constructed engaging both experts and stakeholders" because traditional processes no longer function effectively. In the lowlands, problems lurk at murkier depths, involving matters of social preferences and values. Rittel and Webber offer ten distinctions between wicked and tame problems:

1. *There is no definitive formulation of a wicked problem.* There is no consensus on how planners frame heritage protection, define poverty, describe sustainability, or characterize economic development.

2. *Wicked problems have no stopping rule.* In a chess match or solving a mathematical equation, the player or mathematician knows exactly when the match has finished and is solved. A site manager can never know exactly when the site has reached sustainability, surrounding communities cured of poverty, and endangered species sufficiently recovered and protected from all threats[7].

3. *Solutions to wicked problems are not true or false but instead more or less useful.* Visitor carrying capacity generates an apparently objective, discrete, "correct" number of people in order to avoid damage to resources (true) or a site can manage for an "incorrect" number (false). Yet one of visitor carrying capacity's fatal flaws is the belief that impact can be prevented. Visitors always leave an impact, and so we decide how much impact we find acceptable, making the solution more or less useful rather than right or wrong (Outside the Box 3.1).

4. *There is no immediate and no ultimate test of a solution to a wicked problem.* With tame problems, we know exactly how good the solution is: if we raise entrance fees by $2, then we generate X more revenue; if we pave a trail, we can measure exactly how much erosion we reduce; if we heighten a fence, we can see

that deer cannot jump into the regeneration area. "With wicked problems, on the other hand, any solution, after being implemented, will generate waves of consequences over an extended—virtually an unbounded—period of time." An education campaign increases awareness so that locals in India place greater value on Bengal tigers, but the campaign financing may reduce the number of park wardens. Managers invite reporters to the Historic Center of Sighişoara in Romania so they offer better coverage about a proposed Dracula theme park, but they also publish negative stories about its potential impact. Managers in Glacier National Park (US) write rules to reduce impacts from horses, but equestrian enthusiasts then ride into the adjacent Great Bear Wilderness and damage trails there.

5. *Every solution to a wicked problem is a "one-shot operation"; because there is no opportunity to learn by trial and error, every attempt counts significantly.* We cannot call microfinance loans back to the bank without effect; we cannot delete the educational campaign from people's memory; we cannot pretend that reporters never arrived. We can guess how to improve these interventions, but we will never know what would have happened had we done them differently or not at all.

6. *Wicked problems do not have an enumerable (or an exhaustively describable) set of potential solutions, nor is there a well-described set of permissible operations that may be incorporated into the plan.* Unfortunately, we cannot say only five possible solutions exist to poverty in the same way a chess master can say that there are only five possible stratagems to checkmate his or her opponent.

7. *Every wicked problem is essentially unique.* "Part of the art of dealing with wicked problems is the art of not knowing too early which type of solution to apply." Tame problems readily submit to established research protocols and prepackaged solutions; wicked problems resist them. While poachers afflict parks throughout the world, each location has a different history, culture, environment, target species, set of laws, actors, and other problems that also require treatment. Thus each case ultimately proves unique, linked only by common lessons and similar conditions.

8. *Every wicked problem can be considered a symptom of another problem.* We can consider wildlife poaching as a symptom of general moral decay, weak park enforcement, market demand, poverty, or whatever causal explanation most

excites us. The level at which we attack a problem depends on our self-confidence in understanding the problem and cannot be decided on logical grounds. That is, we can deal with ape bushmeat poachers in Gabon by intercepting them with armed patrols. We can improve their family diets so they do not need to hunt. We can strengthen the local economy so they have money to purchase food, reducing regional and international demand for bushmeat so no one will pay them to hunt. Or we transform the entire capitalist system so there is no market economy in which to sell bushmeat.

9. *The existence of a discrepancy representing a wicked problem can be explained in numerous ways. The choice of explanation determines the nature of the problem's resolution.* We can explain poaching by citing not enough park guards, too many criminal poachers, inadequate laws, too many loose military weapons, cultural deprivation, increasing demand, deficient opportunity, lazy livestock farmers, and so on. Each explanation demands a different strategy.

10. *The planner has no right to be wrong.* Scientists propose hypotheses that later other scientists shoot down. The scientific community does not punish scientists for proposing faulty hypotheses as long as they play by the rules of the scientific game. Wicked problems grant no such mercy for managers, whose goal is to improve conservation and resource use of protected areas. Managers must answer for any consequences their choices provoke. Every decision a manager makes affects different people who care very much about the consequences, such as the Cave Creek disaster in New Zealand's Paparoa National Park, where an inadequately constructed overlook collapsed under the weight of visitors, killing fourteen (*Commission of Inquiry into the Collapse of a Viewing Platform at Cave Creek Near Punakaiki on the West Coast* 1995). Consequently, New Zealand's park system implemented entirely new construction standards.

One thought as to why protected area planning around the world grows increasingly ineffectual is that planners operate as if they were in the PLUS highlands, viewing problems as tame and isolated events when in fact they are wicked, connected, and messy. Ackoff (1974) uses the term *messy* to apply to ill-structured problems lacking social consensus on their framing when he observes, "Every problem interacts with other problems and is therefore part of a set of interrelated problems."

Wicked and Messy Problems Are Part of a Larger System

As several of our examples have implied, and as Ackoff noted earlier, the problems we face are not isolated events. When we dive deeper along the iceberg we see that how one protected area is managed affects what happens in those nearby. What services a community offers impacts how tourists interact with a protected area. If Yellowstone National Park limits snowmobile use, then the economy of the town of West Yellowstone experiences the consequences of that choice. When Kruger National Park fails to repair the high voltage fence around it, elephants rampage through the holes to stomp on local villagers' crops. If the Ministry of Lands and Resettlement in Namibia designates some area as suitable for farming, then farmers may compete with wildlife.

These connections all mean, as Ackoff noted years ago, that "solutions to most problems cause other problems." In these situations, we need to recognize the basic interconnectedness of heritage sites—they are coupled to other sites, local, and even distant communities. They may be linked to central government, policies, and constituencies living continents away, such as the animal rights groups that forced the South African government to change its policy on elephant culling in parks.

Together these interactions create a system. A system is more than the sum of its parts, and as a result, it has properties that none of its parts do. For example, as Ackoff observes, a human body can write or run, but its individual parts, say a kidney or a finger, cannot; a brain can think and solve problems, but a neuron cannot; a historic monument's landscape provides opportunities for transformative experiences, but a single reflecting pool probably not. Systems contain other systems, moreover, linking problems in a massive, complex, interconnected whole. Because we are dealing with a system, we can only understand the parts if we understand how they connect to other parts—for instance, we can best describe the steering wheel of an automobile by describing how it relates to wheels and the hydraulic system and to the purpose of a car itself.

For heritage sites, we could say the following is not a list of unique problems:

- climate change

- economic instability

- pollution and consumption (hunting, fishing, growing)

- poverty

- criminality (violence, drug trafficking, tomb robbing)

- technological advances (bioengineering, genetic engineering, nanotechnology, robotics, and artificial intelligence)

- connectivity and political participation

- leadership and organization

- overpopulation

- political messiness

- peak oil sovereignty and management capacity of nation-states

- international security

- weakened ecosystems

- public perceptions and attitudes

- management paradigms

- human nutrition and health

This list rather is just one problem composed of variously nested or different facets of the same greater system. All these problems spin at different speeds and spaces, seen by observers using differently colored eyeglasses. As astrophysicist Stephen Hawking (1988, p. 11) said, "If everything in the universe depends upon everything else in a fundamental way, it might be impossible to get close to a full solution by investigating parts of the problem in isolation."

System components may be either tightly or loosely coupled. In tightly coupled systems, changes in one component directly relate to effects in another component, such that effects occur only after short delays: when we press the "A" key on a computer keyboard, the "A" appears immediately on the screen. If resource extraction occurs, we can see effects relatively quickly as resource users graze sheep, cut thatching grass, or harvest fish. When longer delays between causes and effects occur, when multiple causes lead to the same effects, or when great distances separate causes and effects we have a loosely coupled system (Weick 1976). When people harvest timber, graze sheep, or catch fish, other effects take a longer time to become visible, and we may find that these effects have other causes as well. Loosely coupled systems prove especially difficult to understand. So while we blame rhinoceros poaching on the market value of its horn, beliefs about sexual bolstering thanks to horn powder, who holds these beliefs and how strongly, how they express them, and the connection with a regional Asian horn distribution system are loosely coupled components of a complex system.

To understand a social-ecological system, composed of at least one biophysical and one human component, we build a mental model that depicts these components and their interactions. Anderies et al. (2004) have done just that (Figure 3.1). In the PLUS World, we build models to control and predict the system. In the wicked and messy twenty-first century, model building cultivates our understanding of how the system works; the benefit of modeling comes from the learning that arises through the modeling process (Sterman 2002)—more so than any predictability.

Figure 3.1 | *A Simplified Representation (Model) of a Complex Social-Ecological System (after Anderies et al. 2004)*

In this system, a protected area is represented by Box A. Arrows 1–6 represent positive and negative feedback loops that determine how the system functions and its resilience in the face of disturbances from outside the system, represented by Arrows 7 and 8. The "external" forces act upon resources (A), such as heritage values, but also on resource users (B)—constituencies—public infrastructure (D), and infrastructure providers (C). The number and character of relationships in a system lead to complexity and uncertainty.

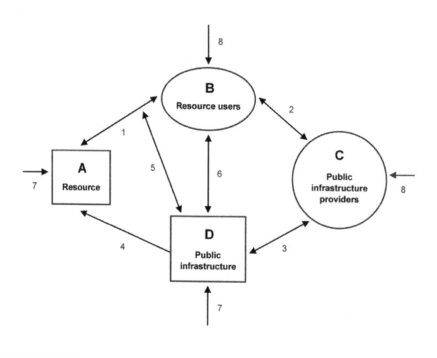

The model contains four major components: (1) the resource—the values, materials, and services provided by the biophysical system or the cultural values of a historical site; (2) resource users—the people who extract materials and services, such as a tour operator, from the system and the people who use those systems for recreation, spiritual, and cultural ends; (3) infrastructure—the physical, policy, and management infrastructure needed to facilitate and manage access to the area and extraction of materials and services; and (4) infrastructure providers—government and NGOs that plan and manage the heritage area, other agencies with jurisdiction, legislatures, and parliaments that develop use policies for the area. These four components connect through various and principally loosely coupled relationships and feedback loops. The whole system is embedded within larger social-ecological systems.

For example, Etosha National Park (the resource) is managed by the Namibia Ministry of Environment and Tourism (infrastructure provider) under policies established by the Namibian Parliament and the Minister's office (infrastructure provider). The park contains numerous roads and rest camps (infrastructure) so that visitors (resource users) may enjoy viewing wildlife (resource). Levels of visitation, however, are influenced by larger-scale systems, such as the global financial system, which has its own four components. Changes anywhere in the system—such as the US Millennium Challenge Corporation granting money to the ministry for construction of a new lodge—changes other elements, such as visitor use patterns. The new lodge, a response to an economic development problem, creates new challenges for infrastructure and infrastructure providers, as more automobile use on roads now creates a demand for higher levels of road maintenance, increases potential for collisions between wildlife and automobiles, and requires upgrading and staffing of an entrance point.

Because the system links several different levels, changes in the larger social-ecological system percolate down to impact processes at lower scales and vice versa. For example, growing affluence in the West enables the public to travel more, thus becoming exposed to a variety of heritage and cultural values in the East, enhancing their awareness of ecosystem-based services, and how past political events shape today's newspaper headlines. These lessons in turn affect values, beliefs, and priorities, sometimes resulting in political pressures to change public policy on heritage protection. Such changes precipitate new demands, mental models, policies, and management actions. Coupling is very loose, however, which makes understanding the system elusive.

Relationships (Arrows 1–6 in Figure 3.1) among subsystems shape structure and function of social-ecological systems. Changes in one component, such as use limits at the Alhambra World Heritage Site in Granada, Spain, inevitably lead to changes in other components, such as the lodging and transportation infrastructure.

Social-ecological systems are impacted by processes and decisions occurring at larger scales, both biophysical (Arrow 7) and in public infrastructure and social-economic conditions (Arrow 8). What happens in the larger context does matter.

Ecology connects with society through information, energy, and material flows. Changing climate therefore affects distribution of vegetation, which in turn affects not only efforts to protect rare plant species but also food availability. These influence how society responds and adapts—sometimes through mitigation, sometimes with adaptation, sometime not at all. Many civilizations, such as the Maya, collapsed because they did not respond well enough to change.

This model of a social-ecological system is of course an extreme simplification. Yet simplification helps our minds deal with a complex world rather than collapse in frustration, enabling us to function effectively, whether just getting through the day, constructing a plan for a cultural landscape, or figuring out how to reduce rhino poaching. When we simplify, of course, we make mistakes, sometimes ignoring important variables or discounting significant social or ecological processes. As complexity communicator Juergen Appelo has argued (2011), "You can try to simplify a system to make it understandable, but you cannot linearize the system to make it predictable."

From the Lowlands, Another World Challenges PLUS

According to Kuhn (1962), in order to overthrow a paradigm in science, the paradigm must face a competitor. Otherwise, guardians of the old paradigm simply twist its rules and arguments to explain away all anomalies. Fortunately, the PLUS highlands have an overwhelming adversary. That adversary comes from the swampy lowlands. It is a world that has always existed but has never been seen, even by those who lived there. It is emerging, however, through exploration and discovery, and, as luck would have it, this world behaves very differently from the PLUS World because it can better describe and integrate wicked problems and messy situations. Enter the DICE World. As with the PLUS World, this acronym's initials correspond to principal assumptions of the paradigm. Also, of course, the name is only a placeholder to represent the full gamut of traits that distinguish this new place (Inside the Box 3.1).

Inside the Box 3 | *Difficulty of Managing Wildlife in Yellowstone National Park*

The same swampy lowland difficulty occurs in managing wildlife. The late science-fiction thriller novelist Michael Crichton, author of *Jurassic Park* and *Congo*, gave a speech (2005) based on his research for his controversial book, *State of Fear* (controversial to environmentalists at least who did not like his criticism of them for ignoring complex systems). Crichton described the challenges of managing wildlife at protected areas, Yellowstone in particular (quotes below are Crichton's).

Despite Yellowstone being the most precious gem in America's national parks crown; 809,000 hectares with a long, storied history; one set aside in 1872 by President Ulysses S. Grant as the first formal nature preserve in the world; one lauded by John Muir and President Teddy Roosevelt alike, Yellowstone was not preserved.

> On the contrary, it was altered beyond repair in a matter of years. By 1934, the National Park Service acknowledged in a report on wildlife management in national parks that white-tailed deer, cougar, lynx, wolf, and possibly wolverine and fisher are gone from the Yellowstone fauna.

The National Park Service, according to Crichton, did not acknowledge that it was solely responsible for the disappearance of these animals. For decades park rangers had been illegally shooting them. Supposedly they believed their understanding to transcend "any mere law" (Crichton's words).

To understand what happened requires tracing the problem back to the 1890s when park folks believed that elk were headed to extinction. Thus they fed and protected them, and their population exploded. By 1914, 35,000 elk romped in the park. The park also introduced and encouraged rainbow trout, a good recreational species that crowded out the native cutthroats. Bears, moose, and bison increased in numbers. But even President Roosevelt in 1915 expressed concern that the elk not only romped but overgrazed.

Eventually antelope and deer declined, and the elk overgrazed aspen and willow to the point where they could not regenerate. To compensate for lost grazers, rangers killed predators, without public knowledge.

> They eliminated the wolf and cougar and were well on their way to getting rid of the coyote. Then a national scandal broke out; studies showed that it wasn't predators

that were killing the other animals. It was overgrazing from too many elk. The management policy of killing predators had only made things worse.

As predators disappeared by 1930, so did the once plentiful aspen trees, which the beavers needed to make dams. Without dams, meadows dried out in summertime, stressing and eventually eliminating yet more animals.

Some sighed relief when in the 1960s rangers had sightings of wolves coming back. Persistent rumors, however, alleged that rangers were trucking them in. In either case, the wolves vanished again. Without beavers, their populations could not be sustained. Soon the Park Service decided to prove that the elk numbers were not responsible for park problems, "even though they were." A decade-long public relations campaign ensued during which time bighorn sheep also virtually disappeared.

In the 1970s, bears became a problem as did litigation threats. So rangers shipped grizzlies to remote areas of the park where they quickly became endangered. At first, the park would not let scientists study them, but once listed as endangered, they went in.

Sneaking in wolves did not work either, so the Park Service officially brought them back to the protests of local ranchers. With this Crichton concludes:

> As the story unfolds, it becomes impossible to overlook the cold truth that when it comes to managing 2.2 million acres of wilderness, nobody since the Indians has had the faintest idea how to do it. And nobody asked the Indians, because the Indians managed the land very intrusively. The Indians started fires, burned trees and grasses, hunted the large animals, elk and moose, to the edge of extinction. White men refused to follow that practice, and made things worse.

> To solve that embarrassment, everybody pretended that the Indians had never altered the landscape. These "pioneer ecologists," as Steward Udall called them, did not do anything to manipulate the land. But now academic opinion is shifting again, and the wisdom of the Indian land management practices is being discovered anew.

> Now, if we are to do better in this new century, what must we do differently? In a word, we must understand complex systems.

This World Is Dynamic—Characterized by Continuous Change, Activity That Is Nonlinear or Discontinuous

The DICE World makes life for PLUS-based planners exponentially difficult. The DICE World never stays still. Even when things appear stable, on some time scale they change dynamically. Dynamic change is nonlinear, discontinuous—even revolutionary in some ways. Science does not evolve in a predictable manner. For instance, Copernicus's notion of heliocentrism did not slowly evolve among scientists of the time but rather was an inspiration, a bolt of lightning. $E=MC^2$ was a complete break from the Newtonian physics of the past.

One reason changes can occur quickly is because small changes in one factor can lead to large changes in another. For example, a ball placed at the top of a hill may roll down one side or another depending on tiny grass tufts at the peak. A slight change in the chemical composition of the sealing cement in an oil drill rig in the American Gulf of Mexico in 2010 led to the Deepwater Horizon oil spill, the most devastating environmental disaster in the country's history. Nonlinear change is less predictable and often involves discontinuities, leading to unintended consequences, or "surprises." Similarly, human populations can overshoot and collapse. In the ancient Easter Island (a World Heritage site in Chile), local people completely deforested the once biologically rich island, and the lack of anchoring tree roots then caused soil erosion. The tree loss also allowed for both increased ground wind speed and more rain to hit the soil, which worsened erosion yet again. As soil eroded, food production dropped and streams dried out, further reducing production. Without logs, residents could no longer move their famous statues. And, because people crafted much of their fishing equipment from wood, fishing production dropped off, reducing food supply even more and eventually kicking off a precipitous die-off of Easter Island humans. Human population peaked around 10,000 people in 1600, but as natural systems degraded, all tree species went extinct, people reverted to violence and cannibalism, and perhaps 2,000 people remained by 1786. By 1972, only 111 people remained. More contemporary explanations for the population plummet include European slave raids and a subsequent smallpox epidemic also brought by the Europeans[8].

As mentioned in chapter 2, exponential growth, one form of change, can start slow and then explode way beyond anything planners could have imagined. When insect pest populations, such as locusts, are not controlled at an early stage, almost overnight their population can blow up and cause tremendous damage to vegetation. For example, during massive plagues, desert locusts can appear over a land area of nearly 30 million square kilometers in Africa—comprising more than 20 percent of Earth's land surface.

Yet exponential growth is one of the simplest behaviors of changing systems in the DICE World. More complicated systems overshoot and collapse, too. That same plague of locusts over Africa can devastate vegetation for millions of hectares, overshooting the land's capacity to support its airborne invaders, and without food, their population collapses with a massive insect die-off. To avoid collapse, the horde must quickly invade new areas.

Systems can also suffer repeated booms and busts, such as the business cycle and real estate markets. This happens when delays in feedback cause overcompensation in one way and then another, often never reaching a stable equilibrium. For example, when you want to take a shower at a friend's house with old plumbing, you start by turning the shower knob to give a moderate amount of hot water. After a little while, though, the water still is not even warm. So you increase the hot water … and then again. Suddenly scalding water pours over your shoulders and back. You scream, and frantically spin the hot water knob several times. As hot water fails to subside, you turn it down again. Then after a few moments, the water turns icy cold, you scream again, and the cycle starts over, until you either decide simply to apply extra deodorant or, with strength of will, understand the system delay, increase your patience, and reduce your overcompensation to eventually arrive at an acceptable temperature.

Perhaps one of the most famous oscillating biological systems occurs at Isle Royale National Park, a series of islands in the northwest portion of Lake Superior, between Michigan (where the park is located) and Canada. A population dynamics study between wolf and moose there celebrated fifty years in 2008. Because of the island's relative isolation, scientists have had a clear example of an oscillating predator-prey relationship. Using PLUS assumptions, they initially believed that the ecological system would eventually reach a stable equilibrium between wolves and moose, but that never happened. Rather, populations have fluctuated wildly and nonlinearly. A third crucial species, the balsam fir, the moose's main food, complicates the dynamics. When moose overeat fir, its population crashes. This precipitates a crash in the wolf population, eventually creating a bouncing seesaw effect (Vucetich and Peterson 2012).

Tipping points, thresholds, and discontinuities also characterize dynamic, nonlinear systems. A tipping point occurs when slow growth suddenly alters behavior from rare to rapidly and dramatically more common. It could be the moment that a certain kind of clothing popularity takes off such as the Hush Puppy shoes in the United States (as detailed in Malcolm Gladwell's 2002 book, *The Tipping Point*) in the mid-1990s or when a disease suddenly explodes as when Ebola erupted in West Africa in 2014. A threshold for elephant populations in parts of Africa may be reached when they overgraze baobab trees. In terms of climate change, scientists argue that, in another five to ten years, if we do not seriously reduce greenhouse gas emissions, we may shoot beyond a tipping point where climate change transforms into a new behavior (rapid heating acceleration, possibly even a global cooling, or other scenarios) totally beyond human control. This new scenario would alter the species composition of most parks as we currently know and love them.

This World Is Impossible to Completely Understand— Characterized by Not Being Easily Comprehended, Mysterious

Isaac Asimov, in his science fiction Foundation series (2004) describes the fictional science of psychohistory which posits that probability statistics applied to millions and millions of people can predict with great precision future historical events, such as growth and conquest.

As Asimov showed, this science requires PLUS assumptions: the universe is predictable, linear, understandable, and to some extent stable. A powerful psychic eventually violated all these assumptions. He could manipulate human emotions, which he used to forcibly convert people to his desire to conquer the galaxy. This allowed him to disrupt psychohistorical predictions by invalidating the assumption that human emotional responses to stimuli will remain the same. Thus, this ultimate experiment in PLUS predictability eventually succumbed to the uncertainty of the DICE World. Indeed, a changing context injects great uncertainty and drives changes to plans which is a factor leading to plan failure (Turner and Cochrane 1993).

Another threat to PLUS-based planning is that most knowledge is tentative—theories are not permanent, cause-effect relationships are often influenced by factors that we have not yet observed, what once seemed to work no longer does. For example, American foresters thought by aggressively suppressing all wildland fires—even those ignited by lightning—forests would be safer and wood supplies secured. What we found later, however, is that fires got bigger, more expensive to control, and fighting them became riskier because fire behavior grew in intensity as a result of more fuel accumulating on the forest floor.

We conveniently overlook that our minds can only comprehend very simple systems containing just a few variables. Therefore, we create mental models of systems to better comprehend them. Yet many learning barriers stand in the way of our mental models. Most of us have poor inquiry skills; we exhibit numerous defensive routines; we hold extraordinary overconfidence in the veracity of our own opinions; and debilitating misconceptions about systems including specifically delays, complexity, feedbacks, stocks and flows, and diverse system behaviors serve to confound learning.

We expect to see effects of our actions within a short period—say a few years—and we expect those effects to appear conveniently before our gazing eyes. Yet delays in fact characterize systems, as we have observed earlier: the climatic heating we feel today may originate with contamination emitted decades ago, and the emissions we discharge today could very well contribute to sea-level rise on the other side of the planet in future decades. Spatial discontinuities abound: the mass production of corn in the United States runs local Mexican farmers out of business; cars in Europe demand oil extracted from Nigeria where oil companies have run indigenous tribes off their land; and the flapping of a butterfly's wings in Brazil can set off tornados in Texas (or so the metaphor goes).[9]

Even if we could fully understand a system in any given moment, as soon as we attempt to intervene, we automatically change it, often irreversibly. As Rittel and Webber (1973, p.163) remind us,

> With wicked planning problems, however, every implemented solution is consequential. It leaves "traces" that cannot be undone. One cannot build a freeway to see how it works, and then easily correct it after unsatisfactory performance. Large public works are effectively irreversible, and the consequences they generate have long half-lives. Many people's lives will have been irreversibly influenced, and large amounts of money will have been spent—another irreversible act. The same happens with most other large-scale public works and with virtually all public-service programs. The effects of an experimental curriculum will follow the pupils into their adult lives. Whenever actions are effectively irreversible and whenever the half-lives of the consequences are long, every trial counts. And every attempt to reverse a decision or to correct for the undesired consequences poses another set of wicked problems, which are in turn subject to the same dilemmas.

Thus, it is not only very difficult to understand wicked problems, but it may very well be impossible to understand them deeply. Even if we could understand some aspect, it would change soon enough anyway. As Heraclitus said, "There is nothing permanent, except change."

Having said that, once we do integrate inherent uncertainty into our daily thinking and planning, we can plan and manage for uncertainty with greater success, as we will see in the following chapters.

This World Is Complex—Characterized by Interconnected and Interacting Parts, Exhibiting Behavior That Cannot Be Predicted Based on the Study of the Individual Parts Alone; Complex Systems Have Emergent Properties

When most people think of complexity, they think of many parts involved in a system or many factors considered when making a decision: all the variables that keep a skyscraper from toppling onto the city below or the number of variables to schedule thousands of airline flights or the many possible moves to win local community support. Complexity can occur even in simple systems where a few relationships can cause interesting and unexpected effects. In complex systems, each cause can have multiple effects, and multiple effects yield new causes.

Take the English alphabet. It contains only twenty-six letters, but so far they have been arranged in at least a million different ways to form meaningful representations of ideas. So, the alphabet is relatively simple—we learn it in the first year or so of primary school—but the language formed from that alphabet is complex because small differences in spelling (e.g., dog vs. dig) result in major differences in meaning (that is why we had a copy editor for this book!). Words, of course, are arranged in an infinite number of sentences that contain ideas. Those sentences are formed from a few rules about the types of words in the sentence (e.g., subject, object, verb) and rules about punctuation (e.g., periods, commas, etc.). Amazing how those minor things, such as a simple comma, can create completely different meanings:

> Time to eat, Mom.

> Time to eat Mom.

While systems with lots of parts can be complex, what makes the system complex is its behavior. Using models to simplify can be dangerous if they are not based on an understanding of the whole system.

For example, at Tikal National Park in Guatemala, the park's simplistic view of a problem led to ineffectual management actions. During the 1990s, the park suffered from *xate* poaching. *Xate* is a palm used for floral arrangements in the United States and Europe. Local people entered the park at night and cut *xate* fronds. Not only did their practice threaten the *xate* population, but collectors' campfires often escaped control and ignited forest fires.

Meanwhile, the conservation organization RARE Center for Tropical Conservation, specialized in training local bilingual nature guides around parks to improve biodiversity conservation (Kohl 2007a). The program's goal was simple: to select local poachers and try to convert them into ecotour guides. Once guides, they would give up their lives as poachers, thereby reducing pressure on *xate* and forests. This economic substitution strategy was consistent with the park's own systems to monitor *xateros* (*xate* collectors), enforce control over *xateros*, and seek funding to convert xateros into nature guides, small business owners, and sustainable farmers. All these programs worked only with the assumption that a limited pool of *xateros* exists and thus linearly diminishes by one with each converted guide, businessperson, and farmer.

Another related assumption held by many conservationists the world over, whether for *xate*, trees, parrots, Syrian antiquities, or bushmeat, is that local people drip with blame for *xate* (or fill in your favorite threatened resource) extraction. If this responsibility actually lies with other actors in the system as well, distant in time and space, then all the programs, trends, and events change like falling dominoes. Imagine now that our camera zooms out from the local *xate* poacher in Tikal to *xate* distributors in Guatemala City, to thousands of floral arrangers in the United States and Europe, to millions who buy these arrangements for their weddings and do not even know what *xate* is. To manage these actors, to manage demand in the global marketplace, calls for very different monitoring systems, enforcement strategies, incentives, rules, and conservation approaches. Very likely, an institution that truly wants to manage *xate* would seek more effective leverage points (i.e., most change for the least investment) way beyond Tikal's rain forests.

It is very unlikely that any of Tikal's strategies to combat those who harvest *xate* will work because the incentive to become a *xatero* does not originate from within a local community; rather, it originates in a global market structure. Seen this way, for each *xatero* converted into a guide or farmer, another local person will become a *xatero* to fill the vacancy, driven by payments and quotas issued by big-city distributors responding to international demand. (Or the new farmer or guide will continue collecting *xate* to supplement his farming income.)

Reductionism breaks complexity into component parts (*xateros* rather than the more complex economic structure that drives exploitation), but studying parts will never allow us to understand the whole. I may know you very well and your brother or sister very well, but that information alone tells me nothing about the relationship between you two. Further, reductionism will never allow us to understand large-scale emergent properties, such as understanding brain function by studying neurons (see section on emergence, below).

Reductionism has its value in the PLUS highlands where some problems can be solved largely by technical know-how, where the solution is unequivocal, and whose success is clearly defined, such as designing new management planning software, improving a GPS gadget, or better explaining aurora borealis in the ionosphere. In the PLUS World, models focus on prediction and control, in the DICE World we build them to gain insights into why things work which should help to improve our interventions.

Many of our tools and theories related to conventional forecasting, planning, and analysis, however, cannot deal with the dynamic complexity of the DICE World. Following a recipe to spray invasive gypsy moth caterpillars in the northeastern United States, steps to apply for grant money, or taking inventory of a cemetery's residents are not complex tasks, but they may be complicated ones.

We call a system complex when it exhibits the characteristics below (Cilliers 1998), but not all characteristics are needed for the system to exhibit complexity. When the system also self-organizes and adapts, we term it a *complex adaptive system*. Complex systems include the following characteristics:

- They contain a large number of elements.
- The elements interact—a forest contains many trees, but unless they interact, it is simply an aggregation. Interactions may by physical but do not have to be.
- The interactions are rich—that is, any element will influence several other elements, and many elements may influence any particular element.
- Interactions are nonlinear—a small change in one element may lead to a large change in another and vice versa. Nonlinearity is a precondition for complexity.
- Interactions are parts of loops, which provide feedback. Feedback may reinforce an effect or inhibit or control an effect.
- Complex systems are open—they interact with systems at larger scales. As a result, the definition of a system depends on the purpose of the definition or the position of the observer.
- Complex systems are never in a state of equilibrium; change is constant.
- Complex systems have history; their current state is a function of their past. Their current condition is sensitive to an initial point of interest.
- Each system element "ignores" the whole system behavior. Each responds only to information provided from interactions of nearby elements.

This World Is **E**ver-Changing—Not Static, but Changing without Specific Predictability as to Results and all Consequences

Our argument would be well served simply to say the universe changes and every day changes faster. Hundreds of years ago social change occurred very slowly, when people generally expected their children would engage in the same vocation and encounter the same conditions that they themselves did. Nearly every culture in human history has had a nonevolutionary creation story/worldview in which someone or -thing birthed or created or coughed up the world and then a severe case of stability set in, Old Testament included. Today a parent would be naïve to think that many things in their child's life will be the same as how they themselves grew up or what they did for sustenance when even in remote locations the invisible hands of the green revolution, climate change, market capitalism, and globalism have altered everything we could ever consider local and pure. In fact, Alvin Toffler wrote (1971, p. 14), "Change is avalanching upon our heads and most people are grotesquely unprepared to cope with it."

The world also exhibits more than random change like popcorn bouncing inside a popcorn maker. Change on a longer time horizon appears directional. We shared Kurzweil's views on tracking technology that exponentially doubles in power and speed every eighteen months. Change is not just about technology or about the creation of new forms of biological life. The ever-changing, evolving world occurs galactically (stars, galaxies, clusters), geologically (rocks and canyons), biologically (species, ecosystems), culturally (consciousness), economically (scale of economic relationships), politically (forms of organization), and technologically (faster, smaller, starter machines). On a longer scale, the E of DICE may be evolutionary, while on an everyday or shorter scale it is ever changing.

The PLUS World misses or outright ignores the ever-changing nature of the universe with resulting limitations on our ability to know and understand. The world is not stable in the sense of tomorrow being like today. If it were, we would never have to consider the future, which is what the notion of sustainability is all about. The world changes in ways not necessarily predictable: surprises happen both as a result of our own planning actions but also, as we indicated earlier, from actions taken elsewhere by people totally unknown to us. Dvir and Lechler (2004) state that "the essence of changes is even stronger than of planning, and indeed, while plans are not nothing, 'changing plans is everything.'"

We are not the only ones who recognize that changing assumptions about the world leads to new and useful insights. Many other disciplines have their rebels and paradigm challengers.

Outside the Box 3 | *Clash of Paradigms: Managing Visitors and Tourism in Protected Areas*

In our global society, paradigms battle each other on many fronts. Within protected areas, however, perhaps the fiercest of paradigmatic conflicts might be how managers deal with tourism and visitation. The clash involves two powerful mental models, each reflecting fundamentally different assumptions about the real world of tourism and visitor impacts and how to manage them. In one corner, some ask, "How many people can fit in our site?" These advocates stand firmly with the notion that identifying a tourism carrying capacity (TCC) may solve visitor impact issues. The forces in the other corner advocate the question, "Which biophysical and social conditions are appropriate or acceptable in our site?" reflecting serious skepticism of magic numbers. This camp favors a framework called Limits of Acceptable Change (LAC).

The TCC approach represents classic Modernism: including the illusion that it is scientific, mathematical, and "objective," but also enforcement-oriented, expert-driven, reductionist, and focused on symptoms rather than underlying causes. It marches with other tools that provide only the appearance of objectivity and rational thinking. TCC emerged from scientific management approaches to livestock where range managers calculated how many cows a particular pasture could support without apparently degrading it. The notion eventually spread to wildlife biologists who then applied it to other animals—from fruit flies in a jar to moose in Isle Royale National Park.

TCC's problem: it simply does not work. People are much more complicated than cattle. The tool contains many hidden assumptions about the natural world, many of which reflect human values, and requires so many conditions to make it function that on a practical level it fails. Despite its alluring promise of an objective, scientifically calculated number of people beyond which impacts on a resource begin to accrue, impacts—both biophysical and social— are a function of many variables, not just visitor numbers. In addition, the hope presented by TCC relieves managers of the responsibility of using their own judgment in making management decisions: they can simply appeal to The Number as a justification for limiting use. While multiple formulas have been proposed to calculate TCC, few protected areas, in reality, have implemented any. Galapagos National Park tried but eventually needed LAC to make it operational (Cazar 2007).

TCC makes several assumptions that have led some scientists and managers to abandon it as a useful concept:

1. Impacts from human activity such as visitation can be eliminated or reduced to insignificant levels. On the contrary, any level of use, however small, brings impacts.

Leading scientists have noted that low levels of use cause disproportionate larger amounts of impact.[1] Elimination of impact would thus require elimination of tourism.

2. Impacts are a function of visitor numbers. While this is true to some extent, other variables, such as visitor behavior, season of use, soils, management style, vegetation and presence of various animal species affect impacts. We know that one unhappy visitor can wreak more damage than fifty well behaved ones.

3. The world is stable. A carrying capacity is a singular number good for all time. Yet the world is in a state of flux: Ecosystems change, often unpredictably, in response to larger-scale processes. Social systems and preferences change, often unpredictably. Carrying capacity does not recognize complexity and nonlinearity.

4. The issue of impact and its acceptability can be solved by purely "objective" means. Knowing how much impact exists is different from making decisions about how much impact is acceptable (see discussion about Rittel and Webber). But acceptability is a value judgment, subject to and formed by dialogue among constituencies involved in a park's management.

5. The amount of impact can be measured and is subject to mathematical analysis. Its acceptability on the other hand results from negotiation and dialogue. One input is the amount of impact and from what cause. However much biophysical or social impact a park finds acceptable is and always will be a subjective decision.

A consequence of the TCC approach is that managers immediately turn to limiting use levels as a first option to reduce impacts. Limiting use in the face of high levels of demand creates additional and often politically charged challenges, such as selecting which visitors can enter and which cannot. Equity considerations surround how to make this decision and whether the park has staff enough to enforce use limits. While limits on visitor numbers may be an effective tool, LAC advocates argue it is only one of many visitor management tools.

LAC recognizes a DICE World, where uncertainty, multiple constituencies with different values and objectives, limited resources, and complexity require collaborative, subjective, and learning-based processes to produce at least temporary decisions. So how does it work?

In theory, it is simple as long as a manager can shift focus from limiting people to managing conditions. Consider the ever popular trail. A TCC advocate would try to limit the number of people who use the trail daily, based on the assumption that with fewer users there would be less impact, only partially true. A LAC advocate would focus on key trail conditions: soil compaction, trail width, number of secondary trails caused by visitors walking off-trail, number of encounters with other people. Which variables are actually measured would be influenced by constituencies' values.

Then managers decide by working with constituencies on how much impact or change they can tolerate or accept, since, they assume all visitors have some impacts on the site and on each other. This is a "limit of acceptable change." They might decide with input from constituencies that the LAC of the trail should be no wider than 0.8 m, or the number of bird species identified on an average walk by park guards in the morning should not fall below twenty-two, or visitors should encounter no more than two other groups during their walk.

Once they define limits, managers work to keep site conditions beneath that limit, much like water quality managers ensure that fecal coliform counts remain below a particular number. Depending on how close conditions are to the limit managers activate predefined mitigation strategies.

While many academics strongly advocate LAC, it has not won too much ground on TCC because a shift in management paradigms first requires the presence of underlying values of the new paradigm that promote learning in a DICE World. Until those values exist, learning-based tools such as LAC, adaptive management, monitoring and evaluation, and Recreation Opportunity Spectrum, are unlikely to win too many battles in this paradigm war.

1. *Two of the earliest studies that demonstrate this result include Frissell and Duncan (1965) and Merriam and Smith (1974). Since then, there have been dozens of studies, primarily by David Cole, Jeff Marion, and Yu-Fai Leung, which support this finding.*

Managers Expect Surprise and Emergence

The word emergence describes the process by which larger patterns and entities ("emergent properties") arise from smaller and simpler ones. The latter do not share the same properties with the former. In other words, simpler entities combine, forming new relationships with new behaviors never before seen—such as when the right molecular chains combined to sustain life, or the right brain structure and environmental stimulation produced self-aware-ness, or when a culture adopted the use of animals to do farm labor thereby producing surpluses that permitted the rise of hierarchical organizations. Emergence is an inherent quality of complex systems. Chuck Palahniuk, author of the book *Fight Club* (2005), observed about emergence, "All you can do is hope for a pattern to emerge, and sometimes it never does. Still, with a plan, you only get the best you can imagine. I'd always hoped for something better than that."

Most of what we actually see in our heritage areas—Strengths, Weaknesses, Opportunities, and Threats—emerges unpredicted by any plans or SWOT analyses (see Inside the Box 6:

What's Wrong with SWOT? Claiming Participation When It Is Not). Our imagination can only account for a small percentage of what actually becomes reality. If our plans cannot predict or contribute to more than simple, short-term elements, then our planning must do something more than predict. It must manage conditions from which emergence itself emerges.

Implementation then does not begin once a plan has been completed—it begins at that very moment the notion of planning first emerges in a single person's mind. As it arises, it takes the planning process down what will likely be a path of no return.

When the idea first emerges, its originator assumes a perspective: "I will do this, she will do this, we will do this, or they will do this." With that near instantaneous decision, power configurations begin to take shape like cells specializing from a zygote. One path leads to RCP and bureaucratic central control, which may eventually suffocate participation, ownership, and other aspects of social capital needed for plan implementation. The person talks to power brokers, such as donors and government agents, about mounting a planning process because he or she thinks a certain heritage area needs another plan. They compare notes, budgets, schedules, and laws and then muster resources, very often before community actors or even the heritage area staff itself becomes aware that the idea has been born. They share biases such as optimism and systematic errors that cripple plans and projects at the very earliest stages (see the seven deadly sins of project planning, Pinto 2013). This pathway, pulled by the singular gravity of PLUS, emits subtle and then not-so-subtle signals about who owns this process and where control will lie, often independent of any sweet-sounding declarations to be participatory.

Another path leads toward a planning process that recognizes emergence, establishing the conditions for its manifestations to be perceived and cultivated and integrated into the process of transforming vision into reality. When change does erupt, an emergent-friendly planning and managing process is ready with flexible budgets, planning documents that can be easily updated, capability to quickly convene meetings, protocols to forge new contacts and hastily formed networks around emerging issues (Denning 2006; Huston 2006), and a tendency to constantly plow under aging assumptions. According to Bornstein (2007), young social entrepreneurial organizations that eventually achieve success do not in their beginning pay much attention to writing objectives in logical frameworks, formal evaluations with indicators and targets, rigid budget structures that cannot be amended on the fly, or other strategic planning tools usually reserved for more mature and more bureaucratic projects.

Innovative organizations, then, scan landscapes for emerging opportunities such as funding sources, contacts to add to their network, conferences to share their wares, clients to pitch to, and critiques of their work that require rewriting brochures, charters, and mental models. They also scan for emerging threats to prepare for or to nip in the bud. In both cases, such organizations prepare themselves and the conditions for emergence.

Although Faludi had already anticipated the importance of emergence in his revised definition of implementation (Outside the Box 1.1) when he included unplanned benefits as a component of implementation success, few organizations in the heritage management world have yet to take this open and optimistic stance toward the universal process of emergence.

Emergence often manifests as a sudden inspiration or insight that breaks through how we routinely see and do things. Some call these "innovative spurts" (Majchrzak et al. 2006):

> An innovative spurt is a quantum leap in insight. It occurs when parameters are in a state of flux, plans have broken down, and a real-time adaptation is required. It is participatory when it is the product of any and all stakeholders who have an insight to contribute, not just those whose job description gives them the specific responsibility to innovate. An engineer who reframes a problem from building a bridge to affecting the flow of traffic is engaged in an innovative spurt. The Red Cross's redirection during the [Hurricane] Katrina disaster from a direct-service delivery model to an information broker role was an innovative spurt.

It should be clear then that without individuals and organizations prepared for emergence, without their having the power to bring new ideas to the organization and implement them quickly, organizations lose many of these innovative spurts in the noise of everyday troubleshooting.

Managing emergence is a critical part of any Holistic Planning regimen, discussed in the final chapter of this book.

It Is All DICE in Protected Areas

Before you think that this discussion of DICE is academic and hence irrelevant to managers, you just need to look around to see DICE in your own sites. In the old days, parks could simply remove local residents; now they must engage them politically and developmentally. Thanks to globalization and democratization, the nonprofit governmental organizations and citizens' movements have been steadily growing. NGOs have seized the heart of society's social development, employing more than 20 million full-time employees, networked and virtually linked (Hall-Jones 2006). This makes life much more complicated for managers who have to manage many more actors (armed with smartphone cameras) than when they were able to simply "ignore" those actors away.

Managers have to satisfy many more objectives than before by integrating biodiversity conservation, community development, spiritual values, and others. Even wildlife management in Yellowstone proved DICE-y for managers throughout the park's history.

As change speeds up, more and more threats emerge, one on top of another, all mashed together like different colors of Play-Doh after a rough day in kindergarten (Naughton 2007). For example, in June 2009, Mexico suffered multiple misfortunes to protected areas, demonstrating how unpredictable, nonlinear, and complex real life can be for parks. The drop in oil prices required cuts in the national budget (oil is a major export) as well as for the National Commission for Natural Protected Areas that manages federal protected areas. Then the recession struck, cutting into tourism revenues. Then swine flu impacted visitation (Partlow and Booth 2009), and drug violence scared away visitors from many destinations (Ellingwood 2009). The problems just kept piling up for Mexico.

The protected areas community has begun to respond to such pressures of DICE reality. Adaptive management has become a vogue concept, as well as monitoring, limits of acceptable change, co-management, and a professionalization of how we design, manage, and measure conservation impacts, as seen in the Conservation Measures Partnership that pushes the application of adaptive management in biodiversity conservation (Toolbox 3). These different strategies, however, have met limited success for reasons related to the conflict between DICE and PLUS and misconceptions about learning (discussed in chapter 9). Consider the following list of paradigmatic battles going on in the protected area field:

- Managing for activities vs. managing for experiences
- Incremental/ad hoc decision making vs. using a framework
- Focusing on biophysical attributes vs. focusing on values
- Focusing on the average visitor vs. understanding diverse motivations
- Thinking of recreation planning as separate from implementation
- Identifying a carrying capacity vs. identifying acceptable condition
- Site-focused vs. regional-level management
- Conceiving of planning as a technical exercise vs. building capacity
- Destination (end state) is static vs. destination dynamic
- Focusing on events vs. understanding the system underlying the events

In Mexico, moreover, the National Commission's strategic protected areas plan describes its new paradigm is based on two pillars: equity and sustainability, without which real development cannot occur. It calls this vision much more "humanistic" and "pragmatic" than in older (i.e., PLUS) days. In 2009 the Mexican government set up the Conservation for Sustainable Development Program that has worked in 1,900 communities with 68,000 people around its protected areas. It also has a Temporary Employment Program that supports community projects with conservation components and sustainable use of ecosystem resources (CONANP 2007).

Similarly, heritage sites that tried to operate strictly in technical RCP-PLUS terms are discovering that problems do not inhabit the highlands as much as they had thought or hoped. In South Africa's Kruger National Park, for example, growing elephant populations led managers in the 1980s to fear severe impacts to vegetation and other animal populations in the park. So, they made a decision to cull the large-eared animals. In 1994, managers suspended culling because changes in public sentiment demanded alternative, nonlethal controls such as translocation and birth control.

Initially, park managers regarded population control as a strictly technical issue—i.e., what is the most efficient method to reduce elephant numbers? Much of this planning, however, occurred during a period of significant turbulence in South African civil society: the end of apartheid meant that voices long suppressed would now be heard. The growing movement toward democracy also meant that planning, once the domain of biologists, must now be transparent, inclusive, and responsive.

Managers soon discovered that elephant management had more to do with understanding people's values than implementing an efficient mechanism to eliminate them. They found major divisions in society about this charismatic megafauna and that each management alternative precipitated significant social consequences.

The tension between management and society, a tradition of collaboration between science and management, and the desire of SANPARKS (the parastatal authority that manages national parks in South Africa) to remain relevant to South Africans, led to the notion of strategic adaptive management—a different way of thinking about management, which included opportunities for reflection and learning (Biggs et al. 2003; Nkhata and Breen 2010). Strategic adaptive management, as practiced in South Africa, begins with constructing a vision, a pro-

Toolbox 3 | Miradi *Software and the New Conservation Science*

For many years biodiversity conservation organizations not only adhered to PLUS-based assumptions but also reported to donors any kind of positive outcomes. Consequently, as resources dwindled in the donor community, donors demanded greater accountability for their limited dollars, and others sought new ways to instill greater accountability. In this context, the nonprofit Foundations of Success (FOS) emerged to agitate for a conservation science revolution to conservation practice (Salafsky et al. 2003). Following best practices revolutions in public health and other fields, FOS applied the scientific method to conceiving, designing, implementing, and evaluating conservation projects. Based on its classic 1998 book *Measures of Success* (Margolis and Salafsky 1998) as well as efforts in other fields to promote more accountability, FOS and partners co-led the development of the Open Standards for the Practice of Conservation, the Conservation Measures Partnership (CMP), and the *Miradi* Adaptive Management Software for Conservation Projects.

The software[i] and CMP's approach in general applies adaptive management to conservation practice, whereby practitioners subject conservation objectives to continuous experimentation, trial and error, and assumption testing to feed back into project design and kickstart a learning cycle that hopefully keeps on spinning. So the software, based on the Open Standards, encourages conservation planners to follow a step-by-step software wizard to consciously define and make explicit their mental models (and component assumptions) in order to understand the conservation situation, identify conservation threats and targets, objectives, and strategies that ultimately improve the conservation status of the targets, as well as indicators to assess the effectiveness of the whole project. [ii]

i. The software exists as well as an online version, Miradi Share, *that allows teams to combine data and roll up and assess program-level data across multiple projects. www.miradishare.org*

ii. It is worth mentioning that the most widely used conservation planning software in the world is Marxan *(Ball, Possingham, and Watts 2009)*

cess that requires substantial deliberation involving people with different value sets. This is done prior to considering management actions.

No site will successfully sail a ship or plan its future focusing only on parts. To be relevant and effective, managers must navigate their craft carefully around partially submerged limbs, dense vegetation, and biting gnats of the swampy lowland, otherwise their efforts amount to little more than rolling DICE in a real-life game of craps.

Because DICE World Conditions Change Quickly, Learning Is Paramount

A boxer who enters the ring with a few set moves may survive for a while, but eventually his opponents will learn those strategies and throw new punches and moves at him. The boxer stuck in a paradigm box of his own construction will soon hit the mat with a bloodied nose. A boxer, however, who can learn and adapt during the competition, block and offer new punches as conditions change, may very well be fit for a shiny new belt. Right now heritage areas resemble far more the boxer with a bloodied nose.

One case in point comes from a different part of South Africa, the former Natal Parks Board in KwaZulu-Natal. It entered this world with its mission focused on recovering game populations and thus adopted a military culture to protect species. It succeeded for a while, like our boxer. In the meantime, society's expectations about the role of parks moved, and the board grew increasingly irrelevant as it did not change its strategies or mission. If it suffered any change in purpose, it was to survive as an institution; after all, the first goal of a bureaucracy is to survive. In the end, the board broadened its mission, cooperated with communities, and shared financial benefits with them. It learned a few new punches.

If conditions always change, knowledge is mostly tentative, and we cannot fully understand problems, our one hope for survival pivots on our ability to learn to duck those punches quickly enough with innovations and strategies to meet the challenges of the times. In other words, we must experiment, reflect, learn, and adapt at a pace that exploits our wonderful capabilities of being human. This proves true for all of society, not just heritage areas.

As Arie de Geus (1988), a former Shell executive and noted leader in organizational learning, says, "The root source of all competitive advantage is an organization's relative ability to learn faster than its competitors." In this modern day, a business's competition can usually imitate its products within a very short time, so its best hope for survival is to accelerate its ability to innovate, learn, and create new products—faster than the competition can. In protected areas, we still manage rising complexity with PLUS-age, dinosaurian assumptions; this stance will lead first to irrelevance and second to disintegration. We must learn, rather, to develop innovative management strategies and perspectives faster than the DICE World can throw jabs and undercuts at us (Holling 1978). This, of course, will not always be possible.

This uncertainty, this rapid change has increasingly led academics to question strategies generated from PLUS assumptions, such as Rational Comprehensive Planning, as being one-way routes to the precipitous edge of a flat world. As high seas threaten protected areas, managers must chart a new course forward into the future. As with any explorers, there will be risk and miscalculation along the way. Fortunately for those who look toward chapter 4, a first glint on the sand offers hope for a New World.

> *Successful problem solving requires finding the right solution to the right problem.*
> *We fail more often because we solve the wrong problem than because we get*
> *the wrong solution to the right problem.*
>
> —*Russell Ackoff*

Integral Theory: Charting a New Course for Heritage Planning

You can never Plan the Future by the past.

—*Edmund Burke*

THE OTHER
SIDE OF
COMPLEXITY

EVENTS

PATTERNS

STRUCTURES

MENTAL MODELS

Expanding Consciousness to See
the Other Side of the Iceberg

Although Isaac Newton devised the laws of gravity, his consciousness of nature fell way short from our perspective of nearly 400 years later. Only when Einstein arrived would we realize how limited Newton's awareness was. He only perceived a very small range of all velocities possible in the universe (much like the rest of us), and thus his laws only applied to a narrow portion of physical reality. Einstein's theory of special relativity, however, explained the behavior of matter and energy at all velocities, from zero to light. Because he enjoyed a much broader awareness, Einstein had an entirely new understanding of space-time, energy, and matter, things that Newton never even saw. Interestingly as we wrote this book, a physics experiment in Italy shocked the scientific world by announcing that neutrinos could move faster than the speed of light (Brumfiel and Nature 2011). This was a direct violation of Einstein's theory. Was it time for even this great paradigm to cede its throne of scientific dominance? The challenge to Einstein's supremacy, however, failed as scientists discovered the following year that the anomaly resulted from equipment error (Brown 2012). Maybe the next anomaly will be the paradigm-changer.

In simplest terms, consciousness is an organism's ability to perceive and react to stimuli.[10] A bacterium perceives some stimuli (light, heat, pH) and has certain behaviors with which it can react (retreat, divide, wither). A mouse has yet greater awareness of its surroundings (time of day, mice in heat, hungry cats) and a vastly increased number of behaviors (investigate, run, hide, sniff, and see). A human adult is far more sophisticated and enjoys much greater capacity than a mouse. The difference in awareness between one person and another also varies a lot. Obviously, an adult is much more conscious than a child, while the consciousness of the Dalai Lama is greater than that of average people. Another way to understand consciousness is the degree to which someone can see through others' perspectives. The more perspectives or lenses one can see through, the more limits they can see beyond (Inside the Box 4.1), and the more consciousness they have.

As far as this discussion may seem from planning, though, the evolution of consciousness will in fact be key to understanding where heritage planning has come from and to where it may go.

Inside the Box 4 | *Boundary Lines in the Sand*

From park borders to zoo cages to museum exhibits to artifacts inside glass boxes to historic city centers, heritage management has traditionally concerned itself with cordoning off, encaging, zoning, and boxing in heritage. Although separation ostensibly protects valued heritage from untrustworthy hands, just below the surface lurk PLUS assumptions. Formal boundaries are very PLUS. They are predictable in function, linear in form, easily understood in law, and highly stable in time. As Modernism seeks simplicity and methodical, categorical, and universal understandings of nature and society as part of its quest to decipher nature's secrets, the protected area boundary provides heritage managers with unambiguous, clear-cut criteria for making management decisions.

Just consider the conventional zoning system found in protected areas around the world. Zones most often regulate uses by creating borders that separate different uses, supposedly increasing management ease. Such single-use, segregated zoning first began in the early 1800s to separate urban industrial activity such as glue factories and slaughterhouses from residences (Russell 1994). While that was an important function then, the separation of residential from commercial and industrial areas has contributed in large measure to sprawl, a car culture, deterioration of community, obesity, and other social ills (Hirt 2007; Gerckens 1994; Jacobs 1961). Despite these and other criticisms, this nearly two-century-old urban industrial paradigm extended to wildlands, where managers zone off and separate human uses such as tourism and agriculture considered a threat to biological and cultural diversity conservation from heritage areas. This became the global model for protected areas.

Yet the DICE World respects not what PLUS draws in the sand. The new worldview presents the notion of heritage site boundaries with a deep philosophical challenge: boundaries might not move, but everything else does (Bandarin 2014).

As change accelerates, we see area boundaries grow more porous and fuzzy. This Inside the Box concept actually leads to not only challenges but conflicts. Boundaries try to stop those who have historically moved through the space, whether indigenous Maasai tribes or migrating elephants. They can be used to freeze lost-era villages in time by drawing a line around them and declaring them heritage. Modern-day humans regularly cross heritage area boundaries whether local fishermen, villagers en route to market, or militiamen and narco-traffickers.

Financial, economic, political, and most every other social force affect protected areas without consideration to legal boundaries. But climate change perhaps most of all now illustrates how heritage site boundaries are not the stable fixtures that traditional protected area planners once thought them to be. All sorts of organisms now move out of one territory into another thanks to changing temperatures and climate patterns, whether insects, mammals, birds, and even trees.[1] If the very animals for whom humans created protected areas disrespect boundaries, then one has to question what the future of protected areas might look like.

Some see the future of natural heritage protected areas as integrated back into society as many city parks do today, without definite boundaries, pocked by multiple entry points, interlinked by wildlife corridors, and respected by neighbors both human and nonhuman who desire no fences. On a landscape stage with ever more dancers, site boundaries dashed in the sand may not last too much longer.

1. There are many reports and literally thousands of published studies on the changes to species biogeography due to climate change. Inkley et al. (2013) and Dudley (2003) are but two.

Integral Theory Helps Explain Worldview Change

For most of human history, people lived inside just one culture with no knowledge of how others see the world. If you were born a Viking, that is all you ever knew, and all your parents had ever expected for you. Today, however, through archaeology, anthropology, and other studies, we have access—almost universal—to all of the human cultures, wisdom traditions, and sciences that ever existed. Now with the Internet, most are only few clicks away.

For nearly the first time in human history, we can ask if it is possible to integrate all the different forms of knowing and perspectives into one framework to understand reality. Can we take a global tour of cultures, selecting essential insights and truths and fuse them to give us a comprehensive map of human potential? For years, American philosopher Ken Wilber and others have been doing just this. They studied the legacy of human thought, especially theories of development from ancient shamans and mystics, to today's breakthroughs in cognitive, developmental, and astrophysical science. Wilber integrated more than 100 developmental models in the "Integral Map," a holistic framework or lens that allows us to understand forces that influence any phenomenon (Wilber 2000).

If we lay this Integral Map on the floor, we see that it has five principal components which is why he calls this map the AQAL model (pronounced "ah-kwal"), which stands for "all quadrants, all levels, all lines, all states, and all types."[11] We can experience each one, all available to us at all times, if we know where to look.

States

States are temporary conditions such as states of weather (cloudy, rainy, sunny), states of matter (liquid, gas, solid), or states of consciousness: We are all familiar with three states of consciousness: waking, dreaming, and sleeping. Others exist as well, such as meditative states (yoga, meditation), altered states (drug-induced), and peak experiences (making love, walking in nature, listening to music). As Wilber points out, the great Wisdom Traditions (Christian mysticism, Vedanta Hinduism, Vajrayana Buddhism, and Jewish Kabbalah) hold that these different states can help us build great spiritual wisdom. That is, through meditation, for example, people can experience fundamental aspects of reality inaccessible any other way. Even on a daily basis, we often find motivation, meaning, and drives in these states, such as a sudden "Aha!" moment. (Note: Although states are important for understanding reality, that topic remains beyond the purview of this book.)

Levels or Stages of Development

While states of consciousness come and go, levels stand as permanent milestones of growth. For example, once a child has developed language, the child will have that capacity forever. Language is not a fleeting state but rather an enduring achievement. People can also achieve higher levels of consciousness, emotional maturity, morality, cognition, and other qualities. Each stage of whatever quality represents a higher level of organization than the earlier stage. Consider how people evolve and expand their self-identity from egocentric (me-centered) to ethnocentric (us-group-centered) to anthropocentric (us-humanity-centered) to worldcentric (all of us–centered, human and nonhuman). Each level transcends and includes the previous. That is, people who are anthropocentric also understand the ethnocentric perspective because they held that perspective at some point in their lives. Developmental psychologists agree, moreover, that no one can skip levels, although different people pass through them at different speeds, and people reach different levels in their lives.

Researchers have focused on many aspects of development, but the concept of levels remains the same whether a Padawan Apprentice→Jedi Knight→Jedi Master or an atom→molecule→cell→organism→species→community. Later, we see evolving stages of consciousness that explain the origins of the PLUS and DICE paradigms. Some famous developmental researchers—Jean Piaget, Clare Graves, Robert Kegan, Jean Gebser, and Lawrence Kohlberg—study how morality, cognition, rationality, ethics, emotions, aesthetics, consciousness, and many other aspects develop in all of us (Figure 4.1). AQAL incorporates them all.

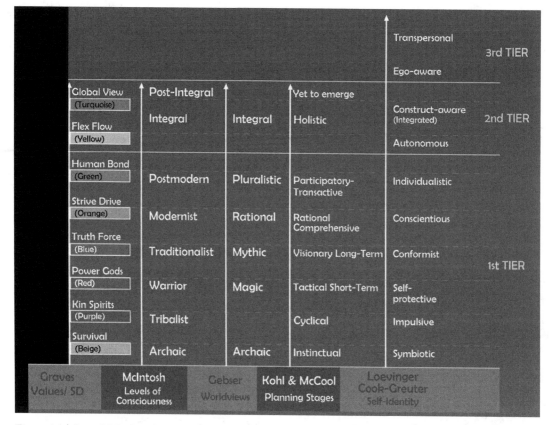

Figure 4.1 | *Some Major Development Lines (redrawn from Wilber 2007, p. 69). This figure shows various famous lines of development. Notice particularly the line of McIntosh with the level names of consciousness used in this book as well as corresponding levels for planning identified by us.*

Lines of Development

Howard Gardner's multiple intelligences (2006) popularized the idea of stages and lines by arguing that each person develops through stages along eight psychological lines, each largely independent of the others. For example, some people excel at math or music or relating to other people or controlling their physical body. While these people may rise to celebrity along one line of intelligence, they may remain below average along another.

Each line then marks development throughout a series of stages (Figure 4.1). The above-mentioned example of Jedi levels unfolds along a line that could be called Jediism or Order of the Jedi. The examples of egocentric, ethnocentric, and so forth, could be on a line called "compassion," where at each stage the person has compassion or identifies with a larger group. As they develop along the line, their compassion grows broader and they identify with more and more of reality. Try to recall your own level of compassion from childhood to the present day. How many stages have you passed through?

As we discuss later, many additional lines might be relevant to planners, such as participatory facilitation skills, empathy for community members, and mental complexity to create more meaning to manage heritage in an increasingly DICE World.

Types

Types are horizontal classifications, not vertical stages of development. They can exist at any stage. Types simply describe a category with multiple variants. We have male and female gender types, personality types, blood types, body types, and, of course, planner types: spatial, urban, rural, business, and heritage area planners.

Quadrants

Wilber described in his study of wisdom traditions that throughout history, philosophers and cultures made dozens of references to three principal dimensions through which we see reality. Sometimes this grouping appeared as the Beautiful, the Good, and True; or Nature, Culture, and Self; or Science, Morality, and Aesthetics. He noted that these dimensions corresponded to different perspectives, also encoded in most major languages as different person perspectives, including First Person (I), Second Person (You), Third Person (Him), and their plural versions ("we" is first person plural, for instance).

So Wilber built these universal perspectives into his Integral Map. Rather than using three, however, he split Third Person into singular and plural, giving us four (Figures 4.2 and 4.3), calling them quadrants.

	Interior	Exterior
Individual	**Upper Left (UL)** **Psychology** "What I experience" *Aspects of Reality Revealed:* "I," subjective realities, e.g., self and consciousness, states of mind, psychological development, mental models, emotions, will	**Upper Right (UR)** **Behavior** "What I do" *Aspects of Reality Revealed:* "It," objective realities, e.g., brain and organism, visible biological features, degrees of activation of the various bodily systems
Collective	**Lower Left (LL)** **Culture** "What we experience" *Aspects of Reality Revealed:* "We," intersubjective realities, e.g., shared values, culture and worldview, webs of culture, communication, relationships, norms, boundaries, customs	**Lower Right (LR)** **Systems** "What we do" *Aspects of Reality Revealed:* "Its," interobjective realities, e.g., social systems and environment, visible societal structures, economic systems, political orders, natural resource management

Figure 4.2 | *Standard View of the Four Quadrants (Brown 2007). This view shows the basic four quadrants, their corresponding perspectives, and a brief description. For this book, however, we will focus only on the human social system of planning and development.*

UL	UR
Psychological and Spiritual	**Physical and Behavioral**
• Awareness, thought, feeling	• Physical health and well-being
• Attitudes, values, beliefs, intentions	• Skills and abilities
• Inner health and well-being, self-esteem	• Activities
• Sense of safety, trust	• Program participation
• Sense of connectedness, responsibility and caring for others and the environment	• Consumer behaviors
• Creativity, innovation, artistic expression	• Diet, fitness
• Motivation and experience of participation and contribution	• Actions toward others and the environment
	• Skills and opportunities for participation and contribution
LL	**LR**
Cultural	**Natural and Social Systems**
• Worldviews	• Natural environment, ecological systems
• Shared meaning	• Built environment, human systems
• Collective norms, ethics	• Community institutions (schools, health, authority, justice system, religious institutions, etc.)
• Shared attitudes, values, beliefs	• Programs and services
• Shared vision and goals	• Laws, policies, protocols
• Shared history, customs	• Organizational systems and structures
• Shared language, symbols, art	• Community infrastructure (transportation, housing, social planning council, etc.)
• Co-creativity	• Governance systems and structures
• Culture of participation and contribution	• Economic system
	• Systems and structures for participation and contribution

Figure 4.3 | *An Integral Map of Community (Lundy 2007). As communities are very broad concepts, they can be broken into many different, but not exhaustive, factors across the four quadrants.*

In the **Upper Left/UR** (I), which deals with the psychological or interior-individual, we find our own immediate and interior thoughts, including awareness, beliefs, feelings, values, intentions, self-esteem, motivations, mental health, spiritual orientation and consciousness, and overall interior experience. Standard lines include cognitive, moral, emotional, interpersonal, self-identify, and spiritual. In planning, the mental state of community participants can greatly influence planning outcomes, a point recognized by Friedmann (Outside the Box 4.1).

Outside the Box 4 | *One of the World's First Integralist Planners?*

John Friedmann may have been one of the world's first Integral planners. Friedmann, a professor of urban planning at the University of California–Los Angeles, entered the planning world while classical Rational Comprehensive Planning was not only often failing to achieve its objectives but was also disrupting lives of hundreds of thousands of residents in urban "renewal projects."

Because of planners' technical training and specialized language, a gap separated planners and citizens they tried to serve. This gap generated misunderstanding, failed projects, and project opposition. According to Friedmann, planners could only jump this gap of knowing through a series of "transactions"—dialogues occurring in small groups between planners and citizens. The dialogues must have authenticity that eventually would lead to social learning occurring in group processes. Once citizens and planners understood each other, they could jointly agree upon and pursue societal action. This three-component process (dialogue, social learning, and societal action) he termed the Transactive Theory of Planning in his classic, *Retracking America* (1973).

Certainly, Friedmann's proposal responded to the ills of RCP, and as such, represented not just an incremental departure from the dominant paradigm of the 1970s, but a radical departure. Our view of planning in this book through the Integral lens of four quadrants evolves from his giant step. Dialogue and social learning represent the LL. The implication that a new view and internal mental experience of citizen engagement was needed was a UL departure from the norm of the times, demanding both new skills (UR) and paradigms (LL). While Friedmann did not really engage the LR, certainly transactive planning would have required new institutions, such as new forums and policies that would allow this approach to flourish.

The **Upper Right/UR** (It), or the behavioral or exterior individual, addresses the physical result of what happens inside an individual's mind. For example, we see the physical health and well-being, skills and abilities, and activities and behaviors of individuals. For nonhuman elements, we find physical components, whether atoms, molecules, and cells or different parts of the brain. For planning, the physical comfort level during workshops as well as the planning skills of participants (for example, how to facilitate a conflict without a fight) can influence planning outcomes.

The **Lower Left/LL** (We), which emphasizes the cultural or collective interior, deals with how a group thinks, such as shared meanings, worldviews, paradigms, myths, collective norms, ethics, values, visions and goals, customs, history, language, and organizational culture. Standard lines include consciousness and worldview. The community's perception of power greatly influences its use during planning events. This is the quadrant that represents ideas that groups or communities of minds have built together.

In the **Lower Right/LR** (Its), or the social or exterior collective, we find the physical forms of our culture. This is what our collective ideas build in the physical world. They include social-ecological systems, institutions, programs and services, laws and policies, infrastructure, governance structures, and economic systems. Standard lines include the collective social systems (foraging, agrarian, industrial, informational) and human organization (survival clans, ethnic tribes, feudal empires, early nations, corporate states, value communities, holistic commons, and integral meshworks). For planning, plan design, and technology influence its implementation. The overriding point here, as emphasized by Wilber (2007b, p. 68), is that

> every event in the manifest world has all three of those dimensions. You can look at any event from the point of view of the "I" (or how I personally see and feel about the event); from the point of view of the "we" (how not just I but others see the event); and as the "it" (or the objective facts of the event). Thus, an integrally informed path will take all of those dimensions into account, and thus arrive at a more comprehensive and effective approach.

It is important to realize that within quadrants, we can represent the other four elements of the Integral Map. Because for our purposes, lines of development are the most important, we include Figure 4.4 which shows that all quadrants have lines and corresponding levels.

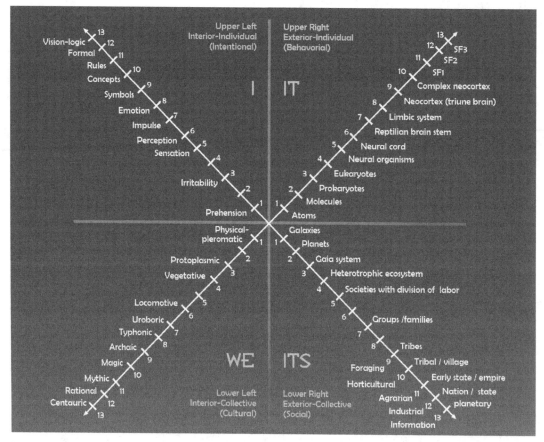

Figure 4.4 | *The Ascending Levels along One Line in Each Quadrant (Wilber 2007a). This figure shows one line in each quadrant and its corresponding levels. In the LR, a second line describing human societal organization is superimposed on the same line starting at point 9 (groups).*

Practitioners can use Integral Maps for any kind of problem or issue to better understand forces that contribute to that situation. Here, we analyze planning barriers and our response to them, based on IT. In the meantime, Figures 4.5 and 4.6 show applications to sustainability.

I
Psychological Influences

Individual-interior: Self and Consciousness
The subjective, internal reality of an individual

Context: self-identity and consciousness, intentions, personal values, attitude; religious or spiritual beliefs; commitment (e.g., cognitive, emotional, moral); cognitive capacity, depth of responsibility; degree of care for others and the environment, etc.

Examples of areas addressed: psychological health and development; educational level; emotional intelligence; motivation and will; understanding of one's role in the community and impact on the environment; personal goals; the practitioner's mental model, and self-knowledge; a city-dweller's disconnection from the natural world.

Tools for transformation: e.g., psychotherapy, religious or spiritual counseling; Enneagram analysis; Myers-Briggs testing, phenomenological research; self-questioning; body scanning; introspection; prayer, meditation; journaling, goal-setting; emotional literacy training, increased exposure to wild nature; vision quest; compassion practices.

IT
Behavioral Influences

Individual-Exterior: Brain and Organism; Actions
The objective, external reality of an individual

Context: biological features; brain chemistry; bodily states; physical health; behaviors; skills; capabilities; actions; empirically measurable individual qualities; physical boundaries or surfaces, etc.

Examples of areas addressed: energy level and physical health of a practitioner; nutritional intake; pre and postnatal care; conduct toward environment or opposite sex; routines; response to rules and regulations; birth control use; money management; computer skills; acidity or toxicity of a water source; metabolic response to pollutants.

Tools for transformation: e.g., diet, hygiene, medication; exercise, weightlifting, preventative, allopathic, and/or complementary medicine; skill building; clear rules, regulations, and guidance from a respected authority; use of sustainability technologies such as pollution filters, drip irrigation, solar panels, or a GPS system; use of litigation to enforce regulations or the Freedom of Information Act (in the USA) to acquire governmental data.

We	**Its**
Cultural Influences	**Systems Influences**
Collective-interior: Cultures and Worldviews The intersubjective, internal realities of groups	**Collective-exterior; Social Systems & Environments** The inter-objective, external realities of groups
Context: Shared values and worldviews; shared meaning; mutual resonance; cultural norms, boundaries, and mores; language; customs; communication; relationships; symbolism; agreed upon ethics, etc.	**Context:** Visible societal structures, systems and modes of production (economic, political, social, informational, educational, technological); strategies; policies; measures; work processes; technologies; natural systems; processes and interactions in the environment; etc.
Examples of areas addressed: Cultural "appropriateness;" collective vision; relationships between practitioners and the community; relationship among community, family, organization members; stigmas; language differences; collective interpretation of power, class, race, and gender inequities; collective perception of the environment and pollution	**Examples of areas addressed:** Stability and effectiveness of economic and political systems; legal frameworks; strength of technological, educational, and healthcare infrastructure; poverty alleviation; actual power, class, race and gender inequities; job creation and trade; corporate regulation; organizational structure; food security, health of local biota or global biosphere; climate change; restoration, protection and sustainable use of natural resources; feedback loop efficiencies, bio-accumulation in food chains
Tools for transformation: e.g., dialogue, community-directed development; inclusive decision making; consensus-based strategic planning; organizational learning; support groups (religious or secular); trust-building exercises; participant-observer techniques; community visioning; cooperative participation; storytelling; collective introspection; group therapy; meme developmental propagation; language skills development; communication skills development	**Tools for transformation:** e.g., policy-making; organized protest; shareholder activism; capacity building; systems thinking; complexity, chaos, and cybernetic theories; "upstream" strategies; organizational re-engineering; micro credit and micro-enterprise; pollution taxes; subsidies; regulations; natural resource recreation and management systems; geographic information systems; natural environmental changes, populations changes

Figure 4.5 | *The Territory of Sustainability Revealed by Each Quadrant (Brown 2007). This figure focuses on human social development in general, identifying areas that can be addressed and transformative tools to help the dimensions of each quadrant evolve.*

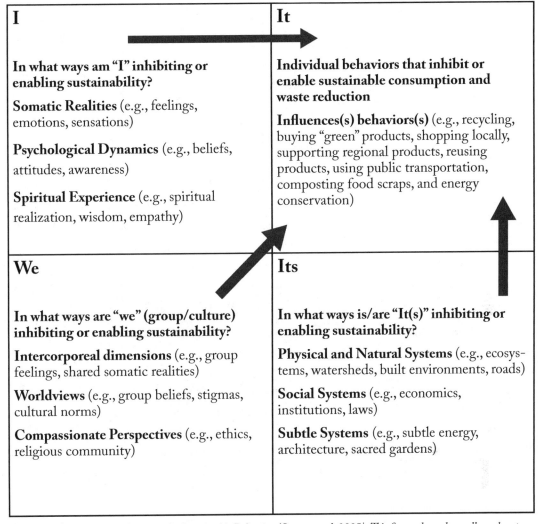

I	**It**
In what ways am "I" inhibiting or enabling sustainability? **Somatic Realities** (e.g., feelings, emotions, sensations) **Psychological Dynamics** (e.g., beliefs, attitudes, awareness) **Spiritual Experience** (e.g., spiritual realization, wisdom, empathy)	**Individual behaviors that inhibit or enable sustainable consumption and waste reduction** **Influences(s) behaviors(s)** (e.g., recycling, buying "green" products, shopping locally, supporting regional products, reusing products, using public transportation, composting food scraps, and energy conservation)
We	**Its**
In what ways are "we" (group/culture) inhibiting or enabling sustainability? **Intercorporeal dimensions** (e.g., group feelings, shared somatic realities) **Worldviews** (e.g., group beliefs, stigmas, cultural norms) **Compassionate Perspectives** (e.g., ethics, religious community)	**In what ways is/are "It(s)" inhibiting or enabling sustainability?** **Physical and Natural Systems** (e.g., ecosystems, watersheds, built environments, roads) **Social Systems** (e.g., economics, institutions, laws) **Subtle Systems** (e.g., subtle energy, architecture, sacred gardens)

Figure 4.6 | *Barriers and Supports for Sustainable Behavior (Owens et al. 2005). This figure shows how all quadrants can contribute to overcoming barriers and supporting sustainable behavior (UR). The arrows indicate the direction of influence from each quadrant into the UR. In place of "sustainable behavior" we could easily put "participatory planning behaviors."*

Quadrants and levels of consciousness are the most useful features of AQAL to analyze heritage planning and lay down a path toward Holistic Planning. Each of chapters 5 through 8 deals directly with a quadrant of AQAL and its role as a practical pillar of Holistic Planning.

Leave Out a Quadrant, Leave Out Forces That Work Against Us

Sonars detect oncoming torpedoes. Radars detect missiles. What happens when we turn off our sonar or drop a sandwich over half the screen? This is what many in the development world do when they do not consider all quadrants. It should be clear by now that when planners or program developers fail to consider certain perspectives of the AQAL, they drastically increase their chances of program and plan failure. How do we influence these invisible forces if we do not even recognize they exist? In the realm of planning, we can see that interventions most often focus on skills and tools necessary to make and implement plans (UR) and maybe institutions, budgets, and incentives for planning (LR). In both cases, program people usually focus on external aspects of planning and mostly ignore internal ones. In fact, Brown (2007) studied eight major books about sustainability and found that they overwhelmingly discussed solutions in the LR quadrant, with vastly reduced attention to other quadrants. To produce successful change, our chances greatly increase when we identify major forces in all four quadrants and address them. If we ignore a force in one quadrant, that unseen force could sink our ship.

Note that these quadrants do not work in isolation. They constantly interact with one and another. For example, in planning, local planners may feel excluded from the planning process (UL) because of the bureaucratic top-down mindset (LL). This results in local planners' lack of motivation (UL), resulting in passive participation or even sabotage of the planning (UR) (Naughton 2007). The institution then might offer incentive policies to participants such as paying for transportation and hotel stay (LR). It may as well conclude that its own staff is not skilled enough to manage planning and thus set up systems for hiring nonstaff consultant planners (LR). An institution hiring consultants may lower staff self-esteem (UL), which reduces motivation to learn planning skills and consequently lowers skill levels still more (UR).

The interplay between interior and exterior dimensions as well as between individual and collective dimensions enriches and complicates planning. To make matters more interesting, as worldviews and paradigms change, new phenomena emerge in all four quadrants. For example, leadership evolves in all quadrants: UL—strong ego belief that "I will save the day" to "I will help others lead;" UR—behavior of top-down command and control to group process facilitation; LL—belief that the top is where the smartest and most capable reside to the belief that all levels are important for success; LR—huge salary compensation for leaders to financial incentives for other levels as well.

A most important line in both interior dimensions is consciousness, and its evolution has been speeding up.

Consciousness Is a Principal Component of Integral Theory

Wilber focused on twelve theories of consciousness (Wilber 1997) in creating the AQAL. Consciousness, he discovered, evolves not just for individuals but for collectives as well, although through different mechanisms. Thus over human history, consciousness has been evolving with no signs of stopping. So where, then, did consciousness begin, and where is it going?

Wilber describes a hierarchy of consciousness levels within which each higher level arises through conflict. Each level or worldview arises from tension between people's perceived external life conditions and their internal values. This tension between negative external conditions and positive values drives people to develop or evolve solutions that reduce the tension and bring external reality into greater harmony with internal values. This tension drives all kinds of development. For example, physical challenges drive children's increased use of body and brain. Interpersonal challenges create opportunities for teenagers to learn to deal with others. Existential challenges help adults to mature—for example, how to deal with a midlife crisis, death of a loved one, or the traumatizing destruction of a giant Buddha statue in Afghanistan. Threats to heritage drive planners to innovate new solutions for its protection.

Throughout human history, then, one level of consciousness has evolved into the next. Each level is conscious or aware of a greater portion of reality than the previous, and we all experience multiple levels throughout our lives (as we do with so many other psychological qualities).

In effect, a person or group has an average center of gravity that is more descriptive of the level at which their behavior and values function. Although a person might be studying Integral Theory, he or she remains anchored in Postmodernism, and perhaps that person's fascination with professional sports reflects the Modernist value of competition. Finally, although that person does not practice religion, she identifies with her Jewish roots, especially when she hears about anti-Semitism, harking back to her Traditionalist days. Remember that evolution transcends and includes, but does not discard its component parts. Similarly, in any given society there will always be people from different levels of consciousness, although societies will vary overall.

Here, then, follow the worldviews whose names come from McIntosh (2007).

Archaic

The earliest human consciousness corresponds to preculture, which relied mostly on basic instinct to survive. This level of consciousness marked hominids for millions of years. Today we can only find this level in infants or adults who have regressed due to severe cerebral injury or illness.

Tribal

For tribal peoples, spirits inhabit all aspects of nature, whether rocks, skies, or animals. These spirits exert power over people sometimes gracing them with favors and others times bullying them. The animistic mystery of this world fills tribes with fear. They survive by forming tightly knit, cohesive tribal groups in which everyone does everything possible to support the group. They follow rituals to appease spirits, believe superstitions that explain spirit behavior, and subjugate themselves to the words and eternal wisdom of shamans.

The Tribal worldview barely distinguishes itself from surrounding elements, blending objects and subjects—the ultimate in closeness to nature. Its organization in small, tightly integrated tribes remains close to their body and has been a stable and successful strategy for millennia. Eventually some tribes became very successful in this context, bringing their external conditions into greater coherence with internal values. The energy once dedicated to solving the spirit problem was rechanneled into longing for change. Higher needs and values awakened. Some tribes began to reject complete submission of individuality, subjugation to the group. They expressed their own individuality, motivation, and personal ideas. They accumulated wealth and developed new technologies, setting the ground for a more warlike worldview.

In general tribes do not need to plan as most of their behavior is prescribed by eternal cycles and traditional wisdom orally passed down through generations. For daily matters they use a lot of trial and error.

Warrior

The Warrior worldview marches forth from oppressive tribal control. Warrior-minded groups see the world as insecure and threatening, but this time they can do something about it as individuals. They strive to maximize individual positions, gratify immediate needs, and they crave honor and fear shame as they fight for what is theirs in a jungle of predators. Warriors excel or fall because of personal strength, initiative, intelligence, and charisma. Their numbers include

Mongols, Vikings, barbarians, and even contemporary terrorists, street gangs, and warlords of Afghanistan and Somalia.

They are much more individual-oriented than Tribals; they are egocentric, trusting none but themselves. As Tribal consciousness contributes closeness to nature, strong kinship, and individual self-sacrifice to the human legacy, Warriors offer individual expression, initiative, and creativity. Nevertheless, the energy invested in fighting for their share of the cookies increased wealth in some groups, which liberated that energy to pursue desires not yet experienced in human history: to be free from a brutal and chaotic life and to create something bigger than small Warrior groups.

Warriors must plan attacks, where they will set up houses, plant crops for next season, and make other short-term, tactical decisions. Because they rely on personal initiative and creativity, their behaviors are no longer commanded by generations of experience.

Traditional

Traditional consciousness rejected Warrior chaos and violence, short-term thinking, and insecurity. They labeled it an "evil" that required salvation, law, and order to vanquish. Thus, each level of consciousness develops new technologies to meet their needs, to harmonize unfavorable external life conditions with positive internal values. The Traditional mindset invented the written word so that it could document and encode the new law and order revealed by higher powers and mediated by elites who could read and write.

Thus to conquer the Warrior mentality, Traditional consciousness created hierarchies based on unquestionable codes of law. Although these codes required faith and loyalty, in exchange, Traditional peoples enjoyed not only liberation from Warrior culture but also the benefits of advanced organizations and division of labor. They essentially created civilization, fabulous works of art and architecture, specialized professions, and, of course, law and order.

As with Tribal societies, Traditional ones valued self-sacrifice for the greater good. Their followers received salvation through obedience and faith in a clearly defined right-and-wrong, a black-and-white, unambiguous story about how the world works. The energy used to defeat the Warriors and elevate their own groups—whether the Roman Empire or the Catholic Church—resulted in a strong group affiliation, then ethnocentrism, dogma, and patriotic nationalism, which became the pathology that every successful worldview eventually produces, planting seeds for the next worldview to germinate.

Nazi Germany would prove an excellent transitional example between the required obedience and belief in Aryan-based, hyper-ethnocentric supremacy and the Modernist military and scientific machine that blitzed across Europe.

Traditional collectives need long-term planning to build cities and conquer vast lands. The systems in which they operate may not be so complex, but their plans can often span generations.

Modernist

Ancient Greeks had already turned in blind faith, dogmatism, and mystical understandings for rationality, meritocracy, and social progress. For good or ill, though, the Greeks could not sustain their Modernism against the advance of the Roman Empire. It did not reappear again in long-lasting form until the European Enlightenment, a millennium later.

In both times, people began to reject rigid, obedience-based, right-and-wrong codes of Traditional cultures. Early Modernism instead yearned to advance in social status and standard of living based on individual merits, on the power of individual minds and hands. It dumped faith for rationality. It subordinated permanent, heritable station to upward mobility based on personal capability. To do this, Modernists invented science, which depended on the power of mind more than any religious dogma. It championed new values of individual liberty to justify people's rights to excel in their own best interest.

Science then stripped spirituality from nature so that natural resources could be freely converted and transformed, allowing people to create their own future. Modernism added the values of progress, empiricism, and technology to their toolbox and as a result created or professionalized many of today's great institutions, including democracy, science, university education, modern medicine, bureaucracies, capitalism, modern militaries, industrialization, multinational corporations, and professional sports.

Although Modernist thinking contributed many positive innovations to the human legacy, its drive for self-improvement brought with it its own pathology. Its emphasis on scientific empiricism meant that anything that could not be measured did not exist. As such it stripped spirituality and meaning from places and nature. To be successful required that one compete. That meant (as with the any majority-takes-all democracy) that there had to be losers. Those losers included everyone who wielded less power, whether women, minorities, indigenous peoples, or a commoditized nature itself.

Modernism invented the PLUS World paradigm necessary to use concepts of science, technology, and progress. The world was supposedly composed of interchangeable parts, a giant machine that could be fixed when broken or replaced when outmoded, used most notably in modern medicine.

Modernism sows the seeds of the next stage in three ways. First, its own scientists have discovered that PLUS assumptions could not explain the DICE World that their own science was revealing. Second, Modernism's own achievements have left behind so many discontents that these would transform into the next—and very unsatisfactory—perceived life conditions of those who would reject Modernist "success." Third, the Modernist central economic system has been shaking (neoliberalism in particular), maybe even toppling, inciting people to question some of its fundamental values (Gerzema et al. 2010).

Modernism now faces an increasingly complex world, and its plans have been growing in sophistication. Modernist planning has been developing tools to make the world more simplistic, understandable, and predictable, according to PLUS thinking. Modernists created the first professional planners and planning schools. Yet in the face of the DICE World, modernist planning has been suffering a rocky but sure transition to Postmodernism (McGrath 1998, Sancar 1994).

Postmodern

For all that Modernism contributed to civilization, it also left behind an oily record of industrial pollution, oppression, meaninglessness, placelessness, greed, sexism, and weapons of mass destruction. In the 1960s many Modernists had had enough, turned in their badges, and evolved a Postmodern consciousness.

In only a few short decades Postmodern thinking has championed all the leftist, liberal, socially conscious causes under the sun, dedicating itself to bringing back excluded points of view of oppressed people as well as the importance of wildlife and environment. The intention is to bring down oppressive hierarchies, bring up world's cultures, bring everyone over to the consensus table, bring an end to war, and bring back everything good and natural that Modernism had stomped into spiritless soil.

Postmoderns in their zeal to include all those who had been excluded by the modernists, believe that everyone boasts a valid opinion; all perspectives are of equal truth and validity. People furthermore have great potential to mature spiritually and as part of a growing egalitarian community. Postmodernism champions organic food, meditation, intentional communities, green living, and adds a meaningful, spiritual, interior dimension to DICE that Modernism missed when scientists first began to untangle complexity, chaos, and quanta.

Although worldcentric, highly sensitive, and inspired by many noble socio-environmental agendas, Postmoderns have already laid the tracks for the arrival of the next stage of consciousness. Its drive to include and defend all individuals, its focus on the individual ego has become what Lasch (1979) called a "culture of narcissism." Because it dislikes political, religious, and economic hierarchies that oppressed minorities, it extends its ill will to all kinds of hierarchies, including intellectual, moral, aesthetic, and spiritual. This rejection even of natural hierarchies created by evolution (for example, atom-molecule-cell-organism) erects a tall barrier to social and spiritual development. The elimination of traditional sources of meaning such as religion have left Postmodernism without any spiritual reference—in effect, leaving it to narcissistically focus on the only thing that remains: itself.

Even more, Postmodernism has claimed to be sensitive and egalitarian, yet loathes values of Modernist and Traditional groups, waging a righteous culture war with them. By giving equal value to all people and all points of view, in other words, value relativism, Postmodernism has sacrificed its ability to judge the quality of different strategies and perspectives, whose careful selection is critical to defend against titanic threats to civilization.

Postmodernism has only been around since the 1980s. But even in this brief period, worsening life conditions of people around the world combined with value relativism and culture wars that play out in daily newspapers, the ground had been set for the emergence of Integral consciousness.

Postmodernism has all the complexity of Modernism—plus it recognizes the world is not simply PLUS. It also pushes to make planning collaborative, participatory, inclusive, and bottom-up.

Integral

Postmodernism, despite its idealism, has triggered many battles: alternative and modern medicine, conventional and organic agriculture, top-down leadership and dispersed networks, equal rights and religious hierarchy, socially responsible investing and profit maximization, and so on. These tensions have led some people to note that the battles represented a set of values organized into hierarchical, evolutionary waves.

Integral consciousness was the first to realize that human culture in fact consists of different stages of consciousness. It understands that consciousness evolves as do biology and technology. As with all evolution, the process transcends and includes simpler forms—elements, cells, planets, and earlier forms of consciousness—preserving their properties while at the same time incorporating them into larger wholes. Integral mindset can see how each stage builds on earlier stages, bringing forward positive aspects and values as well as pathologies. It knows, as developmental psychologists point out, that stages cannot be "skipped" because each lays the groundwork for the next. We cannot have molecules without atoms, words without letters, or identification with all animals without first identifying with all humans. We do, of course, evolve through levels at different rates, and we all reach different stages during our lifetimes.

For Integral Theory, evolution and consciousness top the tree of values. All human problems have a consciousness component, and Integrally minded people dedicate themselves to speeding up evolution to overcome problems generated by earlier stages. They understand the spiritual, interior component of development and the cyclical, systemic nature of evolution.

To deal with problems involving people at different levels of consciousness requires conversations that invoke values relevant to those levels. Barrett Brown describes how Integral practitioners can either transform or translate values for different levels of consciousness. Many heritage managers dream that if only neighboring communities enjoyed greater consciousness or more environmentally friendly values, the site would suffer less deforestation, looting, or vandalism. What managers are really saying is, "Oh, if only we could transform their values to ones at a more evolved level." As Brown writes (2005): "Changing someone's values—achieving this shift in consciousness—is normally very difficult." See Toolbox 4.

Kegan (1998) notes that it takes about five years for an adult to shift to a completely new way of seeing the world, and only if a number of conditions are present. However, many people freeze in their development, seeing the world with the same core values for decades.

Integral planning builds on Postmodernism by integrating processes that strongly consider interiority It diagnoses situations using an Integral lens. It also recognizes that any given situation has a mix of consciousness levels with different values and life conditions that must be considered in decision making.

Since levels of consciousness greatly influence our values, how we use power, reflect our life conditions, and detail future needs, the kind of planning we need to survive is also affected. As change accelerates, humanity confronts new challenges and requires new forms of planning, such as Holistic Planning.

Toolbox 4 | *Translation Beats Transformation on the Road to Sustainability*

People of different consciousness truly use different value lenses to see the world. People of earlier levels have not experienced values of higher levels and thus cannot understand them. So often, those of one level try to transform others. They try to convince them of their values, say a Postmodern arguing to a Modernist about animal rights or a Modernist arguing to a Traditional about economic growth, or a Traditional arguing to a Warrior about God-ordained law. These arguments simply do not resonate with values that others hold.

A primary Integral tool, then, is translation that frames arguments in terms of the audience's values, not the communicator's. Barrett Brown, expert in Integral leadership, writes (2005) this about translation with respect to sustainability:

> Fundamentally, translation is a way of truly honoring people where they are, without trying to change them. The process is to carefully frame a sustainability message in a way that resonates with someone's worldview, with their deepest values and motivations. If framed well, and supported with the requisite prompts and reinforcements that help people establish habits, behaving sustainably can become a part of people's everyday living.

A project that worked with local farmers in Bosra, Syria, had to translate sustainability to their values. Maalouf says that sustainability implies long-term planning and vision, which makes little sense to poorly educated people with daily struggles to find a job and make ends meet. So they chose an example that makes sense (Human Emergence Middle East n.d.): "The Bosra amphitheater is a great example of sustainability. Their ancestors kept it intact for more than 2,000 years by burying it in the sand and building an Ummayad fortress around it." Translations more common to heritage managers might include these values:

- To translate the Postmodern values of heritage conservation for a Modernist, we might focus on the economic benefits of tourism revenues or conserving ecosystem services.

- To translate heritage conservation to Traditionals, aside from protecting God's creation, some heritage highlights achievements of certain groups favorable to the Traditional.

- To translate heritage conservation to Tribals, we might focus on indigenous territorial rights, hunting grounds, protection of sacred spaces.

Transition to a New Worldview Changes Many Paradigms

Kegan (1994, p. 351) defines Integral consciousness as, "the capacity to see conflict as a signal of our overidentification with a single system." To not overidentify with any single system in any quadrant, a person must see that system, converting the previously hidden system (which was part of the self) into an object, seen and recognized from the outside. This is how people advance from one level of consciousness to the next—this may be how a person develops and matures to see clearly what was formerly invisible. This also means that Integral thinking can take advantage of any previous stage to handle different life conditions. If conditions require, an Integral mindset can create solutions that are nonhierarchical, consensus-based forums or solutions that are top-down and hierarchical—for example, police-like control of looters in an archaeological site. This power to create solutions using values and tools of different worldviews will become important as we define what planning and management might look like.

Of course, according to Integral Theory, it, too, will develop pathologies that feed the emergence of post-Integral stages. McIntosh (2007) thinks that characteristics such as elitism, impatience, insensitivity, and the allure of post-Integral culture will carry Integral consciousness up the evolutionary spiral.

As worldviews evolve, so, too, do the forests of paradigms that grow from their soil, nourishing them with values and assumptions. Paradigms themselves are people's solutions to perceived challenges in the external environment. Paradigms can go extinct or actually pass between worldviews, but they often change as they do in response to new values. For example, environmental education, adaptive management, and heritage interpretation are all fields born during Modernism in response to environmental problems caused by Modernism. To reverse this history of environmental problems, each field began with Modernist assumptions focused on science, rationality, and the objectively measurable facets of reality. Environmental educators and interpreters therefore taught and interpreted about nature and science. Adaptive management advocates used the problem-solving scientific method to learn and improve management. These approaches all safely remained within Modernist boundaries.

With the arrival of Postmodernism, these same fields adopted its ideas about the spiritual, ethical, and political aspects of environmental destruction. They argued for more participation, considered human rights, community involvement, inclusiveness, other forms of knowing, value relativism, and so forth. In effect, they transcended and included their Modernist versions, by expanding on them, adding new perspective and values to those of their Modernist colleagues.

Of course, many social, cultural, and technological paradigms die a slow death as worldviews change. Diffusion rates and tipping points vary for different paradigms, cultures, and organizations. Various paradigms are currently on their way out, such as the internal combustion engine; cancer treatment that burns-cuts-poisons the body; antibiotics; fortress conservation; command-and-control, top-down organizations; and teacher-centered memorization-based teaching. In science, of course, new paradigms destroy old ones; none just linger around. Science cannot function with two contradictory, mature paradigms. Heliocentrism destroyed geocentrism, and Darwinism destroyed Lamarckianism without the possibility of prolonged coexistence. Regardless, whether totally replaced or only improved, paradigms set the stage for their evolved replacements.

We can now see how the PLUS World and Rational Comprehensive Planning (RCP) paradigms rose from the soil of Modernism. Both paradigms depend on Modernist assumptions of a world that is an understandable, predictable, and fixable machine. The world must operate this way or else a methodical, controlling science could not be possible. Without that, progress and technology would not promise humanity hope to overcome our problems (which we have not overcome anyway) and drive civilization forward.

Modernism still dominates conventional planning in heritage areas. We still approach plans with large helpings of rationality, technicality, empiricism, and a craving for discrete, implementable solutions. We can also see now how Modernism's own scientific process, by discovering quantum, relativity, complexity, and chaos theories, has reduced PLUS to describing fewer and fewer real-life situations, at least among physicists and systems modeling folks. Many of the rest of us still lag pretty far behind. RCP has been retreating in other fields of planning, including urban planning (Bandarin 2014) and business planning, although it remains strong and tall like a canopy tree in the protected area forest.

This argument does not ignore progressive Postmodern contributions to protected area management, such as increased public participation, human development, animal rights, multiple forms of knowing, and spiritual values of place. Planning paradigms evolve in response to the changing character of the context—or at least our changing perceptions of the context. It does so like all aspects of society, at times incrementally and at other times with big leaps. Protected areas specialist Jim Barborak, recalls incremental advances in his own work (pers. comm. 2009):

> I do not believe that there has been a Stephan Jay Gould–type punctuated equilibrium situation with protected area planning, but rather a gradual process of

evolution from one person to teams to interdisciplinary and interinstitutional, from no consultation to broad consultation with stakeholders, from looking from borders inward towards landscape and seascape approaches, and similar thinking on other themes has evolved. I was already doing public participation workshops at La Tigra [National Park] in Honduras in 1977; we already had proposed a formal buffer zone for the area, and in the early 80s in La Amistad [Costa Rica]; we already had social scientists on our multidisciplinary, interinstitutional team and did our best to consider landscape issues, altitudinal and latitudinal connectivity, indigenous issues, watershed issues, etc.

Onaran and Sancar (1998) note that Postmodern planning has allowed new themes to enter discussion. We can now speak not just of spaces but also places and place identity, sense of place, caring, uniqueness, authenticity, stories of the land, and symbolic values. Places are no longer only "natural or cultural resources"—they can even be home.

We regularly talk about sustainability today, where before Modernists only talked about scientific management, rational use, maximum sustainable yield, and protectionism, because for them, resources, inputs, and material building blocks have no moral endowment.

The third major theme that has been chipping at Modernist planning has been participatory democracy rather than traditional authoritarian, technocratic, expert-driven, and formal control.

Protected area planning has also just begun to include other, nontechnical points of view and ways of knowing. For example, when technicians of CATIE worked on the management plan for the territory of the Kuna Indians in Panama (Inside the Box 2.1), the Kuna easily understood the modern concept of protected areas because their culture already had botanical "parks." These areas of virgin forest found on the mainland coexisted with nearly all Kuna communities. The Kuna left these *boniganas* or spirit sanctuaries untouched, even ones very apt for agriculture, because malevolent spirits could rise up and attack communities if their lands were disturbed. No Kuna can farm within the boundaries of the spirit sanctuary, and certain larger trees may not be removed because the spirits string their clotheslines among tree branches. Felled trees would make them very mad as well as it would sully their clothes. Interestingly, these sanctuaries are true botanical parks because medical practitioners may gather herbs there. North American Indians often have similar sacred protected areas such as burial grounds, mountain peaks, and geological formations like Devil's Tower in Wyoming.

As another conservationist, Allen Putney, said at the 2006 Latin American Parks Congress in Bariloche, Argentina, protected areas managers still do not accept traditional knowledge as part of a rational comprehensive process, except in the context of indigenous peoples. We would also be hard pressed to see strategies in management plans based on intuitive, experiential, collective, or spiritual ways of knowing.

As Integral Theory points out, the goal should not simply be that Postmodernism make deeper inroads into the Modernist forest—Postmodernism has also been unable to solve society's problems. It still suffers from a rampant fragmentary approach to dealing with different issues. It depends greatly on financial, political, and power institutions formed by Modernism in order to operate (e.g., World Bank). Its value relativism slows the selection of options that work best. It fights with the values of both Modernism (hierarchy, power, capitalism) and Traditionalism (ethnocentrism, definitive right/wrong, nonscientific explanations). It is narcissistic, focused on self-indulgent egocentric rights and techniques. Yet if Postmodernism cannot offer salvation from Modernist ills, then we must look now to Integral consciousness for help.

Integral thought expands and deepens our consciousness by adding an interior, multidimensional aspect to evolution that no previous level can see. Integral theorists such as Wilber like to say that Integral consciousness is the first stage to realize that all prior stages have one thing in common: they think their way of seeing the world is the correct way. An Integral thinker, however, realizes that different stages and their survival strategies correspond to different life conditions and values. It also points out that each stage contributes something to our human legacy. It would be as silly to criticize Traditional cultures as it would be to say that cells are an unworthy and outdated part of the more evolved human body. While Postmodernism can imagine a world without Traditional folk, can it really imagine it without highways and democracy?

The Integral Map Points Us toward Possible Futures for Heritage Management

Integral Theory and the Integral Map offer us deep insight not only into why site plans fail to be implemented but also why management and sustainable development in general very often fail to meet expectations, despite millions of dollars, people-hours, and credibility invested.

If indeed we can view any event from four fundamental perspectives, then if we use only one or two our understanding of reality must really suffer. In that case, as Brown (2007) points out, we leave out important aspects of reality from our understanding and hence our programs. Just because we ignore forces that influence implementation does not mean they go away. On the contrary, they work against us below the surface, out of sight and out of mind. Until it is too late.

For example, some university and nonprofit organizations train site staff to use adaptive management. This focus on individual skills comes from the Upper Right (UR) perspective (see Outside the Box 4.1). Yet to implement adaptive management, practitioners need to have a certain level of appreciation for the value of learning (UL). There are cultural beliefs that influence the implementation of adaptive management such as the role of leadership in a learning context or about the kinds of knowledge acceptable (LL). There are institutional forces (LR) that influence implementation of adaptive management such as incentives to learn, budgets for learning programs, safe spaces in which open dialogue can take place, and so on. So, a focus only on technical skills has little chance of improved staff performance when forces in the other three quadrants also push and pull, well beyond the reach of limited training programs. Never mind that forces from these four quadrants all endlessly interact!

Thus in chapters 5 through 8, we consult our AQAL to dive deeper down the iceberg. We pay particular attention to the evolution of consciousness, which helps us see where planning has come from and where it may go.

Chapter 9 integrates all four quadrants and offers a definition, principles, and hands-on techniques for making Holistic Planning a reality. In so doing, this final chapter takes us from the dark oceanic depths toward the other side of the iceberg, into the light on the other side of complexity.

> *What often happens if you study this Integral Map is that it begins to make room in your psyche, in your being, in your soul, for all the parts of you that were disowned, whether by society, your parents, your peers, whomever. An Integral approach even makes room for those who did the disowning to you.*
>
> —Ken Wilber

Part II
Holistic Planning Responds to the Challenges of a Changing World

The triskelion or triskele represents the emerging vision of Holistic Planning. This ancient symbol has appeared in many ancient cultures dating back to Malta (4400–3600 B.C.). The three interlocking spirals set on a stone plate resting on a green field represent the Big Three fundamental perspectives of all reality upon which Wilber (1996) founded Integral Theory. The circle represents holism and the irreducible cyclical nature of reality and development. The integration of this symbolism evokes the creative impulse of all evolution.

Part II of this book discusses how these notions apply to Holistic Planning.

CHAPTER 5

Managers' Minds Influence the Plans They Write

> *No pessimist ever discovered the secret of the stars, sailed to an uncharted land, or opened a new heaven to the human spirit.*
>
> —*Helen Keller*

THE OTHER
SIDE OF
COMPLEXITY

EVENTS

PATTERNS

STRUCTURES

MENTAL MODELS

Mind the Mind

Numerous professions work almost entirely within the experience of the mind. Magicians such as David Copperfield fool the audience's mind into believing illusions. Clinical psychologists calm patients' emotional and psychic storms. Criminal profilers and investigators such as Sherlock Holmes teleport themselves into the mind of the bad guys to reenact and solve murders. Novelists control every detail as they guide a reader's internal experience from first to final word. Captains, too, must manage their sailors on long, forlorn voyages.

One might expect that almost any profession that works with people would strongly involve their inner experience. Yet conventional planners—like many Modernist professionals—often peer outward to the physical world, missing the psychocultural aspects of individuals and groups. They at times undervalue beliefs, emotions, experiences, motivations, thoughts, and fears of the very people they intend to serve. This irony enlarges still more when we think that everything we plan and do ultimately emerges from the mind.

To avoid confusion, we should be clear that some theorists regard "mind" differently from Integral thinkers. The former understand mind to include a person's skills and behaviors, which the Integral framework focuses squarely in the Upper Right (UR) (see Outside the Box 4.1). This difference hardly explains the already well-discussed preference of conventional planners to focus on the physical, material, and measurable. And traditionally, planners have actively avoided the political domain, envisioning themselves as recommending, not deciding, actions (Ferguson 1994; Ferguson and Lohmann 1994).

Being apolitical is entirely consistent with the PLUS World in which Modernists see themselves as technicians, not politicians. Yet heritage site planners, like most planners, play in a hotly political environment. There they propose policies and respond to political pressures, misinformation, and hidden agendas. Forester (1989, p. 27) talks about the political challenges of rational comprehensive planning: "Planners often have had little influence on the implementation of their plans. Those painstaking plans have too often ended up on the shelf or have been used to further political purposes they were never intended to serve." How to deal with politics—fueled by interior motivations and values—has always been a source of great confusion for conventional planners (Baum 1988).

Conventional planners often downplayed or denied meaningful public participation as unimportant, as "regular" people simply are not qualified to contribute to technical planning discussions. What do local farmers in Bhutan, after all, know about land use zoning in Jigme Dorji National Park, or a Kenaitze Indian teacher in Alaska about maximum sustainable yield of salmon runs in the Kenai River? If stakeholders do not have technical expertise, then rational comprehensive planners likely do not think they can contribute to planning in any substantive way. Alternately, conventional planners assume that politicians—also nontechnical people—will make the "best" decision based on the technical alternatives that those planners lay out in their plans. Baum (1996), however, states emphatically that theorists maintain this assumption, however unrealistic it might be.

Modernist bureaucracies often do not consider the Upper Left (UL) (as described in chapter 4, the UL refers to the realm of the interior individual experience consisting of one's thoughts, values, emotions, and so on) of their stakeholders.

Ignoring the mind can generate major trouble, often leading to unintended consequences confronting unsuspecting protected area staff. Such side effects could lead to the failure of multimillion-dollar World Bank development projects. These failures in turn further impoverish poor people, according to Ferguson (1994), referring to management plans that languish on shelves

Exclusion from planning and policy development can provoke local resistance, ranging from arson in Andringitra National Park in Madagascar (Kull 2002) to revolts against the New Forest National Park Authority in the UK (Savill and Mole 2008) to simply a bitter lack of support that has paralyzed Prokletije National Park in Montenegro, leaving it without staff, infrastructure, or even a management plan (Vugdelic, pers. comm. 2010). Scott (1987, 1992) writes about how locals, peasants in particular, may resist or sabotage government efforts rather than mount open and unwinnable revolutions. In many cases, locals also battle to protect protected areas from higher levels of government, such as those who opposed a secretive proposal to build a motorway from Moscow to St. Petersburg right through the Khimki Forest Park (Chirikova 2010).

It should be evident that forces do emanate from the UL that are capable of influencing planning and implementation success. Of course, according to Integral Theory, all quadrants reveal different forces, like a radar that scans all directions for blips of incoming missiles. This information about forces helps planners decide where to spend limited effort and money, which forces to confront, and which ones can be set aside. We can, of course, ignore these forces, but that ignorance does not eradicate them; it merely obligates those forces to conjure their debilitating magic offstage and out of sight.

Most heritage site development, as with development in general, focuses on the right-hand column (UR, LR): the external, objective, material, empirically measurable world. Conservation and site development programs continue to invest heavily on guard, interpretive guide, and technical trainings (UR). Funding agencies aim their monies at large, visible institution building projects (LR), such as visitor centers, financial management systems, and, of course, management plans.

Our comments do not imply that no conservation efforts consider the left-hand column. In fact, most likely do to some extent, but not enough. A precious few, however, such as the World Wildlife Fund (WWF) Dialogues (Outside the Box 5.1), bestow on the left-hand column their primary focus, investing energies in interior realities that affect the success of conservation.

Outside the Box 5 | *WWF Aquaculture Dialogues Work Especially with Interior Realities*

Retaining the Problem at Belize Shrimp Farms

When the World Wildlife Fund (WWF) team arrived at the Royal Maya shrimp farm in Belize, Eric Bernard, a French shrimp farm specialist, nodded at what he saw. "There are no feed bags lying around. The water color is the same everywhere. The aerators are being maintained, no barnacles, dirt, and in good shape." But he knew there was much more to managing a sustainable shrimp farm, even one partnered with WWF like this one. If he could sum up such management in one word, it would be retention.

To control polluting sediments (especially shrimp poop and uneaten food) that leak from shrimp farms, the trick is to slow their descent down waterways, giving them time to settle out before they reach ecologically valuable wetlands and the ocean. Settling ponds, recycling water, mangroves to trap sediments, and dams and canals can all slow the flow. In this case, sediments meander their way to Placencia Lagoon, a major seagrass bed where juvenile fish such as barracuda, bonefish, snook, groupers, and others grow before migrating to Belize's World Heritage barrier reef. The Nature Conservancy has wanted to have this lagoon declared a protected area due to its ecological importance, but even if it had, it would not mean much if upriver shrimp farms like Royal Maya didn't take care of their waters.[i]

WWF Leads Global Dialogues to Reinvent Industry Standards

In the case of Belize, WWF can do little more than monitor and coax farmers to adopt best sustainable practices; fortunately, the world's largest conservation organization has its eye on a much bigger fish. Working with Packard Foundation support, WWF labored to establish the first global, credible, and voluntary sustainability standards for shrimp, salmon, tilapia, mussels, and other species. To do this, it set up global Dialogues, multistakeholder consensus-based forums for hammering out standards. But what's different about these Dialogues is their focus on the left-hand quadrants.[ii]

"Conservation in the past has had little to do with multi-stakeholder agreement building. It has been more about NGO groups identifying and pursuing their agendas. They typically followed a 'name and shame' approach…" asserts Merrick Hoben (pers. comm. 2011), head facilitator for several Dialogues and employee of the Consensus Building Institute (CBI), hired by WWF to serve as impartial facilitators for the Dialogues. "It is still practiced by a lot of small and large organizations. More sophisticated conservation groups, however, realize that getting objectives met needs multi-stakeholder agreements and buy in by those affected; otherwise you will not get implementation of those agreements." It doesn't matter where in the world or what kind of ecosystem, stakeholders always decide whether agreements and proposals prove better than doing nothing at all. In the negotiation world to determine whether and how to engage, that is the gold standard.[III]

The premise underlying these Dialogues argues that if a few of the biggest players in the industry of commercializing each aquaculture commodity adopt these standards, eventually consumer expectations and preferences become greener, and the rest of the industry shifts behavior toward sustainability.

Forging Consensus Requires an Integral Approach

But to forge a consensus between wildly diverse stakeholders, such as farmers, distributors, conservationists, community activists, academics, and government officials—each of whom places on the negotiating table a briefcase full of different interests, values, and levels of consciousness—does not happen easily. Although conservation work has traditionally worked mostly in the right-hand column, the Dialogues have employed a more integral approach to building ownership and commitment in order to implement these standards in the marketplace, and keep them clean of the plans-on-shelf syndrome so common in the conservation world.

Just consider that WWF and CBI build skills of stakeholder steering committees (UR) to think in a certain way and have a certain interior experience (UL) so that together they can create a problem-solving culture (LL), build trust and choose commitment to ultimately establish new industry practices (LR). Let's see how they do this.

First Assemble the Right Team

The primordial building block that holds up the Dialogues must be a credible steering committee. Credibility derives from a diversity that reaches out to all participants in the industry across geographies, sectors, and areas of expertise. To strengthen these groups during negotiations, Hoben strongly encouraged WWF to search for missing voices.

But not just any voice can serve in the core group, effective group decision making requires engagement of people with the capacity to not only identify and articulate their own needs (UL), but who value the need to understand other stakeholders' interests (UL) and explore jointly and widely (LL) more elegant solutions that meet everyone's needs.

Once a core group has been assembled, participants must prepare to work together and problem solve. To have a functional, high performing group (LL) requires the right players trained to together forge meaningful agreements. But this first requires that they agree on how to agree. They must jointly develop and commit to implementing ground rules of conversation and consensus building. Before they jump into the crossfire of debate, they absolutely must have this kind of alignment.

Then Get All Interests on the Table

Negotiation success demands that participants place all interests on the table when they enter. "If these interests are not transparent and on the table, if they are not made part of the conversation, they transform into a big hidden agenda that shadows and shapes participants' negotiating behavior—unexplained arguments morph into fixed positions. If they are not understood, they are misunderstood." Then Hoben hits a key point in Integral Theory: "You can't expect them to be fully aware of all those forces on their thinking at all times, so it requires developing a group culture of people who prepare themselves before they come to the table by identifying their interests, how to explain them, figure out how to navigate potential obstacles to getting them met, and how to meet interests of the other side in ways that are good for them while satisfying the concerns for their counterparts." This approach echoes distantly from our normal experience of thinking only about our own priorities.

One notable example, perhaps surprising to many conservationists, concerns a primary interest of conservation groups involved in the Dialogues. At first glance, an outsider would guess that conservation groups' primary interest would be to conserve in a sustainable fashion places such as Khao Sam Roi Yot National Park in Thailand which has been devastated by shrimp farming.[iv] But a primary concern for these groups is actually their reputation in the eyes of colleague organizations.

"Standards are a proxy for scientific integrity of an ecosystem management approach. If colleagues perceive that standards are weak, then their reputation can be damaged. That influences those NGOs to set a very high water mark for each of these standards," notes Hoben. "They are concerned if they compromise any more then, by association, they may be seen as associated with a greenwashing initiative."

Science Supports but Does Not Dominate Dialogues

Although WWF and partners insist on firmly rooting all standards in science, unlike their more Modernist-tilted colleagues, science does not dominate. CBI keeps in clear view of what it calls Joint Fact Finding: Technical Rationality does not substitute for the sociality of negotiation. Dialogue participants, rather, devise technical questions that they need scientists to answer. Scientists then feed requested data back to steering committees so that they may make the tough value-laden decisions and trade-offs that empirical science cannot (Naughton 2007). Thus, we witness a jump in consciousness between Modernists, who believe all problems are technical in nature, and Postmoderns and Integrals who also fit politics and social realities into the decision-making puzzle.

Standards Offer Hope Back on the Farm

On the boat ride through Placencia Lagoon, the local WWF ecologist points out to Eric and others that 83 percent of the nutrients that shrimp farms dump into the Mango Creek estuary does not make it to this lagoon, and none makes it to the reef. He points to the water. If they did, they would destroy critical nursery habitat, smothering sea grass under anoxic sediments. Turning back to the audience, he says that WWF aims to reduce nutrient loading, turbidity, and water exchange at farms and recover 100% of sea grass in the lagoon. "I think that we can do this in five years."

1. *Information about the visit to the Royal Maya comes from Kohl (2008).*

2. *For additional resources on the Dialogues, visit http://cbuilding.org/publication/article/2009/supporting-global-standard-setting-sustainable-aquaculture and www.worldwildlife.org/what/globalmarkets/aquaculture/aquaculturedialogues.html.*

3. *Hoben studied at the Harvard Negotiation Project, the same institution that produced the classic* Getting to Yes: Negotiating Agreement without Giving In *(Fisher et al. 1991).*

4. *According to Jim Enright (2011), Asia Coordinator for the Mangrove Action Project, the park, which is Thailand's first coastal park and eleventh Ramsar site, "could be the most devastated park in Asia caused by shrimp aquaculture....The mangrove loss in the park probably is not the [largest] loss but the park lost extensive areas of other habitats including salt marsh, salt pan and fresh water marshland which was probably the most devastating ecologically." Also see Alexander (2011).*

While most forces that emanate from the depths of the UL do not require high-end techniques like Vulcan mind-melding to manage, they do require identification. Could the WWF Dialogues really build consensus and implementable standards if all participants did not identify and share their interests and motivations? Can any site make significant inroads into improving community-based conservation, poverty reduction, visitor security, or plan implementation if participants' hidden interests morph into hidden agendas that then sabotage site plans? To address these questions, Table 5.1 describes general categories of UL forces that can influence planning and other areas of development. While not an exhaustive list, the reader should be able to visualize the mindscape of possible forces.

Table 5.1 | *Forces That Influence Planning Implementation*

I

Perceptions, Values, and Attitudes

- Sense of self, level of consciousness (egocentric to worldcentric)
- Sense of responsibility, loyalty, and affect toward planning agency, its mission, constituent community, and managed resources
- Sense of trust, transparency, and fairness within agency and constituent community
- Attitude toward participation and rights of other constituents in planning process (levels: none, EIS, collaborative, DNA) (McCool 2000)
- Affect toward people who inspire and guide (priest, respected site manager, president who asks for the plan, foreign donors, friends)[1]
- Perceived behavioral control to act (such as plan), also known as perceived locus of control (Ajzen 1991)
- Role of self in planning (planner, facilitator, core member, peon, other stakeholder) and power to influence planning decisions
- Feeling of recognition[2]
- Visions and dreams of the future

Beliefs, Knowledge, and Experiences

- Past experience in similar processes or local participants
- Anticipated costs of participating in planning process (time, money, risks such as disappointment or loss of face or power)
- Alternative planning approaches known
- Mental model held about the nature of transformation or change (role of science, God, individuals, systems, intuition, luck, destiny, revelation, steady evolution or punctuated equilibrium, etc.)

It

Chapter 6

- Collaborative experience held to achieve common or joint objectives (i.e., Dialogues)
- Purpose of plan (bureaucratic requirement, just for funding, prestige, or to change the world)

Intentions

- Individual goals, interests, and motivation to participate in planning process (see Dialogues)
- Intentions to implement plan and related attitudes[3]

Cognitive Capacities

- Emotional or interpersonal intelligence to work with others in processes[4]
- Capacities to analyze data, understand issues, generate conclusions, focus attention, develop personal vision, maintain discipline, and think critically
- Personal mastery includes rapport with subconscious, integrating reason and intuition, continually seeing more of our connectedness to world, compassion, commitment to the whole.[5]
- Level of loop learning (single, double, triple, and quadruple)[6]

We	Its
Chapter 7	Chapter 8

1. The Theory of Planned Behavior (Ajzen 1991) indicates that there are three predictors of intentions to act: attitude toward the behavior in question (values), subjective norm (that is, other people who affect positively or negatively the intention to act), and perceived behavioral control (the belief whether one actually has control to act). These three influence or predict intentions which are predictors of behavior. The theory also recognizes that external forces can intervene causing us not to act on our intentions. For example, we have the intention to recycle, but due to the lack of a recycling program in our town, we do not recycle.

2. So much has been written about people's deep need to be recognized and that such recognition often transcends salary as a motivation for work. A Google search will instantly reveal dozens of articles on this theme.

3. One's intentions to implement, how optimistic one is with regards to implementing, and similar task-completion predictions all influence our ability to actually complete tasks of any kind (Koole & Spiker 2000).

4. To learn about the full range of skills implied by the term "emotional intelligence," see Goleman (2006).

5. Personal mastery is one of the five disciplines of a learning organization; it is the one that refers most to individuals rather than teams. The other four include systems thinking, shared visioning, team learning, and managing mental models (Senge 1990).

6. There is extensive literature on single- and double-loop learning. Kim (2005) spoke about triple- and quadruple-loops. These loops are also referred to in this book in the wildfire cases (Fire Boxes) that appear in chapters 1, 2, 7, and 8.

Important Questions for Quadrant Forces

Once we have identified forces in any of the four quadrants, then what? Questions follow that planners would ask of any force.

What Conditions or Factors Create This Force?

It is one thing to identify a force, another to understand from where it arises. In the case of the Dialogues, Hoben and colleagues (pers. comm. 2011) argued that conservation groups worry greatly about their reputation in peers' eyes (UL force). This concern, however, has several contributing factors, such as a powerful liking for technical solutions. Effective technical solutions enhance one's reputation, and reputation is critical for obtaining funding.[12]

Similarly, some community members may suffer a general lack of motivation to attend planning meetings or take responsibility for tasks. An analyst without a sense of interior forces might view them as lazy or incapable of seeing their own best interest. With an Integral perspective, however, we ask which forces affect this apparent lack of motivation. Is it a belief that they will be excluded from real decision making? That the entire planning process is just a circus show? That they are not smart enough to participate and would suffer embarrassment if they appeared? Or, that they have a physical or mental illness that might lead to depression (Inside the Box 5)? Or, is it because meetings are so poorly designed or managed that people would rather be home watching a local soccer match on television than attending another boring meeting?

Inside the Box 5 | *Managing Suicide in Japan's Aokigahara Forest*

At the end of Seichō Matsumoto's 1977 mystery novel, *Kuroi Jukai* ("the black sea of trees"), that took place in Japan's Aokigahara Forest on the lower slopes of Mount Fuji, the leading lovers, in order to avoid extramarital blackmail, committed a double suicide in what is known throughout Japan as the "Suicide Forest." Thanks in part to the book's inspiration, the spiritual (and haunted) location, and a literarily inclined as well as suicide-prone economically depressed Japanese society, the dark forest has become one of the world's most popular suicide sites. Since the 1950s more than 500 people have died there.

The park could define the suicide problem in various ways: spiritually inspired, mental health-related, as a Japanese social phenomenon rooted in unemployment, culturally (suicide is still considered an honorable way to go), law enforcement deficiency, suicide education deficiency, deficient infrastructure to prevent suicides, or perhaps as no problem at all (rather the problem belongs to society or individuals). The Yamanashi Prefectural managers eventually defined the problem as a lack of psychological counseling for suicidal citizens, thus underlying the high connection between mental state (UL) and behavior and physical welfare (UR). Consequently, officials deployed signs in the forest, urging those who have gone there to end there not to kill themselves, that family loves them, and they should seek help. Unfortunately, and despite security cameras at the forest's entrance, we'll never know for how many people these last-resort signs prove their suicide solution.

How Does This Force Promote or Inhibit Plan Implementation?

Many UL forces can be grouped in terms of their effect on implementation. These forces, if accommodated, have the power to inject energy and enthusiasm into project planning and implementation where participants dance with excitement and the thrill of contributing to a cause larger than themselves. On the contrary, if planners ignore these forces, then people may not only lack enthusiasm, energy, and motivation to implement but may even muster the motivation to sabotage the very project which requests their participation. In 2009, bureaucrats in Paris proposed turning the Calanques—the stunning cliffs that plunge down to the sea west of Marseille—into France's tenth national park. Chantal Jouanno, the environment secretary, declared, "The idea of the park is a wonderful opportunity ... it will be the most beautiful [park] in France." The locals, who had been excluded from the planning process, however, thought otherwise.

Bitterness bubbled up from fishermen who would be pushed far out to sea to fish. Local environmental groups complained that the park's true purpose was merely to extend capital power, not protect nature, and many people worried that a flood of tourists would end their traditional right to quietly spend afternoons doing very little. One fisherman said to a local newspaper, "They should leave us alone. I'm not against a national park in theory, but we haven't had any serious information about what it will mean" (Burke 2009). This, of course, is just one of innumerable examples of parks imposed by a well-meaning but technically oriented central government. Such good intentions, however, often awaken an unseen UL dragon that breathes fire on rational processes.

How Does This Force Reverberate in Other Quadrants?

Integral Theory quadrants are not isolated from each other; they interact in many ways. In the Calanques example, one could easily imagine that the government proposal stirred up UL interests causing them to speak out (UR), develop solidarity (LL), and form a resistance movement against the park proposal (LR). Caught by surprise, the environment minister travels to Provence (UR) to offer incentives (LR) to people to change their minds (UL) in order to support the park (UR). Of course, the people have "a long tradition of rebellion (LL) stretching back to hatchet-wielding peasants and burghers of Aix-en-Provence who in 1630 took on the government of Louis XIII" (Burke 2009) (LR) and thus harbor a justifiable suspicion of Parisian promises. Instead of pocketing the incentives, they interpret them as an attempt to buy them out. Their response: solidify their resolve (left-hand column) to resist (right-hand column). In real life, however, the government established the park in 2011 in spite of local concerns.

What Solution Most Directly Deflects or Redirects This Force toward Plan Implementation?

A solution always involves doing something in the physical world (right-hand column), which then can affect any quadrant. Thus, a solution could be compensation to the Maasai for loss of grazing land in Amboseli National Park in Kenya (Lindsay 1988). It might be a conservation education program to change locals' attitudes toward the golden lion tamarin in Brazil (Matsuo and Boucinha 2005). It might be a cable car (LR) to connect marginalized slums on the border of the municipal Arví Park to the main transportation hub of Medellin, Colombia, so that people feel more connected and thus improve self-dignity (UL) (Chaves 2008). Every solution ripples across quadrants.

The Lesson

Do not leave home without your quadrants. If planners and project implementers do not consider implementation from all four perspectives, submarine forces may torpedo their projects.

Conventional Planning Generates Various Mind-Based Barriers

Now that we have described forces that work for or against plan implementation, this section considers how conventional planning generates UL implementation barriers. Each of the following chapters will build upon these barriers until chapter 8 offers a full model of barriers that arise from RCP. (Note that chapter 2 presented a list of barriers organized around a more conventional categorization.) Now we take those same barriers and reorder them through Integral eyes (Figure 5.1).

I

- Participants feel no commitment nor choose responsibility because they express needs and problems but do not co-create

- Ownership in plans drops when management leadership changes between or as a result of elections

- Expectations in plan unfulfilled leading to loss of motivation, disappointment, disillusionment

- Low stakeholder involvement due to premium on expert knowledge and minimizing subjective variables, means low power sharing and thus low feeling of stakeholder ownership

- Bureaucratic nature results in low trust, transparency, or sense of fairness to build commitment and voluntary responsibility to implement

- Bureaucratic institutions for various reasons often fail to inspire loyalty and affect, reducing motivation to participate.

Figure 5.1 | *UL Barriers to Planning and Implementation*

Participants feel no commitment nor choose responsibility because they express needs and problems but do not co-create. A conclusion arising out of the Dialogue Movement[13] is that people do not choose to commit or take responsibility for efforts they did not help to jointly create and over which they have no control. People cannot jointly create when leaders marginalize them by stealing their power and giving it to those already powerful. Site managers fail to realize how they slash their own plan's Achilles tendon when they only minimally involve those affected by their plans. Arnstein (1969) created a typology of levels of participation ("Ladder of Citizen Participation"), in which only the top three of eight rungs would constitute the empowerment needed to jointly create implementable projects. Indeed, in chapter 9, we see that Holistic Planning results in a redistribution of power, just as the notion of sustainability does when it recognizes preferences of future generations.

Ownership in plans drops when management leadership changes between or as a result of elections. In competitive politics, when a new administration enters, it often throws its predecessor's pet projects and priorities to the lions. A feeling of "oh, no, what do they plan now" occurs, followed soon after by a jaded "so what" as constituencies feel that promises are as never-ending as they are unimplemented. This happens frequently in the heritage world, especially in countries that appoint personnel politically rather than encourage career-track professionals. Lane (2003) studied implementation barriers for Honduran park management plans and found transitioning governments among the top ten reasons management plans did not get implemented.

Expectations in plan unfulfilled leads to loss of motivation, disappointment, and disillusionment. Most everyone hopes that plans lead to positive change. If that wish did not remain so, sites and their allies would not expend so many resources for their creation. Since RCP sees planning as a nonroutine, discrete event that occurs only once every five to ten years, that rare planning moment raises all sorts of expectations. Further, diligent effort by constituencies to create such a plan elevates their hopes even higher. It should be little surprise, then (although it usually is), that when plans end on shelves after their ritual celebration, people become disappointed with site planning and enact at least a subtle form of sabotage similar to that of many stakeholders: *it's not worth my time to attend more planning meetings.*

Low constituent engagement because of a premium on expert knowledge creates barriers to a sense of ownership needed for implementation. Since RCP places such a high premium on science and expert knowledge, it does not allow meaningful involvement of nontechnical folks or take advantage of the experiential knowledge they may hold. Caron (2014) says stakeholders are actually the greatest source of knowledge in a project. Thus, planners restrict participants—and their ownership in the process—from climbing up the rungs of the citizen participation ladder.

A focus on expert based knowledge often results in low trust, transparency, or sense of fairness needed to build commitment and voluntary responsibility to implement. Aside from the general lack of trust, transparency, and fairness, agencies often engage in activities that degrade relationships. For example, the Fisheries Act of 1986 declared on Union Island, part of St. Vincent and the Grenadines, a marine conservation area. Birdlife International in 1998 also declared it an Important Bird Area. These distinctions owe themselves to the fact that the lagoon has all the primary components of a lagoon–coral reef ecosystem, including a long stretch of outer reefs, a shallow protected inner lagoon, abundant seagrass beds within the lagoon, and a large area of mangroves (largest remaining mangrove forest in the country), as well as salt ponds along the shore. Despite its protected status, a foreign developer proposed an ambitious marina smack in the middle of the lagoon. Its environmental impact study predicted that the marina would inflict significant and irreversible damage.

In spite of these anticipated consequences, politicians permitted the project to proceed, and after a year, the developer declared bankruptcy and disappeared, but not before it had damaged the lagoon much as the study had predicted. Local fishermen could not fish there, local tourism operators could not operate, and local swimmers could not swim in stagnant, algae-infested waters where once a pristine lagoon had reflected a blue Caribbean sky (Sorenson 2008). Acts like these go a long way toward eroding trust, transparency, and a sense of fairness in the community.

Bureaucratic institutions for various reasons often fail to inspire loyalty and affect, reducing motivation to participate. Because conventional bureaucracies, heritage sites or otherwise, treat employees as interchangeable parts of a machine, they pay them to execute one technical function. They require them to do, not necessarily to think. They require obedience to established protocols. They punish errors and blame individuals. They discourage learning, self-expression, and may not recognize work well done. This kind of behavior hardly inspires loyalty or a warm heart either for the formal employees or those who must work with them (Wilson 1989).

Techniques That Integrate the Mind and Improve Plan Implementation

The following section offers techniques that planners and managers can use to prepare minds for planning and execution. We must be careful, however, that users do not regard these techniques as magical answers. Modernism has taught us all to expect, even crave, "correct answers" from higher authorities, leaders, and experts (such as book authors). Indeed, during our professional careers, all classes of formulas, recipes, templates, methodological manuals, routines, and other embodiments of expert wisdom rain down upon us.

If people have any chance of advancing in management, they must take responsibility for their own actions; they must think, experiment, and learn, otherwise the DICE World will consume them and their protected areas in an endless series of surprises and conflicts.

Reaching either the individual mind (UL) or the collective mind (LL) requires that practitioners take actions in the objective, physical world. They may offer training workshops so people develop learning skills, such as those of the Society for Organizational Learning's Leading and Learning for Sustainability course given to the US National Park Service. They may finance continuing education (UR), such as the Colorado State University's or the University of Montana's International Seminar on Protected Area Management. They may allocate institutional funds to create dialogue spaces (LR), such as what WWF and Packard have done. These actions, if well planned and integral, yield positive results in the left-hand column. See Table 5.2.

Table 5.2 | *Strategies to Involve the Upper-Left Quadrant*	
I	**It**
←	**Respect Stakeholder Beliefs, Attitudes, Values, and Fears** Rapid Rural Appraisal, Participatory Rural Appraisal, Participatory Evaluation (Jackson and Kassam 1998), Appreciative Inquiry[1] **Prepare Stakeholders for Co-Creation in the Planning Process** • Orientation, explanation of how process works, as with the Dialogues • Teaching new ways to think as with the Society for Organizational Learning • Warm ups and games for mental awareness and readiness in the moment • Storytelling, prayers, singing to establish mood • Visioning, individual and collective, to create direction and bond the group • Meditation, introspection, contemplation about own role and that of others • Exemplary, symbolic, or model behavior to establish culture (such as leaders who voice constructive criticism; listen deeply; share their emotions, defects, vulnerabilities, and mistakes[2]) • Block's five techniques of engagement (Toolbox 5)

	Promote Stakeholder Empowerment and Psychological Development
	• Myers-Briggs testing, emotional intelligence training, psychotherapy, religious or spiritual counseling
	• Long-term training and education
	• Mentoring
	• Promote the inner game[3]
	• Presencing[4]
	• Teaching about different ways to look at planning before planning
	• Training people to think better, be more aware, whether using systems such as Personal Mastery (Senge), Emotional Intelligence (Goleman), or other learning skills such as reflection-in-action (Schön)
	• Gail Hochacka: as development workers (planners, managers) we have an obligation to attend to our own mentality and consciousness first, before working with others
	• Senge identifies some learning skills
	◊ Recognizing "leaps of abstraction" (noticing our jumps from observation to generalization)
	◊ Exposing the "left-hand column" (articulating what we normally don't say)
	◊ Balancing inquiry and advocacy (skills for honest investigation)
	◊ Facing up to distinctions between espoused theories (what we say) and theories-in-use (the implied theory in what we do)
We	**Its**

1. These approaches encompass many specific tools such as open-ended interviews, focus groups, community mapping, journaling, community transects, community cycle/seasonality mapping, etc. The point here is to involve people in the research of themselves, to discover and empower as well as generate information about the wide range of values, interests, and perspectives in the stakeholder community. The central book for appreciative inquiry is Cooperrider and Whitney (2005).

2. Senge in The Fifth Discipline quotes several leaders on this new outlook. For example, Ed Land, founder of Polaroid had a plaque on his wall that said, "A mistake is an event, the full benefit of which has not yet been turned to your advantage."

3. www.theinnergame.com. From the website: "A phenomenon when first published in 1974, The Inner Game was a real revelation. Instead of serving up technique, it concentrated on the fact that, as Gallwey (1999) wrote, 'Every game is composed of two parts, an outer game and an inner game. The former is played against opponents, and is filled with lots of contradictory advice; the latter is played not against, but within the mind of the player, and its principal obstacles are self-doubt and anxiety.'"

4. Presencing is a skill proposed by Senge et al. (2004) to listen deeply, be open to emerging realities, and be present in them. According to experts in spiritual matters, presencing is not too different from meditation and other spiritual practices, but for the business world, this non-materialist notion is a major breakthrough.

Respect the Beliefs, Attitudes, Values, and Fears of Our Constituencies

One of the first steps in planning is for the core planning team to understand participants at a much deeper level than ever before. Planners want not only to avoid ignoring hidden forces that later surface as disinterest, resistance, sabotage, or even mutiny against planners and managers, but also to truly integrate constituents' interior experience in the process, culture, and solutions that emerge from planning.

Fortunately, a fairly rich history of participatory research in international development can be traced back to the 1970s and includes toolsets and perspectives such as applied social anthropology, farming systems research, rapid rural appraisal, participatory rural appraisal, participatory action research, participatory evaluation, and appreciative inquiry.

This thinking establishes opportunities where community research can actually even benefit the researched communities. By being participatory, participants often come to understand themselves, their role, and their knowledge in new ways that empower them.

Gail Hochachka, an Integral development specialist, has worked extensively in El Salvador. Interviewing Salvadorans in her research site (2005, p. 11), she writes of her experience:

> To truly engage with inhabitants in community-directed work, the development practitioner must be able to "meet people where they are," both in terms of their value-systems and their ways of "making meaning," building a bridge between existing worldviews and the emerging ones (as described by Kegan, 1994). Combining support and challenge … was significant in creating the conditions for health at each stage, and for growth through the various stages, of personal and collective development. In all phases of the methodology, honoring the interior dimensions of the process enabled us to create connections between people and between groups that, in turn, facilitated working with the exterior aspects of arriving at outcomes and carrying out solutions.

Rather than a research project like Hochachka's, Stephan Martineau (2007, 2008) used an Integral perspective to establish a community forest concession in British Columbia's Slocam Valley (Canada), a historically conflictive and densely forested region. The government had repeatedly failed to reach resolution among First Nations, miners, loggers, homesteaders, descendants of a former World War II Japanese-American internment camp, Vietnam War dodgers, and other Postmodern American transplants. Through the use of what he calls Integral

Mediation, which attempts to fully understand the perspectives and values of all actors and contributions that each can make, his core team visited all community members for four years, without ever bringing them all together, to construct a consensus of how they would manage the community forest concession.

He points out that ideally everyone on his core team would have an Integral perspective but admitted the difficulty in finding enough such people. Instead, he identifies five lines of psychological development found at all levels of consciousness. That is, these lines do not depend on a person's worldview. If one can populate a core team with people highly developed in these areas, that core team can apply an Integrally informed approach. These qualities, attitudes, and capacities follow:

- Natural inquisitiveness, an ability and willingness to listen to others

- Integrity and reliability; actions are aligned with words

- A voice of reason to offer to their respective constituency; being respected and carrying a certain influence

- Flexibility: not too entrenched in a particular value system, not too vested in one's own position—personally, socially, or professionally

- An inherent quality of being that includes personal growth as part of the life process, even if only unconsciously

- Motivated by a care and concern for the greater community and ready to seek its betterment, even if the reasons are ultimately personal

Prepare Constituencies for Joint Creation in the Planning Process

An important result is for planners to prepare the constituent community (which includes scientists and managers) to jointly create the plan and implement it. Planning participants may feel they have little influence on the planning process because

- they do not hold the skills, power, or respect of sitting bureaucrats;

- they distrust that planners will actually share power or information or worse feed them misinformation; or

- they feel they are misunderstood and ignored.

Participants holding these feelings will experience at best little motivation to participate or at worst lots of motivation to trip up the process.

Planners can offer a variety of activities to help change these perspectives and attitudes in the short term. The WWF Dialogues team, for instance, recruited participants by explaining consensus-based processes and how their role would directly impact results. They also explained the mutual benefits of having aquaculture standards. In many cases, just the demonstration of the consensus-building process has been enough. In other cases, such as that of Hochachka, simply allowing local people to state their mind, to feel recognized, and to have a dialogue helps to build their self-esteem, which might have otherwise inhibited them from taking any sort of leadership position in activities to come.

Many practitioners agree that dialogue has the power to unleash not only people's creativity but also create bonds and trust and a sense that their contribution to the creation of something new is real and significant (Toolbox 5).

Toolbox 5 | *The Road to Implementation: Block's Five Techniques of Engagement*

People choose to commit to a decision based on emotion, feelings, intuition, trust, hope. These become the playing field for change... The decision to support change is not just based on logic and reason; we need to help our clients deal with attitudes and feelings as well. A core strategy for building emotional commitment to implementation is to design new ways for people to engage each other... Implementation of any change boils down to whether people at several levels are going to take responsibility for the success of the change and the institution.

Peter Block comes from the private sector and offers five strategies to engage participants (2000), whether a product development team or people creating a community park. The goal, he says, is for people to be emotionally committed to implement and to choose responsibility (not just compliance, which is what employees in a bureaucracy do) for doing so. This requires first that there exist trust, transparency, and a sense of fairness.

1.   The Presentation-Participation Balance

At conferences, in board rooms or the cafeteria, the more one person speaks, the less others participate. Even more, the speaker can dominate transmitting the message that he or she is the expert and the only one with something important to say. Even worse when organizers allot no space for real questions, when the speaker cannot even see the audience, or when the speaker recites a scripted and lifeless talk. "All of these practices are more appropriate for a monarchy than a workplace." Indeed, bureaucratic Modernist culture teaches us to listen to and revere leaders and experts.

To even the playing field and share more power, planners will minimize speaking and maximize participating. They realize the important conversations are those that occur between participants. Participation, power sharing, exchange of ideas, and free choice to move in a certain direction that lead to co-creation and engagement. Not talking heads.

2.   Transparency, Full Disclosure, and the Public Expression of Doubt

Anyone who has worked in a bureaucracy, regardless of whether a heritage management agency or toy factory, knows that many things cannot be spoken in the open. Mistakes must be hidden. Criticisms silenced. If workers want to declare what they really feel, they often have to do it in bathrooms, at lunch, or create anonymous avatars in virtual social networks. But as Hoben pointed out, interests and opinions unshared become hidden agendas that warp workplace behavior, tempting sabotage of processes in which people feel excluded. "If we cannot say no, our yes has no meaning."

Expressing one's doubts in public is political power. To redistribute this power, every time people meet, they must have the right to share their thoughts with others. "The truth spoken in public is a rare commodity in most institutions. The success of an implementation strategy will depend on the quality of the conversation that begins it. And the more public the setting, the more powerful the impact," asserts Block.

3.   Placing Real Choice on the Table

In many sites, employees comply — they do just enough to avoid punishment. Compliance is necessary when employees enjoy little motivation to build someone else's pyramids. The leaders may threaten with punishment or dangle carrots, either way, inducements to do what people otherwise would not do. But the more people join in co-creation and shaping a project, the more responsibility and accountability they choose. "Even in this age of self-management and participation, our implementation strategies tend to be packaged long before they are presented. Often the only choice left to people is 'how are you going to support this project?'"

People care for things that they control. When presented with real choices whose decisions result in real consequences, people must learn about the options, discuss them, and then own the result. Under these conditions, true participants become true implementers. In order that those who implement also own that implementation and be accountable for it, requires that leaders redistribute power downward so that implementers can participate in real decision-making and have some control in the decisions.

4. Changing the Conversation

Most conversations echo with déjà vu, that we have heard them before. Often people frame problems the same way as always and the solutions come right off the protected area shelf (perhaps the same one where unimplemented plans lie). We need

- Better monitoring

- More money, time, personnel, information, and political will

- To hire a consultant

- More buy in from local communities

- To reorganize for greater efficiency

- Another plan

Who has not heard these? Notice how these are all expressions of helplessness, placing both blame and solution elsewhere. We disempower ourselves without even realizing it. Our conversations are often guarded where people feel they must protect or hide their true opinions and feelings. By doing this, they avoid key issues and avoid deeper connections with other people that comes with being more vulnerable, personal, and taking risk.

Ultimately our meetings breed cynicism. We feel reluctant or drained at the thought of going to the next meeting, and when the choice exists, we do not go at all. "Sorry, got the flu; sorry, out of town that day; sorry, tired of your damned meetings." Block proposes some ground rules for new conversations.

- Discuss the personal impact the change has on me and us.

- Discourage discussion of anyone not in the room.

- Be careful about discussing history.

- Postpone discussion of action plans as long as possible.

- Discuss what part we have played in creating the situation.

5. Caring about Place

We often say that the message is the medium and then think medium refers to communication technology. Rarely does the room in which we meet constitute that medium. Because if it did, then planners would realize that auditoriums, hotel rooms, or other spaces with institutional lighting, no windows, no plants, and seats all lined up in neatly arranged rows facing forward exude messages of efficiency, hierarchical status, bureaucratic culture, restraint, power, and minimal engagement.

Most office and hotel meeting rooms are designed for persuasion and instruction, not dialogue, feeding expectations of standard meetings, standard results, standard yawns. Where do we often go when we want to do real work? We go to informal locations like someone's house, often with side or outside lighting, comfortable furniture, lots of vegetation, freely available food and bathrooms, and we sit in circles where everyone is equal and can easily talk with each other. Try sitting in a circle with no table in the way and close enough for knees to brush each other to feel what a different kind of conversation might feel like.

Thus we must seek and create spaces that radiate the message of engagement.

Promote Constituency Empowerment and Psychological Development

In the longer term, we can help our constituencies and ourselves grow along a variety of UL lines, such as self-esteem, systems thinking, consciousness, new values, and emotional maturity, to name a few. These often take more time. Often they can occur when institutions commit to longer-term education, mentoring, and simply participation in project design and implementation.

UR Describes What People Do to Plan and Implement

Now that we have glimpsed the forces of the mind that act on the success or failure of site planning, we investigate in chapter 6 what planners and constituent communities do that also affect the same. What we experience in our mind directly affects what we do and how we behave in the material universe. And, it is not always what we think.

> *We can easily forgive a child who is afraid of the dark;*
> *the real tragedy of life is when men are afraid of the light.*
>
> —*Plato*

CHAPTER 6

Managers' Well-Being, Behavior, and Skills Influence Plan Implementation

A man who does not think and plan long ahead will find trouble right at his door.

—*Confucius*

THE OTHER
SIDE OF
COMPLEXITY

EVENTS

PATTERNS

STRUCTURES

MENTAL MODELS

People's Behavior, Competencies, and Welfare Flow from Mental Experiences

While external factors—such as the sudden eruption of a forest fire that incites us to run or a reflex to avoid a falling branch—influence our behavior and welfare, much of our behavior, competencies, and even physical welfare trace directly to our minds. In other words, what goes on in the mind gets imprinted on physical reality as behavior, competencies, actions, and physical welfare.

Mind of course is no synonym for brain. The mind produces our subjective experiences, which cannot be measured or experienced by anyone but ourselves. On the other hand, a cognitive brain scientist can measure brain waves and a surgeon can open up the skull to directly examine gray matter. Thus these electrical-physical aspects of the brain fall into the UR while our thoughts, beliefs, attitudes, and emotions, known only to us, reside in the UL.

Because many interventions such as education, activities, and trainings directly affect the mind, we will see some overlap here with chapter 5. While that overlap serves to reinforce the idea of dynamic interaction between quadrants, this chapter focuses instead on how planners influence UR factors that in turn influence the UL.

Multiple Forces Influence Planner and Constituency Behavior, Competencies, and Welfare

All four quadrants contribute forces that influence planning, whether people's feelings, experiences and beliefs (UL), culture (LL), actions (UR), or institutional factors (LR). Even physical health and welfare (UR) directly influence planning outcomes. If people must dedicate effort and time to deal with health, security, or environmental conditions, they will not attend to higher needs required of planning, such as problem solving, creativity, and a concern for resources and other people beyond the self (Maslow 1943). How effective could planning participants be when hungry, hot, stressed by costs of traveling to a meeting, or even fearful for their own lives, such as park guards killed in Virunga National Park in the Democratic Republic of Congo by rebels in 2011 (World Heritage Center 2011).

Such an understanding would not be complete without the obvious mention that people's competencies and the actions they undertake affect their contribution to or interference with any planning process. Planners' choices and what motivates them means the world to the outcomes they generate. See Table 6.1 for general categories of UR forces that influence planning.

Those who support planners and planning situations, whether NGOs, foundations, or government programs, focus more on UR than any other quadrant. This quadrant includes the overt skills needed to manage protected areas and thus implies the trainings and interventions designed to enhance technical competencies. In its attempt to do so, however, conventional planning generates barriers that trip up even the best-trained planners.

Table 6.1	*Forces That Influence Planning Implementation*
I **Perceptions, Values, and Attitudes** • Sense of self, level of consciousness (egocentric to worldcentric) • Sense of responsibility, loyalty, and affect toward planning agency, its mission, constituent community, and managed resources • Sense of trust, transparency, and fairness within agency and stakeholder community • Attitude toward participation and rights of other stakeholders in planning process (levels: none, EIS, collaborative, DNA) • Affect toward people who inspire and guide (priest, respected site manager, president who asks for the plan, foreign donors, friends) • Perceived behavioral control to act (such as plan), also known as perceived locus of control • Role of self in planning (planner, facilitator, core member, peon, other actor) and power to influence planning decisions • Feeling of recognition • Visions and dreams of the future	**It** **Physical Health and Well-Being** • Health and energy level supports or inhibits participation in plan implementation. These levels are affected not only by above factors, but also by nutrition, medical care, financial state, political culture at local and national levels. **Behavior** • Actions and behaviors promote or inhibit plan tasks, especially working with other participants (opposite sex, local community members, tour operators, people of different status, religions, ethnicity, formality of roles in management, etc.) • Responses to rules and stimuli from management organizations, both incentives and disincentives • Behavior and welfare affected by the built environments, degrees of Biophilia, and structure of meeting spaces **Skills** • Skills and capabilities permit or inhibit participation, planning, and implementation

Beliefs, Knowledge, and Experiences

- Past experience in similar processes or stakeholders

- Anticipated costs of participating in planning process (time, money, risks such as disappointment or loss of face or power)

- Alternative planning approaches known

- Mental model held about the nature of transformation or change (role of science, God, individuals, systems, intuition, luck, destiny, revelation, incremental or big jumps, etc.)

- Collaborative experience held to achieve common or joint objectives (i.e., Dialogues)

- Purpose of plan (bureaucratic requirement, just for funding, prestige, or to change world)

Intentions

- Individual goals, interests, and motivation to participate in planning process (see Dialogues)

- Intentions to implement plan and related attitudes

Cognitive Capacities

- Emotional or interpersonal intelligence to work with others in processes

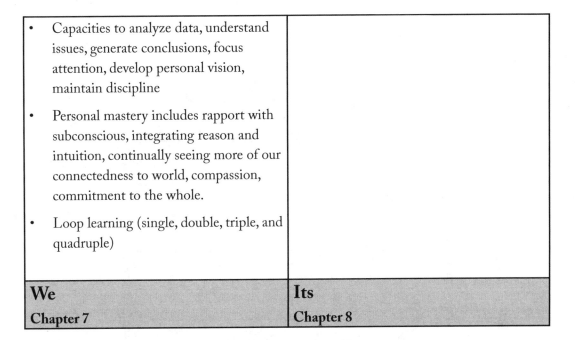

• Capacities to analyze data, understand issues, generate conclusions, focus attention, develop personal vision, maintain discipline • Personal mastery includes rapport with subconscious, integrating reason and intuition, continually seeing more of our connectedness to world, compassion, commitment to the whole. • Loop learning (single, double, triple, and quadruple)	
We Chapter 7	**Its** Chapter 8

Conventional Planning Generates UR Barriers

Investments in Experts over Technical Staff

Conventional managers often invest in consultants to facilitate, think through, and write management plans. They do this because Technical Rationality seeks the best technical criteria and scientific minds that money can buy. When managers invest such resources in consultants, however—whatever their skills or perspectives—these same resources cannot nourish skills and confidence of protected area staff or the rest of the constituent community left behind when consultants depart (Figure 6.1). While a nice plan may result, signed and sealed by consultants, the plan and the community may actually be weakened more than if planning had never occurred in the first place. This occurs because the staff confidence and capability to work inadvertently shifted to the consultant. Systems thinkers say this is an example of "shifting the burden to the intervener" (Chichakly 2010). Sometimes park agencies do not even invest in qualified consultants either (Eagles et al. 2014; Stenseke and Hansen 2014).

This consequence often occurs when an outside intervener enters to accomplish a task for the system, organization, community, or workplace. The recipient system not only can become dependent on the intervener's services, but the system's own capability and confidence to solve the problem can erode. When the intervener leaves, even the prior level of competence to handle the task might have degraded.[15] The costs of reversing the downward spiral could transcend even those of having hired the consultant in the first place. In chapter 9, we propose more beneficial ways of using consultants in a planning process.

It

Investment in Experts over Technical Staff

Management agencies do not invest in staff capacities or skills; rather they dedicate resources to consultant experts. When consultants leave, staff does not have capacity to plan, facilitate, deeply discuss issues, or implement their own plans.

Use of Poor Planning Practices

Lack of investment can result in poor planning practices: constituent community communication; participant coercion; missing components; confused objectives; lack of readiness; shallow reflection; poor facilitation, sterile, unshared vision; many others

Other Behaviors

- People become tired, disappointed, and even depressed when plan produces few results.

- Consultants blamed when process fails.

- Participants sabotage (boycott, do not complete tasks or do so poorly, provoke disputes over interests and territory, ignore plan contents, demand payment for participation) process when they feel no commitment or feel resentment toward it.

- Participants play political and power games to benefit themselves, threaten learning cultures.

- Attempts to manage value conflicts as technical problems.

Figure 6.1 | *UR Barriers to Planning and Implementation*

Use of Poor Planning Practices

A consequence of low investment in staff competencies can result in their use of poor planning practices. Granted, planners can employ ineffective techniques even in a money-rich scenario simply because they uncritically adopt commonly accepted and highly regarded techniques later shown to be lacking. Either way, poor planning practices reduce plan quality and the plan's potential to be implemented.

In protected area planning, many practices are suspect, such as not notifying the public in a timely manner about planning events, limiting comment space to two minutes per person, designating carrying capacity, poorly thought out or vaguely stated objectives (Dvir and Lechler 2004), and writing sterile vision statements that debilitate management plans. Most planners understand that the vision statement, to use one example, articulates a desired future condition for a heritage area. Thus, in pursuit of community participation, facilitators often request favored words and concepts from different participants and glue them together into one general and often uninspiring vision statement.

Some Destructive Behaviors That Can Result from Conventional Planning

Some behaviors destructive to planning and implementation might result from people being excluded from the planning process, as discussed in chapter 5. Such behaviors include plan sabotage, resistance to implementation, and political gamesmanship for personal rather than collective enrichment. Other behaviors might result from the conditions under which planning occurs. These conditions might oblige participants, for instance, to do repetitive, dull, or unstimulating behavior that can cause stress; to work late; to breathe unhealthy air; to take short lunches; to work from a single chair; or to bear loud noises and oppressive smells from a nearby business.

Sometimes planning participants suffer from post-planning stress disorder brought on by disappointment with the process or lack of implementation. Because RCP places so much responsibility in the hands of consultants, managers often find it convenient to blame them when plans fail to meet expectations. Hence shifting the burden to the intervener punishes doubly hard, first by robbing the community of opportunities to plan themselves and second by providing them a comfortable excuse for plan failure, effectively allowing them to avoid self-reflection and criticism of the failure's root cause.

Trainings and Competencies Relevant for Improving Planning

Our competencies begin growing often from our earliest schooling, especially in areas such as language, critical thinking, creativity, and so forth. This development continues through formal university and technical training, which includes the bulk of the nonformal technical training mentioned below. Obviously, the list of skills and trainings could grow very, very long. Our task, however, is merely to paint a cross-section, not build exhaustive lists. We place special emphasis on competencies related to planning in complex and contentious situations, such as those that promote critical thinking, networking, building situational awareness, finding system leverage points, learning, and developing trust, greater participation, and empowering constituencies (McCool and Khumalo 2015). In reality, no one knows which competencies and in what order and combination could prove most valuable in any given context. In fact, Block (2000a, p. 257) issues a warning about institutionalized common training in general:

> The mindset that designs a common training experience is a corollary to the instinct toward common definition ["a wish for everyone to think and act similarly"]. This is not an argument against training; it just questions that value of mandating training... essentially required of large numbers of people. The training may be excellent, but when it is demanded for all, the demand itself becomes another means of reinforcing patriarchy. Common training carries the message that the top, with the help of the consultants, has an answer that all should hear.... The major beneficiary of common training programs, of course, are those who provide them.

Table 6.2 offers four categories of strategies to involve the UR. Note that the strategies emanate from the LR because to offer any kind of intervention—formal education, nonformal training, appropriate food, well-designed spaces, and so on—requires a collective institutional effort. So as we saw in chapter 5 where UR objective strategies affect UL, LR strategies also affect UR strategies.

Table 6.2 | *Strategies to Involve the Upper-Right Quadrant (It)*	
I Chapter 5	**It**
We Chapter 7	**Its** **Physical Health and Well-Being** • In addition to social, nutritional, and similar factors beyond the control of the constituent community, adequate food can be provided at planning events. Events and work conditions can be designed not to exhaust, to allow exercise and mobility, sufficient free time, hygienic conditions, etc., to ensure physical well-being. **Behavior** • Planners choose planning spaces that inspire and energize. To do so requires places and designs that promote engagement, send messages of equity and new conversations, and integrate higher levels of Biophilia than conventional places such as hotel and office conference rooms, auditoriums, and cafeterias, which signal business-as-usual, power imbalances, lack of inspiration and meetings that will change nothing. Such conditions demoralize, reinforce passivity, and reduce creativity and commitment. • Capable facilitation with accompanying communication strategies and participatory design (such as Toolbox 7: Technology of Participation) can elicit community participation much beyond initial expectations or normal inclinations. Poor facilitation can reinforce many barriers to participation such as intimidation; feeling of disempowerment; sense that participant contributions are unimportant; ignorance or suppression of second-language speakers, introverts, quiet, adversarial, or culturally marginalized participants. • Planning institutions that share power, distribute decision-making, and build trust, transparency, and a sense of fairness will promote more engaged and committed participant behavior.

- Investing in the skills and capabilities first in technical staff and then in community members rather than consultants sends the message that such people are important and that the resulting process will more likely arise from the community. These messages promote more engaged and committed behavior to carry on with implementation and management.

- Promote adaptive co-management and organizational learning rather than Rational Comprehensive Planning increases collaboration and empowerment.

Skills Training Media

- University education and other degree-granting programs

- Non-formal coursework offered by a variety of organizations

- On-the-job opportunities such as employee shadowing, paid time for innovation, staff learning teams and networks, pilot projects, prototypes, field trips, mentoring, coaching

- Support for self-teaching and learning on staff's own time such as a library and access to other educational resources, such as high-speed online access

Some Skill Groups Relevant to Plan Implementation

- Thinking and learning

- Group facilitation and community building

- Management and leadership

- Protected area planning

- Communications

Its

Chapter 8

Physical Health and Well-Being

While many factors influence planning success, often planners forget about taking care of their participants. This does not mean coercing or lavishing them with penthouses and fine French cuisine, but consider how food, exercise, free-time, conversations, and bonding, as well as hygienic conditions can augment energy and enthusiasm.

Often these elements, aside from their basic body benefits, carry messages as well. For example, imagine planning situations marked by conversations of ecosystem health, sustainability, organic agriculture, and responsible living, and then comes the lunch served with heaping portions of soft drinks, greasy fried chicken, and calorie-dense desserts. The contradiction in message is apparent and more than simply ornamental—the food symbolizes the organizers' true values. When people speak one thing and do another, others question their honesty, integrity, and conviction. How many meetings hosted by environmental groups have we been to where the groups did not make the extra effort to eliminate disposable plasticware or choose food that cares for people's health or a venue well ventilated and lighted with fresh air and natural light?

In other cases, the message could be about formality and getting things done. For example, when Steve worked with the Bob Marshall Wilderness planning process, they always made sure food was available, and they did this along with other trappings to communicate the informality needed for constructive dialogue to occur.

Behavior

A number of factors influence how participants behave during a planning process. Participants can be inspired and creative, or they can be bored, compliant, and quiet. The following factors discuss how to elicit the best contributions during a planning process.

In addition to inherent messages in the trappings of meetings, the spaces themselves where people meet exert a powerful and underappreciated effect on participants' perception of what they should expect of the meeting. The spaces in which we meet can energize and inspire or depress and demoralize. This force is called biophilia.

Basically humans have an innate inclination or preference toward nature (Wilson 1986), a theory that has been applied to architecture and design (Kellert 2008). An increasing number of studies show that natural characteristics can help heal people faster than those who are not exposed and increase attention, creativity, performance, and improve a variety of other psychological indicators.[16]

Biophilic qualities that planners can incorporate into meeting spaces include views of natural landscapes, lighting, construction materials, ventilation, shapes, imagery, live organisms, water, and many others.

Block (2000) develops the idea of meeting spaces even more (Toolbox 5). Depending on how we arrange spaces, we can affect engagement, send messages of equity, stimulate conversations, and encourage creativity. He writes that most of our common meeting spaces signal business-as-usual, promote power imbalances, stifle inspiration, and reinforce the certainty that nothing is actually going to change. The meeting place sets the tone and structure, and becomes a microcosm of how we will come together in the future. Every meeting that we have is a sample of the future that participants can expect to come.

Capable Facilitation

Capable facilitation with accompanying communication strategies and participatory design can elicit stakeholder participation much beyond initial expectations (Reed 2008). Poor facilitation can reinforce many barriers to participation, including intimidation; feeling of disempowerment; disinformation; sense that participant contributions are unimportant; ignorance or suppression of second-language speakers, introverts, and quiet, adversarial, or culturally marginalized participants. Poor facilitation can also allow many participants and opinions to overwhelm the process and bog it down, causing frustration and failure to meet the event's objectives (Brody 2001).

Investing in Skills of Constituencies

An organization that sees its role as a facilitator working for protected area constituencies may be more inclined to invest in the capabilities and skills of its own staff and also that of other constituencies, wherever in the world they may be, rather than investing limited resources in consultants to do the community's work. Not only does strengthening the community empower its members to assume greater responsibility and ownership in the process, but it also reinforces this result by sending the message that community members are important, and ultimately the protected area's successful management rests in their capable hands (Toolbox 6).

Toolbox 6 | *Holistic, Adult Learning: Making the Training Stick*

In heritage management, lots of training happens (UR). Yet much of that training amounts to little more than one-off bean counting, where the indicator of success is generating the largest number of graduates possible, rather than improving heritage management. Larger international donors often focus more on the quantity of students than the quality of education. Both experience and science show that simply training someone in a one-time, short encounter usually results in poor returns for students, with often rich returns for instructors (Block 2000). Ultimately what matters is that trainees apply what they supposedly learn to improve heritage management and conservation. To get there, training institutions would consider principles of andragogy and holistic training. In 1984 (a, b) Malcolm Knowles proposed four principles which now form the basis of adult education or andragogy:

- Adults need to be involved in the planning and evaluation of their instruction. As we discuss in other parts of the book, people embrace and implement that which they control or co-create. An adult will more readily engage in their education program if he or she had a hand in its design and use.

- Experience (especially mistakes) provides the basis for learning activities. Learning derives principally from making mistakes, corrections, and thus changing behavior.

- Adults are most interested in learning subjects that have immediate relevance and impact to their job or personal life. Since adult learning is mostly voluntary, motivation usually comes from within, and motivation arises from perceived relevance to one's goals.

- Adult learning is problem centered rather than content oriented. Since adult education is usually not compulsory, most adults seek education that can help them directly and immediately. If it does not do this or becomes uninteresting, they will stop participating. For a seminal discussion on the difference between captive (that is, have an external motivation to participate) and noncaptive (internal motivation) audiences, see Ham (2013).

This means that successful adult or vocational training, rather than comprising content- and teacher-driven material, would focus instead on process, be more self-directed, and be dependent on the person's past experience and goals that motivate his or her voluntarily submitting to a training. The training needs to help them overcome problems they face in their lives. Thus trainers need to create authentic scenarios where adults can learn skills they view as valuable and relevant to their needs and be able to make mistakes in authentic and consequential ways, with support of trainers so that mistakes do not get out of hand.

But these principles are not enough, because people accomplish or fail in a social context. To be more holistic (Kohl 2007a, b), these techniques are available:

Shared vision binds trainee to host organization. The organization in which a trainee works must have the same vision for the problem and contents of instruction as do the trainee and training program. Often a trainee learns a skill that has no apparent role in his organization and consequently little opportunity to use it.

Curriculum shows trainee how to integrate new knowledge into larger context. Although there may be a place, say, for nature guiding in the host organization, if the guide does not see how guiding fits into organizational planning or conservation, then guiding may be ineffective in that context.

Trainers adapt material to context of trainees. Each trainee comes from a particular context to which generic training materials need to fit. For example, a course might teach how to do biodiversity surveys using GIS. But what if the organization does not use the same equipment? Can trainers help the trainee adapt to the context?

Prepare context to receive trainee. The training program would work with the host in order that it will utilize the trainee's new skills and perspectives. So often people return from a conference or training with a new idea, but no one at the office has any idea what they are talking about and so that idea does not receive support. Rather, trainers can work with the organization to identify training needs and prepare the supervisor to support the trainee upon her return.

Support network. The training program builds or offers different kinds of support networks, whether a group of similar graduates, direct technical assistance, online materials, or other kinds of follow-up to help graduates achieve program goals.

Promoting Adaptive Co-management and Organizational Learning

Adaptive co-management combines the organizational learning capability of an organization with the power to make decisions delegated from higher levels of government. Adaptive co-management empowers heritage constituencies in two ways: first, by building their ability to learn, and second, sharing with them the power to actually implement identified actions. This empowered collaboration, of course, has much greater possibilities of inspiring responsibility and accountability. (We will talk more about these concepts in chapter 8.)

Skills Training Media

University Education and Other Degree-Granting Programs in Protected Area Management

There exist numerous formal degree-granting programs at the university level around the world. They include those offered, for example, by the University of Montana, Colorado State University Center for Protected Area Management, Autonomous University of Madrid, and the Latin American School for Protected Areas at the University for International Cooperation in Costa Rica.

Nondegree Coursework

Many organizations offer a wide variety of courses and workshops that do not result in degrees but have a strong technical or even university-backed curriculum, such as

- University of Montana in environmental communications and sustainable tourism,

- Foundation of Success's courses on adaptive management,

- CATIE's international protected area management course,

- Rare Pride Campaigns in conservation education (has a degree-granting component as well with the University of Texas-Austin),

- One Sky's Integral Leadership Development Training (Outside the Box 6.1), and

- The UNESCO-affiliated World Heritage Institute for Training and Research for the Asian and Pacific Region.

Outside the Box 6.1 | *Leading from Within: Integral Leadership for Sustainable Development around Cross River National Park in Nigeria*

Cross River National Park began with a story familiar to readers, one of top-down planning in 1991 followed by poor implementation, funds running dry, and locals turning against the park administration (Oates 2002). While this story repeats with painful frequency throughout the world, a different story also has taken place, a story of hope.

The park's 4,000 km^2 of largely primary tropical rainforest is home to sixteen primate species, including the Cross River lowland gorilla and the chimpanzee, but also has numerous threats along its margins, especially poaching. The Canadian NGO One Sky had been working in the Cross River region since 2002, mostly with NGOs to effect social change and biodiversity conservation. But staff grew frustrated with unhindered corruption that often undid well-laid plans. One Sky then decided to work with young leaders to develop their upper quadrant capacities (UL and UR) so that they could promote development in the LL and LR in the region. Consequently, they designed the project "Leading from Within— Integral Leadership for Sustainable Development" to do just that.

The leadership development program recruited people from some thirty regional NGOs to participate in a three-year program based on an integral approach to leadership development. It focused on complementary interior and exterior capabilities.

Integral Leadership Development Curriculum

I **Developing Self**	It **Building Skills**
Leadership Vision and Personal Capacity • Awareness • Perspective taking • Moral development • Self-development	Workplace performance • Writing skills (email, reports, blogging, Internet) • Visioning • Strategic planning • Fund-raising • Media • Monitoring and evaluation

We **Engaging Culture**	**Its** **Influencing Systems**
Organizational Culture and Learning • Interpersonal skills (communication, group dynamics, facilitation) • Conflict resolution • Team building • Diversity and gender	Organizational and Societal Systems • Policy analysis and dialogue • Multistakeholder engagement • Networking • Applied learning of systems theory

One Sky's (n.d. p. 179) integral leadership development program strategically chose complementary interior and exterior capacities to help local leaders help their people shift their worldview for the betterment of social welfare.

The approach consisted of four retreats per year with participants grouped into learning communities of three to five individuals to deepen and apply their learning throughout the year. Later in the first year, Integral coaches from Canada worked with them on their personal growth. Participants then had to carry out "Breakthrough Initiatives" to put their nascent leadership skills into action. All of this had the deeper objective of assisting the development of their existing stage of consciousness or worldview to the next so that they could lead in their organizations toward greater social welfare.

Most breakthrough initiatives had little direct connection to the national park, but one in particular connects the integral leadership training to conservation on the ground. Gail Hochacka (2005) of One Sky sets the context:

> Imagine these forest communities that have been there for millennia. Suddenly someone draws lines and calls it a park. But these villages have relied on that protein source [bushmeat, including gorillas] for a very long time. They are still poaching everything that moves.

A couple of students chose the challenge of reducing gorilla poaching. Emmanuel wrote his project objective:

> For my Breakthrough Initiative, I am going to focus on livestock projects in Boki providing them with livestock and training because 90% are hunters and this will provide an alternative to hunting wildlife and contributing to loss of biodiversity.

And Michael wrote this:

> For my Breakthrough Initiative, I am going to focus on alternative livelihoods with hunters organizing a cooperative on beef production because hunters pressure the flora/fauna of the forest and it is time and energy consuming to have to trek so far for hunting.

Essentially the students with their mentors looked at the problem through an Integral lens. The poaching ("hunting to feed their families" before the park's restrictions took effect) is a behavior (UR) that threatens biodiversity. These people live in meat-eating cultures that have been coexisting with the forest for centuries, so they have nothing against preserving the forest. In other words, they do not need a change of perspective or viewpoint (LL) with respect to conservation. What they needed was a new source of protein to meet their dietary and cultural needs. So the student leaders planned an LR solution that targets the behavior (UR) but not a belief system.

The idea was to train ex-hunters to husband cows in cutover pastures in the rainforest by creating a meat cooperative. The cooperative would sell meat at affordable rates to local families to maintain the system, thereby replacing the need for bushmeat. In a sense, they are evolving an LR line of human production systems from hunter-gatherer to agrarian.

In other words, Emmanuel and Michael had to unblock a behavior (poaching) in order that development could continue, for example, by working with the park and society rather than hiding from them because of poaching. In essence, they took their Integral leadership training and converted it into local training in cattle raising to reduce poaching pressure on protected and rare biodiversity, especially the lowland gorilla, the symbol of the park.

On-the-Job-Training

The private sector in particular has innovated many kinds of employee training, including internal coursework, internal consultants, employee shadowing programs, staff learning teams and networks, paid innovation time, pilot projects, prototyping, field trips, and coaching and mentoring, among others. Even larger protected area agencies sometimes have their own training programs, such as the US National Park Service's family of training centers or Brazil's Chico Mendes Institute for the Conservation of Biodiversity and its comprehensive capacity-building program.

Skill Groups Relevant to Planning and Plan Implementation

In the following section, we focus on thinking/learning skills and group facilitation/community-building skills because training providers most often leave these out of their curricula. We believe that in the DICE World, these skills are essential to good stewardship of heritage resources including planning and management.

Thinking and Learning

For planning to be successful, it must promote critical and reflective thinking that brings planners and constituencies to new places, not just to the same old answers from the same old questions, resulting in plans lying down in eternal sleep.

1. **Visioning.** Defining a person's own vision is a necessary prerequisite to creating a shared group vision. Although it may seem an easy task at first glance, very often people do not spend time or even allow themselves to visualize what they truly want as opposed to what they think they could get, what they think is feasible, or what they think someone else wants them to say.

2. **Problem Framing.** As mentioned in chapter 3, how one defines a problem completely determines the strategy one adopts to solve it. Environmental problems are notoriously difficult to frame, and therefore understand and solve (Bardwell 1991). Is poverty a problem of education, finances, culture, capitalism, or the advent of the Green Revolution? The ability to frame problems from different perspectives enables one to better investigate different possible solutions. Rittel and Webber (1973; see chapter 3) note that rushing too quickly to a solution may result in your discovering that you are trying to solve the wrong problem.

3. **Holding Multiple Perspectives.** Although an increasing level of consciousness allows one to expand their perspectives, there are some who define consciousness as the ability to assume ever more perspectives. It is also a skill that can be developed. Clearly, the more perspectives one can understand, and then maintain while exploring others, increases one's power to see new solutions and comprehend different realities, critical for designing strategies that depend on other people's perspectives. Senge talks about this skill in *The Fifth Discipline* (1990).

4. **Surfacing and suspending assumptions.** To assume new perspectives and explore different assumptions, one first must reduce barriers that one's own

assumptions erect. Again, people can learn to surface their own assumptions so they and others can examine them openly and objectively; they can then choose to suspend those assumptions temporarily while they examine different and often contradictory assumptions. Not only Senge (1990; Senge et al. 1991) talks about this skill, it is mentioned widely in many fields of literature, especially dialogue and community building (see Bohm 2004).

5. **Reflection-in-Action.** Schön talks extensively about this skill in his book *The Reflective Practitioner* (1983). He argues that we act very often without reflection; we act from habit and routine, based on prior knowledge. To generate learning and innovation, however, we must reflect on what we do, our assumptions, and skills necessary to solve new problems and materialize new visions. In other words, practitioners must question and evaluate what they do while they do it in order to improve their practice.

6. **Penetration and forecasting.** Penetration is a planner's ability to see deeper meanings with respect to key causes, restrictions, resources, and contingencies. For example, when new events arise in a heritage site, people can interpret them so as to create new meanings (Fire Box 2 on Double-Loop Learning). Forecasting is the identification of potential future conditions necessary for planning. Both skills may spur creative problem solving in a planning exercise (Osburn and Mumford 2006).

Group Facilitation and Community Building

Most, if not all, planning processes must include some of the following in order to achieve meaningful commitment to change, otherwise planners just produce another idle plan on the shelf. (See chapter 7 for greater consideration of these skills that influence the LL.)

1. Group facilitation in strategic decision-making processes. There are many tools by which facilitators help groups to explore new avenues and arrive at consensus about vital questions. Some include Technology of Participation, Open Space Technology (Harrison 2008), dialogues (Brown et al. 1997), Nominal Group Technique (Bartunek and Murnighan 1984), and SWOT Analysis (Inside the Box 6.1).

2. Large-group methods. While actually part of group facilitation (see above), large group methods have become almost a category unto themselves. They

assume that among any group of people with some common interest, the right process can bring forth their common wisdom, their collective intelligence. Such methods can involve scores or even hundreds of participants (see the classic introduction to large group methods in Bunker and Alban 1996). One of the most well-known methodologies is the World Café.

3. Negotiation. Negotiation or mediation is a process that strives to meet priority needs and objectives of all constituencies at the table in a win-win manner and results in an agreement. For example, as per the World Wildlife Fund Dialogues discussed in chapter 5, the Consensus Building Institute applies its Mutual Gains Approach, aimed at generating shared valued in agreements while strengthening relationships (see Susskind et al. 1999) (Figure 6.2).

4. Small group methods. A large variety of small group methods that promote dialogue, learning, information gathering, trust building, and creating ownership exist. These include discussion groups, task-oriented groups, the Nominal Group Technique, and so on.

5. Dialogue. As discussed in chapter 5, where we cite examples from the Dialogue Movement, real change comes through dialogue that permits stakeholders to understand their respective interests and needs, and to collaboratively address shared problems and challenges. Only through dialogue can a group or community construct a consensus.

Inside the Box 6.1 | *What's Wrong with SWOT? Claiming Participation That Is Not*

As discourse about the importance of participation ascends in heritage areas, managers and consultants often grab the participatory SWOT tool off the shelf as proof of participation, resulting in one of the most used and misused diagnostic tools around.

Leaving aside that SWOT can be used as a simple warm-up activity, the facilitator asks participants to brainstorm the four quadrants of Strengths-Weaknesses-Opportunities-Threats as a preliminary situational analysis. Thus, they have participation.

These same facilitators often do not understand how the tool is really supposed to work, and the results are a table that ends up in the workshop proceedings, often with no further utility, except to prove that participatory processes are alive and well.

As with any participatory brainstorming technique, the SWOT analysis could create a consensus that can be focused toward action. That is, the results of each quadrant should feed into a more specific, action-oriented analysis, rather than just end up in a holding pond.

But the larger issue is claiming participatory when it is really not, about using tools that could promote legitimate participation and climb up the rungs of the Ladder of Citizen Participation, but do not. Consider these common techniques used in the name of participation:

- Inviting people to a workshop where conditions such as intimidating speakers, having to stand up in front of many people, use of technical language, etc., inhibit their speaking and then declaring it a participatory workshop

- Inviting the public to share its perspectives and then disregarding them when the time comes to write the report

- Putting community members on planning teams where high-paid expert consultants intimidate and outnumber them into silence

- Inviting people to planning workshops that are really just platforms for the organizers' promotion of their own viewpoints

- Offering food, transportation, and housing at a nice hotel to entice unlikely participants to attend an event so that planners can take credit for being participatory

Sometimes planners are disingenuous in using these techniques, but likely more often, they simply do not understand the nature of participation and power.

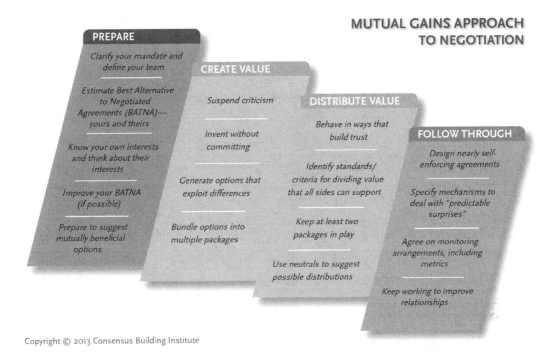

Figure 6.2 | *The Mutual Gains Approach (Susskind and Field 1996)*

Management and Leadership

Any protected area must necessarily consider organizational management. McCool and Khumalo (2015) write that a fundamental purpose of the organization is to enhance the performance of its staff. In this respect, they note that organizations can enable their staff through building awareness and enhancing four powers: (1) employees' access to physical and financial assets, skills, and education; (2) employees' self-confidence or self-efficacy; (3) collaboration among employees, improving the exchange of ideas, developing partnerships, and the potential for collective action toward organizational goals; and (4) employee decision-making power.

In fact, protected area management requires most of the same skill set as that of other major organizations; that is, managing personnel, accounting, leadership, financial management, motivation, innovation and quality control, communication and learning, action planning, organizational structures, strategic planning, diplomacy, and others (Outside the Box 6.1). The business field has hundreds, if not thousands, of individual tools to work with all of these. For this reason, we will not delve into particular areas of organizational management. Any trip to amazon.com, Google Books, mindtools.com, or the local library will reveal troves of options.

Technical Site Planning

In addition, there are many technical capacities, including site assessments, data analysis and presentation (especially GIS), zoning, monitoring and evaluation, logical frameworks, touristic product development, financial planning, work planning, adaptive management, and others.

Communications

Protected area management increasingly involves information management that regularly takes many common forms, such as writing press releases, environmental education, heritage interpretation, social marketing, editing and layout, public speaking, lobbying, diplomacy, branding, feedback between stakeholders, graphic design for interpretive media, architecture, and body language and deep listening. A growing need is to exploit social media in designing communications programs.

Running the Risks of Just One Quadrant

Once again we return to Integral Theory's main lesson: if managers and protected area supporters develop projects without considering all four quadrants, then unseen forces can erupt like balls of fire. Building skills, a UR focus, is commonly the goal of training and technical assistance.

Finally, we cannot ignore the connection between consciousness and technical training. For many years, the United States operated a military training school, first in the Panama Canal Zone and then at Fort Benning, Georgia, for Latin American military officers, called the US Army School of the Americas. The theory or hope was that by training military officers in the skills of military management and warfare, the United States would not only have greater influence over them via military cooperation, but also that those officers would conduct themselves more professionally back in their own countries, such as respecting human rights, both in military and political environments. Of course, the United States was a fully Modernist state trending toward Postmodernism while many countries that supplied the officers had barely even tasted Modernism. Thus the School of the Americas produced several dictators (for example, Manuel Noriega of Panama) who very much took advantage of the technical military skills they learned, but not in the way the US Army may have planned (see pros and cons at Grimmett and Sullivan 2001).

To that risk, Maslow and Stephens (2000, p. 146) had this to say:

> In the hands of a strong and good person, money is a great blessing. But in the hands of weak or immature persons, money is a terrible danger and can destroy them and everyone around them. The identical principle is true for power, both over things and over other people. In the hands of a mature, healthy human being—one who has achieved full humanness—power, like money or any other instrument, is a great blessing. But in the hands of the immature, vicious, or emotionally sick, power is a horrible danger.

We become just by performing just actions, temperate by
performing temperate actions, brave by performing brave actions.

—Aristotle

CHAPTER 7

Our Collective Mind Influences the
Management Systems We Build

The dogmas of the quiet past are inadequate to the stormy present. The occasion is piled high with difficulty, and we must rise with the occasion. As our case is new, so we must think anew and act anew.

—*Abraham Lincoln*

THE OTHER
SIDE OF
COMPLEXITY

EVENTS

PATTERNS

STRUCTURES

MENTAL MODELS

VISION

Together, Our Minds Make Culture

When people put their heads together, a fine line separates groupthink from collective intelligence. The former occurs when everyone in a group thinks the same about a proposed action without critical reflection, such as in a mob, marauding band of teens, or the infamous Borg from Star Trek. As American General George C. Patton once said, however, "If everybody's thinking alike, nobody's thinking."

Or, under the right conditions, the opposite can occur, where minds meld and integrate to produce a collective intelligence and decision making superior to the sum of its human parts (Hamilton 2004). Should several minds suddenly leave the group, the collective to which they contributed may still remain strong. What is this collective product that cannot be measured by counting the yeses of consenting would-be mutineers, brainwaves, or victories on the soccer field?

Whereas the UL (chapter 6) focuses on the experience within individual minds, the LL focuses on the experience that occurs among minds, whether two newlyweds who communicate simply by staring into each other's eyes or the entirety of the human race wherever it may roam. When minds come together, they generate nonmaterial structures that survive generations, grow more powerful as time and membership increases, and allow forever faster integration of new minds. The most common term that defines this collective is culture, but we can also call it shared values, ethics, visions, paradigms, mythology, and legend.

Our species definitely developed culture tens of thousands of years ago. Most definitions suit us here, whether culture is made simply of nongenetic behaviors socially learned from other members, collective solutions and strategies common to particular groups, or shared understandings and assumptions about what the world is and ought to be that determines behavior (Schein 1996). Whichever definition, culture has physical and nonphysical components.

In Zimbabwe, Tribal cultures establish holy groves or ecological reserves, called Marambatemwa ("places that resist cutting") whose boundaries the spirits themselves demarcate. They also enact rules that restrain interference with natural processes of those who enter, such as hunting or felling trees. Rules might include that people can eat fruits on-site but not take them out. Or, that people cannot cut or harvest medicinal herbs. Violation could get one lost, or one might fail to return home—or even be savagely attacked by wild animals. Such taboos arise from the local culture to manage natural areas or enforce other norms that ultimately benefit the group (Gelfand 1979). For other examples of tribal taboos used as conservation measures, see Ormsby and Edelman (2010), Colding and Folke (2001), and Lingard et al. (2003).

In 2013, hunters in Nova Scotia, Canada killed an albino moose. Giddy over their unusual trophy, they then made the mistake of posting their victory on the Internet, at which point a hell storm of protest erupted. The Mi'kmaq Indigenous tribe, which regards all white animals as sacred spirit animals deserving of protection, led the outrage. The hunting taboo—and the fact that the tribe knew of this individual moose for years—says that anyone who kills a white animal will incur bad luck (Tackett 2013). Eventually the hunters gave the pelt (but not the trophy head) to the tribe for a four-day ritual-honoring of the spirit.

This phenomenon does not limit itself to indigenous peoples. Many protected areas in the United States arrived at their protected status because of their spiritual values. Consider President Teddy Roosevelt who, after camping in Yosemite National Park, said, "It was like lying in a great solemn cathedral, far vaster and more beautiful than any built by the hand of man." He also noted: "A grove of giant redwood or sequoias should be kept just as we keep a great and beautiful cathedral."

Perhaps the simplest manifestation of collective constructs would be common understandings, whether early or modern. Jay Forrester, founder of the MIT System Dynamics Group and mentor to many systems thinkers, said this (quoted in Meadows 2008, p. 162):

> It doesn't matter how the tax law of a country is written. There is a shared idea in the minds of society about what a "fair" distribution of the tax load is. Whatever the rules say, by fair means or foul, by complications, cheating, exemptions or deductions, by constant sniping at the rules, actual tax payments will push right up against the accepted idea of "fairness."

Of course, LL collective products can be much more complex, such as those that define paradigms of leadership, organizational learning, communications, and levels of consciousness themselves. All change and evolve depending on perceived conditions affecting the group and the dynamics of how groups' ideas rise and fall. These dynamics are too complex to model in this book, but one force that is particularly relevant to protected area management and planning is how small group conversations illustrate LL phenomena (much of this discussion is based on Brown et al. 1997).

Great changes in human history often trace to small group conversations that eventually scaled up. Small sewing circles and "committees of correspondence" nurtured the American Revolution. The French Revolution erupted from the hush-hush conversations in cafés and salons. The rise of democracy in 1994 for South Africa was stimulated by conversations of political prisoners such as Nelson Mandela working in a small quarry on Robben Island. Even modern revolutions in Egypt, Tunisia, and other North African and Middle Eastern countries began stirring in small groups that quickly expanded via social networks such as Facebook, Twitter, and Al Jazeera reports. These small conversations connected people across countries empowering them with awareness without which said revolutions may never have taken place. Instead a collective desire for values of human liberties, freedoms to choose and publicly express, and social mobility based on one's own efforts and capacity quickly boiled up to throw off the Traditional lid that dictators had locked down for decades.

Wheatley and Kellner-Rogers (1998) pioneered research in self-organizing management systems. They suggest that identity, relationships, and information are fundamental for self-organization (such as revolutionary movements or indigenous management systems) to occur. If true, then conversations about questions that matter are also fundamental (1) to create a common sense of identity and purpose, (2) build relationships among people and ideas, and (3) create richer webs of information.

Based on this observation, Juanita Brown and David Isaacs formed the World Café (Brown et al. 2005), a methodology that uses simultaneous small group conversations to address important issues. These small groups multiply and then scale to larger groups that can discuss former taboos and organizational learning disabilities that can otherwise limit group development. To address earlier problems of poor participation, for instance, Taiwan's national parks used the World Café to discuss their future in the Forum on 21st Century Sustainability for Taiwan's National Parks and contribute to the then newly formed National Parks Commission (Lax 2010). Similarly, Bisina used Open Space Technology to resolve a violent conflict between two ethnicities in Nigeria (2004), and the Institute for Cultural Affairs has been using its Technology of Participation for decades (Toolbox 7).

Toolbox 7 | *Technology of Participation*

The Institute for Cultural Affairs (ICA) is a global community of nonprofits in forty countries advancing human development that has been around since the early 1960s. A while back, it realized that it needed facilitation tools where it worked in small villages, tools that promoted consensus, honored participant perspectives, welcomed diversity, minimized conflict, and pooled individual contributions into useful patterns. Thus was born the Technology of Participation (ToP).

ToP is a family of facilitation methods that started out as tools for ICA and today has grown to become a global network of facilitators and users. The methods include the Focused Conversation Method, the Consensus Workshop Method, the Action Planning Process, and a host of others. In one application, the PUP Global Heritage Consortium worked on Union Island in St. Vincent and the Grenadines.

The objective was to produce a set of interpretive heritage themes that Union Islanders could use for an ecotourism program. The methodology calls first to create a "historical scan" or a participatory timeline that both excites participants as they create a new vision that they hold of their island—as opposed to a version published by some historian on the main island—and to generate material for the themes.

They analyzed the timeline using the Focused Conversation Method or ORID for the natural order of questions from objective, reactive, interpretive, and decisional. It is the same order that human brain uses say when someone throws a rock at it. First the person sees the rock (objective), feels an emotion such as fear (reactive), decides that it could cause damage (interpretive), and moves out of the way (decisional). When the whole group can move together through these stages, it has deeper, collective understanding of the timeline.

Then they used the Workshop Method where participants individually brainstorm significant or superlative attributes about the heritage of their area. As small groups they choose the better examples and as a plenary they group the attributes together, analyze them into emerging themes. A small committee later takes these emerging themes and crafts them into well-written interpretive themes. Community participants then feel some ownership as they all participated in co-creation. Though many protected area managers often feel that the promise of participation has not been met, just as often it is because of poor conceptualization and techniques of facilitating participation (Reed 2008).

Thus, groups construct values, ethics, and culture that greatly influence how planning occurs and is—or isn't—implemented. For example, when planners believe that science reigns over all management decisions in a marine park, there is little chance they will value experiential or traditional knowledge of local New England lobstermen, even if they courteously invite them to sit in at their planning meetings (Ferse et al. 2010). Some planners, such as those in the Osa Peninsula of Costa Rica, believed it better to produce technical management plans than mire themselves in land tenancy polemics and never produce a plan. Other planners may believe it better simply to invite their allies and friends rather than detractors and enemies to planning sessions. Others still may sense weakness in conventional planning but attempt to correct it with yet more money, time, personnel, and data, rather than exhume and reexamine rotting assumptions.

Not only do assumptions and paradigms often remain buried and unseen like a land mine, but the entire lower-left quadrant that deals with the interior collective perspective might remain completely excluded by conventional planning processes. As discussed in previous chapters, Modernist planners barely see the left-hand column of the Integral Map. And, as we have seen in chapters 5 and 6, when forces remain hidden, they contain power much more explosive than when exposed to the warm sunlight and fresh air of open-minded contemplation.

For example, in Galápagos National Park, hundreds of fishermen organized and went ballistic, not once, but several times after a variety of restrictions were unilaterally imposed. In response to the establishment of sea cucumber quotas in 1996, they slit throats of giant tortoises. In 1999, fishermen fired weapons, looted, and took park personnel hostage, this time for lobster quotas (Wyss 2000). While it was likely easy for park staff and media to blame fishermen for suffering a few loose screws in their collective mind, most likely neither park staff nor fishermen had ever discussed what each side believed and had not compared paradigmatic notes— least of all how the government's concessions to initial demands to increase quotas only fed the belief that violence made an effective bargaining weapon. In short, both sides ignored the LL and the fishermen's beliefs never got exposed, instead erupting in violence. Although the abhorrent behavior shocked many observers, these hidden forces finally and predictably surfaced like an oil slick from a ruptured well in the Gulf of Mexico.

Thus, if we aspire to evolve beyond conventional planning to something with more potential to implement, we must explore the LL for core beliefs, assumptions, and worldviews that impede implementation. Being aware is not enough. Heritage sites need to learn to build consensus to survive in the DICE World. In the past, managing agencies had the power both to plan and implement. Today, however, while they retain the authority to plan, the power to implement has slipped through their hands and into those of one or more constituencies. To exclude constituencies from planning and failing to forge consensus often equates to a nice plan that goes nowhere but the bookshelf.

In this light, we continue with Table 7.1, whose initial version we created in chapter 5 and now includes culture-based influences on planning.

Table 7.1 | *Forces That Influence Planning Implementation*	
I **Perceptions, Values, and Attitudes** • Sense of self, level of consciousness (egocentric to worldcentric) • Sense of responsibility, loyalty, and affect toward planning agency, its mission, stakeholder community, and managed resources • Sense of trust, transparency, and fairness within agency and stakeholder community • Attitude toward participation and rights of other stakeholders in planning process (levels: none, EIS, collaborative, DNA) • Affect toward people who inspire and guide (priest, respected park manager, president who asks for the plan, foreign donors, friends) • Perceived behavioral control to act (such as plan), also known as perceived locus of control • Role of self in planning (planner, facilitator, core member, peon, other stakeholder) and power to influence planning decisions • Feeling of recognition • Visions and dreams of the future	**It** **Physical Health and Well-Being** • Health and energy level supports or inhibits participation in plan implementation. These levels are affected not only by above factors, but also by nutrition, medical care, financial state, political culture at local and national levels. **Behavior** • Actions and behaviors promote or inhibit plan tasks, especially working with other stakeholders (opposite sex, local community members, tour operators, people of different status, religions, ethnicity, formality of roles in management, etc.) • Responses to rules and stimuli from management organizations, both incentives and disincentives • Behavior and welfare affected by the built environments, degrees of Biophilia, and structure of meeting spaces **Skills** • Skills and capabilities permit or inhibit stakeholder participation, planning, and implementation

Beliefs, Knowledge, and Experiences

- Past experience in similar processes or stakeholders

- Anticipated costs of participating in planning process (time, money, risks such as disappointment or loss of face or power)

- Alternative planning approaches known

- Mental model held about the nature of transformation or change (role of science, God, individuals, systems, intuition, luck, destiny, revelation, incremental or big jumps, etc.)

- Collaborative experience held to achieve common or joint objectives (i.e., Dialogues)

- Purpose of plan (bureaucratic requirement, just for funding, prestige, or to change world)

Intentions

- Individual goals, interests, and motivation to participate in planning process (see Dialogues)

- Intentions to implement plan and related attitudes

Cognitive Capacities

- Emotional or interpersonal intelligence to work with others in processes

- Capacities to analyze data, understand issues, generate conclusions, focus attention, develop personal vision, maintain discipline

• Personal mastery includes rapport with subconscious, integrating reason and intuition, continually seeing more of our connectedness to world, compassion, commitment to the whole. • Loop learning (single, double, triple, and quadruple)	
We **Paradigms, Mental Models, Assumptions** • Physics (PLUS, DICE, interior DICE) • Relationship between humans and nature • Relationships between planning, implementation, management, power, stakeholders, engagement, research • Diversity of public interests, values, objectives, and orientations of planning • Model of social transformation (focus on individual vs. community, etc.) • Models of capacity building (apprenticing, memorizing, learning while doing) • Protected area planning field's principal stories, myths, texts, language, rules, etc. (components of Kuhn's science paradigm) • Leadership style and decision making • Ethics of public engagement • Role of science in planning (epistemology) • Object of study, sources of knowledge, locus of power • Interpretation of organizational history and meaning • Mutual understandings of planning problems	**Its** **Chapter 8**

- Organizational culture and values (horizontal or vertical, team or only individual learning, adaptive or resistant to change, shared or individual visions, aligned or conflictive members, machine vs. people as caring creative innovators)

- Perception of validity and authority of plan to influence decision making

- Shared visions, goals, consensuses

Engagement and Relationships

Solidarity, trust, transparency, mutual respect, participation, and co-creation or the contrary between people, organizations, communities, and other groups

Communication and Social Learning

- Communication and information sharing within stakeholder community (includes park agency)

- Organizational learning

- Collective intelligence

Collective Consciousness

This field unites us all and serves as the source for collective wisdom, social movements, and self-organizing systems. It includes the Internet to create a collective brain.

Forces That Influence Planning Implementation

Paradigms, Mental Models, Assumptions

These are the most important and obvious products of the collective center on socially constructed beliefs. Bohm (2004) believes it may be impossible to have an original thought, as we individuals continuously access the collective consciousness of thought.

A wide variety of collective creatures influences planning, such as paradigms and mental models about how the world works (DICE vs. PLUS), leadership, decision making, transformation, heritage protection, building staff capacity, and organizational management. We hold beliefs that influence our perception of plans as tools to effect change, suggest risks of involving other actors, bias our perceptions of the importance of science versus participation, awaken us to sources of knowledge beyond empirical science, and others. We also draw on paradigmatic examples, stories, myths, legends, and models from our field, which guide how planners plan the next planning.

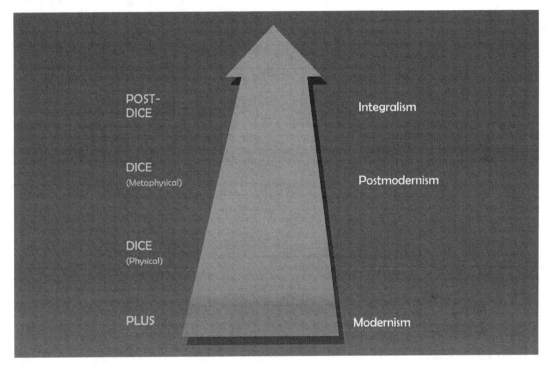

Figure 7.1 | *Evolution of Paradigms about How the World Operates. This figure shows the PLUS World, the physical DICE (exterior focus), and then the metaphysical or interior- as well as exterior-focused DICE World.*

Engagement and Relationships

Another important product of our collective mind is relationships, which are neither physical nor individual. We form relationships with ideas, places, and things—the goal of heritage interpreters. Relationships are collective between those in that relationship, because even if we know two people very well, we do not necessarily know anything about the relationship they have formed. The very notion of heritage involves a relationship between people and places that generates collective appreciations.

Consider the small ironworks town of Völklingen: in 1890, it was the richest city in Germany (Grewenig 2011). After World War II, it began its embarrassing disintegration into a rusting hulk of tangled metal towers, storage tanks, turbine shops, and giant tubes.

While metal recyclers licked their choppers and shredders to demolish the massive iron installations, other minds eventually guided the site to World Heritage status in 1999. Instead of regarding the site as food for the smelter, promoters positioned the site for a very different relationship with society. As Grewenig (2011, p. 46) says, it was the

> only surviving blast-furnace complex which demonstrated the entire process of pig-iron production with this degree of authenticity and completeness, illustrating such a broad series of technological milestones in innovative engineering. The Völklingen Ironworks embodies the industrial history of the 19th Century in general and of the transnational Saar-Lorraine-Luxembourg industrial region in the heart of Europe in particular.

The union of people's minds produces numerous effects. For example, when people clash, a meteor shower of emotions, including fear, hatred, and distrust, rains down. Or, when people do not clash, they engage and build solidarity, trust, transparency, and mutual respect, setting the stage for future creation, shared ownership, and friendship. These feelings not only occur within individuals, they also occur collectively. As well, the relationship between local communities and heritage management agencies can mean everything for plan implementation, regardless of any technical triumphs associated with the final peer-reviewed, polished, and published planning document.

Communication and Social Learning

Several other collective phenomena, including communication and group learning, are only somewhat dependent on individual abilities, as well as collective intelligence (or wisdom) that results from group synergy and produces reflective powers beyond that of its individual members.

Collective Consciousness

No LL discussion would be complete without awareness of the collective consciousness. The notion has been described by authors such as Pierre Teilhard de Chardin, who defined the noosphere as a thinking envelope around the biosphere, or as the sphere of human thought and consciousness (1959); Peter Russell (2008) and Howard Bloom (2001), who profiled the global brain; James Lovelock (2000) who has promoted the Gaia hypothesis; and evolutionary enlightenment teacher Craig Hamilton, who teaches about a post-Postmodern spirituality where our deepest level—the Evolutionary Self—arises from collective consciousness (Hamilton n.d.).

If readers still defend PLUS/Modernism at this point in the book, mention of the collective consciousness could perhaps be a last straw. Advocates often describe it as a field that envelops

We

**The following implications arise from
Rational Comprehensive Planning (Technical Rationality)**

- Emphasis on objective, quantifiable, technical problem-solving methodology, not on building relationships with community members or problems with social, political, subjective, ethical variables which are minimized

- PLUS thinking oversimplifies problems and assumes that plans do not need to be updated with frequency

- Planning assumed to be separate from implementing; once plan is made, implementation will naturally follow

- Agency assumes centralized responsibility to plan and implement, leaving little room for community ownership or participation.

- Because it is a scientifically controlled process, lead agency does not cede power to community members

- Control attitude leads to information guarding and misinformation in the community

- Plan is owned by constituent community; it is owned by lead agency

- Bureaucratic thinking discourages errors, uncertainty risk, and experimentation. Because planning is conceived as a scientific study, there's only one opportunity to get plan right. No need for continuous or ongoing learning

- Leadership based on top-down, command-and control, leader-knows-best, fix-it, Lee Iaccoca model

- Decisions that come from the top and/or outside experts use objective, empirical knowledge, not local or subjective experience or other forms of nonscientific knowledge

- Budget dedicated to consultants' needs, not those of constituents or implementation, thus funds run out after plan is published

- Incentives to produce document, not implement

Since planning and calculating is the tough part, implementation assumed to happen with much less effort.

Figure 7.2 | *LL Barriers to Planning and Implementation*

and connects the consciousness of all in the same way, perhaps, that an ocean envelops and connects all the little surface waves that "fancy" themselves unique.

Integral Theory does speak about how as more people move toward the leading edge of evolving consciousness (now at the Integral level), new cosmic structures in consciousness form in the universe gathering strength and definition, evolving increasingly rapidly toward a possible endpoint, described by Teilhard de Chardin (1959) as the Omega Point, or God.

Conventional Planning Generates Culture-Based Barriers to Plan Implementation

As we have seen in previous chapters, each quadrant offers refuge to forces that erect planning barriers when planners and managers do not see them (Figure 7.1). Many LL barriers arise from interconnected assumptions that underpin PLUS, Modernism, and Postmodernism, and manifest as Technical Rationality and Rational Comprehensive Planning. These beliefs and paradigms that occur at different levels distribute political and planning power in favor of technocratic expertise and economic wealth. They also underestimate the impact of shared values, organizational culture, and institutional design on planning and implementation. This distribution and its biases impede implementation at nearly every turn by avoiding cooperation, collaboration, learning, power-sharing, and by fashioning a plan format willfully resistant to continuous, transparent, and easy updating.

Strategies to Influence Culture and Improve Planning Implementation

To overcome LL barriers, often rooted more deeply than those of other quadrants, planners must recognize that culture, shared values, community ownership, and so forth, influence planning. They must first see the barriers, or all is lost as "the eyes see only what the mind is prepared to comprehend," said French philosopher Henri Bergson. For this very reason, we dedicated an entire chapter to the power that paradigms hold over what we can see in the world.

Assisting planners to see what they previously have never seen may be the ultimate task in transforming heritage planning. Not to discover "the dogmas of the quiet past" will sentence all our sweat and tears to eternal irrelevancy.

So now we survey strategies and tactics that focus on identifying, strengthening, constructing, and modifying shared underlying values, beliefs, paradigms, and organizational culture. An exhaustive survey is not our goal, but Table 7.2 shows that many fields of thought have contributed their fair share of strategies and tactics to confront LL interior-collective realities. Finally, to reiterate a point from chapter 5, efforts to manage forces in the left-hand column manifest as programs and institutional systems in the right-hand column, most notably in the LR.

Table 7.2 | *Strategies to Involve the Lower-Left Quadrant (We)*	
I Chapter 5	**It** Chapter 6
We	**Its** • Apply initial conditions for any of the following categories **Paradigms, Models, Assumptions** • Popular education[1] • Translation and transformation of values from one level to another via communication strategy (Toolbox 4) • PUP Consortium builds trust and integrates participation into planning, moving slowly to a new vision of planning and organizational learning (Kohl 2011) • Paradigm incubation roadmap[2] • Social marketing, environmental education, environmental interpretation[3] • Behavior change and persuasion[4] • Scenario Game Board, among other scenario playing techniques, to develop richer visions based on conflictive perspectives (Sales and Savage 2010) • Crisis management to usher in a new paradigm[5] • Systems thinking changes mental models (Meadows and Wright 2008, Senge 1990) • Public speaking and rhetoric[6] • Positive deviance[7] • Idea diffusion[8] • Training in variety of spiritual retreats, meditation, yoga, etc.

Engagement and Relationships

- Investment in stakeholder community (includes site staff) rather than outsourced planning to increase self-confidence and capacity of community to manage own resources

- Engagement strategies to create new conversations, dialogues, and relationships[9]

- Organizational transformation methods such as those of Generon International (Peck 1998) or Reos Partners

- Strong facilitation to create shared visions and consensus[10]

- Joint planning and power sharing in democratic action

- Organizational leaders modeling exposure of self, valuing errors, and open dialogue (Wheatley and Frieze 2011)

- Short circuiting political and power games[11]

- Large-group methods to foment self-organizing, resilient organizations[12]

- Participatory research to improve community awareness and empowerment, not just extract information (see approaches in chapter 5)

- Voluntary community action

Communication and Social Learning

- Training and application in organizational learning, adaptive management, and collective intelligence (Hamilton 2004)[13]

  o After Action Review (Parry and Darling 2001)

  o Communities of Practice (Wenger et al. 2002)

  o Learning Networks (Brown and Salafsky 2004)

  o Learning infrastructure (e.g., unit to benchmark, study practices)

  o Safe spaces for champions to operate in larger organization

  o Paid time to innovate, experiment and practice

  o Storytelling (Gold and Watson 2001)

- Non-violent Communication[xiv]

- Branding, marketing, and heritage interpretation

- Management of language and misinformation

- Séance, group prayer, and meditation (Hagelin et al. 1999)

1. www.popednews.org/newsletters/definitions.html, Friere says there is no neutral education (2000); all education promotes values and a political agenda. Given this premise he argues for co-creation of knowledge, rather than traditional filling of an empty vessel, with an alternative curriculum that empowers poor, marginalized, and oppressed people.

2. Martin (2010). This model emphasizes how and when to intervene in a paradigm lifecycle. It advises to take advantage of surprise events, or during the suspense phase, get a conductor (architect of change), or manage issue champions, issue tags, etc.; in the critical mass phase, paradigm promoters use facts and logic before power and authority. It privileges charismatic and collaborative over coercive power and brings in issue riders. The constituency phase is for developing constituencies while the consensus and new paradigm phases are for promoting new policies, projects, and innovations.

3. Some useful sources include Andreasen (1995), Tilden (1957) Ham (2013), Beck and Cable (2011); Jacobson et al. (2006), Hungerford et al. (2001).

4. Behavior change, persuasion, and communication fields have been around for decades. Some useful sources include Ham et al. (2009), Fishbein and Ajzen (2009), and Manfredo (1992).

5. Crisis creates opportunity for change. On the society level, WWII created opportunity for new technologies such as oil by smashing the coal infrastructure. President Richard Nixon once pointed out, "The Chinese use two brush strokes to write the word 'crisis.' One brush stroke stands for danger; the other for opportunity. In a crisis, be aware of the danger — but recognize the opportunity." Energy philosopher Rifkin (2003) argues that any great revolution requires a change in energy and communication paradigms. Crises such as war break the hold of previous technologies and allow the emergence of new ones.

6. Jay Heinrichs (2007) pays great respects both to the classics of Ancient Greece as well as very modern techniques and examples. According to him, rhetoric has three goals: To change 1) mood, 2) mind, 3) and willingness to act. While these goals target individuals, audiences also have moods where one's energy influences behavior and energy of those around. Thus there is much communication and collective perceptions and understandings that result from the orator's performance.

7. Pascale et al. (2010). Jerry Sternin has said of large-scale transformation, "You can't bring permanent solutions in from outside. Instead, you have to find small, successful but 'deviant' practices that are already working in the organization and amplify them. Maybe, just maybe, the answer is already alive in the organization — and change comes when you find it." This is a community-based theory to change that takes advantage of those members, whose uncommon behaviors and strategies enable them to find better solutions under the same conditions as those of their peers.

8. Multiple theories explain how ideas spread through a population or stagnate and die. Much research applies epidemiology to ideas: how ideas must attain critical mass, cross a threshold or tip, and then diffuse exponentially such as the H1N1 virus did. At some point in the 1960s touristic carrying capacity tipped and became world famous, as well as SWOT analysis. Park managers tried to use them despite their overall (lack of) effectiveness. Management planning too tipped. The great classic is Rogers (2003). Also see Heath (2007) and Gladwell (2002).

9. Block has three books of interest (2000, 2008) and with McKnight (2010). Also Hochachka (2009) and Ellinor and Gerard (1998).

10. Facilitation can determine success and failure. Consider the World Wildlife Fund Dialogues. Facilitator Merrick Hoben speaks about how the project passed through moments of jeopardy when WWF tried to facilitate itself and not until its donor insisted that the organization hire a professional facilitator did the Dialogues get back on track (Outside the Box 5.1). Poor facilitators, however, run through steps and often fail to lead groups into conversations that matter, that help develop the community, and overcome taboos. Poor facilitation produces plans on shelves, even when all other conditions might otherwise have been ideal. See Spencer (1989). (Several books and manuals on this family of tools created by the Institute for Cultural Affairs exist).

11. Political and power games can debilitate an organizational culture. There are several remedies. Senge says by creating a common vision, people will find motivation to work toward a higher purpose rather than just their own. Schön says that an organization with a learning culture allows teams to discuss what was formerly undiscussable and thus release energy. Forester says by simply recognizing the power games and exposing them, they can be dissipated. He offers lots of preventive measures in his book.

12. These techniques transform meaning and relationships between people and people and organizations. They involve many people, not just leadership teams or hand-picked participants, necessary to transform large organizations. Some examples include The World Café, Open Space Technology, The Conference Model, Whole-Scale Change, the Art of Hosting, and Future Search.

13. See also www.co-intelligence.org, www.collectivewisdominitiative.org, www.community-intelligence.com.

14. Center for Non-Violent Communication (www.cnvc.org), nonviolentcommunication.com.

Initial Conditions for Changing Organizational Culture

Organizational change does not simply plummet from the sky. Many conventional work environments resist novel ideas faster than Genghis Khan could muster his horseback warriors. New ideas require special conditions to foster growth despite dominant forces around them.

Mammals could not ascend to dominance until the dinosaur reign ended. An organization cannot break free from bureaucratic control and adopt a learning stance until certain conditions also exist. Those conditions are a matter of considerable debate.

We jump in with the following conditions:

- **Frustrated with conventional planning and management.** Managers would have already exhibited their frustration with the current planning approach. They may not have a better idea, but they have become conscious that a paradigm in some way contributes to unyielding stoppages in plan implementation. This frustration opens their minds and motivates them to seek new ways to plan.

- **Evidence of Postmodern values already in action.** Managers already believe in cooperation and collaboration, honor different forms of knowledge (Berkes 1999 talks about the value of traditional knowledge for conservation), respect community members, and in general adhere to Postmodern social and environmental values (see chapter 4). These people usually find the ideas of Holistic Planning, organizational learning, and adaptive co-management attractive.

- **Attracted to ideas of managing adaptively, organizational learning, monitoring and evaluation, and limits of acceptable change.** Sites that have contemplated or attempted to use learning-based approaches on their own rather than be coerced through external financing already find their paradigm transition way ahead of conventional thinkers.[17]

- **Motivated to initiate planning from the periphery—constituencies—and not imposed from the center—donors or politicians.** When large multilateral donors or central governments place planning on their annual to-do lists, more likely than not that planning will execute well-worn protocols and end in disuse. When the desire to plan, however, arises from the lower levels of a management agency or from other people or organizations perhaps not expressly endowed with formal authority to plan but without any extraordinary funding to plan, that constitutes an opportunity. When leaders recognize the dominant conventional planning paradigm hinders rather than facilitates achieving goals, the agency is primed for a paradigm revolution. In such cases, authentic interest rather than external money drives more participatory and engaged planning that can alter the course of site history.

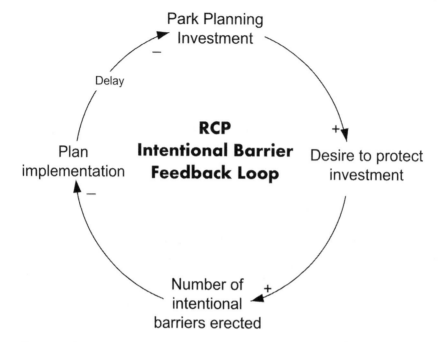

Figure 7.3 | *RCP Intentional Barrier Reinforcing Feedback Loop. This loop can be read as (starting arbitrarily at the top): As park planning investment increases, the desire to protect that investment also increases (positive correlation indicated by "+"). This leads planners and administrators to erect more barriers to protect that investment from subjective change. These barriers by protecting plan results from change reduce plan implementation (negative or inverse correlation indicated by "-"). After a delay of, say, five years, lower plan implementation precipitates in an increase in park planning investment as a new planning cycle begins. Relationships link all elements in this loop, based on assumptions that may or may not be accurate. These relationships, then, drive behaviors, such as planning. Of course, in this case, this loop would interact with various other loops to describe park planning. Forrester (2006) argues that these loops or cycles control all phenomena in the universe. This denotation is a tool called Causal Loop Diagramming, used widely in the systems thinking field.*

- **Existence of champions.** Often times bureaucratic entities call for planning. If planners or outside assistance can identify internal champions passionate about new ideas and approaches and who have the connections and energy, those ideas and approaches, such as a new form of planning, have a much better chance to drop roots (Pinto and Slevin 1989). Kuhn (1962) notes that when scientific paradigms change, the paradigm pioneers tend to be young (not yet invested in the paradigm) or from the outside (those who do not know paradigm rules and boundaries or just do not care about them). And sometimes those are from inside the organization.

- **Ready to manage, plan, and learn.** Despite all the above points, if a site suffers from aggressive staff firings by a new president, invasions by squatter hordes, massive hurricane clean ups, computer hacking scandals, or lobbying campaign to dodge major budget cuts, it simply cannot focus on anything new—especially an effort that requires constituencies to think outside the box and navigate resistance to the new and innovative.

Theories of Paradigm Change

Theories of change abound and every field seems to have cultivated its own share, whether popular education (championed by Brazilian Paulo Friere in his classic *Pedagogy of the Oppressed* [2000]),[18] sociology (Paradigm Incubator Roadmap [Martin 2010]), communication psychology such as GreenCOM behavioral approach (Academy for Educational Development 2004), business management, crisis management, systems thinking, or rhetoric. Of course Kuhn (1962), too, has offered us a valuable theory of paradigm change in science. Table 7.2 surveys a variety of change theories.

Engagement and Relationships

Subtract relationships and the universe collapses into its pre–Big Bang state, before time began. Relationships are more fundamental than things. In systems terms, feedback loops represent interrelated relationships (Figure 7.3).

Others have commented on the nature of the universe, including theologian Thomas Berry who said that "the world is a communion of subjects, not a collection of objects." American poet and political activist Muriel Rukeyser said that "the universe is made of [collective] stories, not [individual] atoms."

One of Descartes's greatest contributions has been the philosophy of reductionism, that by studying parts we can understand wholes. Where are relationships in this view? "Putting the pieces together," as physicist David Bohm (2004) said, "is like trying to assemble the fragments of a broken mirror." A management plan ripped in two is not two plans; it is not even one. It is very easy to miss the whole and its relationships—our culture teaches us how to be reductionist every day of our lives; we spend far fewer days in "class" understanding the whole.[19]

Consider some of the relationship elements in Table 7.2.

Invest in Constituent Communities Rather Than Outsource

As we have already discussed, planning that has any chance of implementation invests in relationships with all concerned heritage constituencies. After all, planning is a facilitated conversation, and powerful questions that promote community and self-organization are personal, ambiguous, and stressful, according to Peter Block (2008).

The Cerros de La Carpintera Protected Zone in Costa Rica went through its first management planning experience in 2010. Because nearly the entire protected area is privately owned, significant conflict erupted between landowners and those calling to convert the entire area into a national park. Similarly, the zone has suffered depressing and incessant encroachment from squatter communities on its flanks. The management plan, however, avoided these major community relations problems—that is, avoided investing in relationships—instead opting for an easier, less confrontational and technical path to nonimplementation.

Engagement Strategies to Create New Conversations, Dialogues, and Relationships

As discussed above, dialogue directed by meaningful questions forms the basis of self-organizing human systems. Effective dialogue then strengthens community constituencies to operate together by reducing the incoherence of thought (Bohm 2004) so patently observed in the Galápagos uprisings. Hochachka (2009, p. 121) says,

> The domain of dialogue/process is important for negotiating values and ethics, arriving at a common vision, and deciding on appropriate actions. This can be done using various communicative processes, participatory frameworks, and social capacity building activities. By including dialogue in development, local people become active subjects in, rather than passive objects of, the development process. This not only fosters political empowerment, but also ushers in personal empowerment by creating a space to explore concerns, ideas, and goals, and to really hear each other's situation, values, and stories.

Organizational Transformation Methods

Many methodologies exist to enhance organizational performance and quality. Heritage sites could employ organizational development consultants, although they rarely do. In 2009, however, the US National Park Service enjoyed the assistance of Peter Senge and the Society for

Organizational Learning during a Leading and Learning for Sustainability Workshop (Grand Canyon News 2009). The private sector has been a rich cauldron of approaches. Some of the more famous in the business world include Lean Production (Jones and Womack 2003), Total Quality Management (Arguayo 1991), and Six Sigma (Pande and Holpp 2001).

Organizational Leaders

Leaders demonstrate values that organizations can follow. Their model can later become part of its culture. How can employees embrace perceived risky behavior if their leaders do not? If leaders can be personal, vulnerable, and exposed, then everyone else is free to be as well. As Gandhi reputedly said, "Be the change you want to see in the world."

According to Senge (1997) and Wheatley and Kellner-Rogers (1998), leaders create opportunities, advocate, motivate, promote communication, create spaces for innovators, set organizational vision, network different kinds of leaders, and give credit for the entire team. Executive leaders can be champions that protect and reduce the threat of new initiatives. Senge (1997) identifies three types of leaders, each with its own function:

1. Local line leaders can undertake meaningful experiments to test whether new learning capabilities actually lead to improved results.

2. Executive leaders provide support for line leaders, develop learning infrastructures, and lead by example in the gradual process of evolving the norms and behaviors of a learning culture.

3. Internal networkers or community builders can move freely about the organization to find those ready to bring about change, to help organizational experiments, and aid the diffusion of new learning.

Training and Application of Organizational Learning, Adaptive Management, and Collective Intelligence

After Action Review

This learning strategy, formally developed by the US Army, consists of debriefings after the action to answer what happened, why, and how. Marilyn Darling, a foremost After Action Review (AAR) promoter, says in Saposnik (2005):

An After Action Review (AAR) is a tool for continually improving your results by discovering and applying lessons before, during, and after a project, and for applying those lessons to similar projects in the future. Many people believe that the main purpose of AAR is to capture lessons for the benefit of other teams. But our belief is that the team itself is the first, best customer for what is learning, and the best time to apply "lessons learned" is in the current project itself. What a shame to wait until the end of a project to hold an AAR and gain an insight that might have helped improve the results of that project!

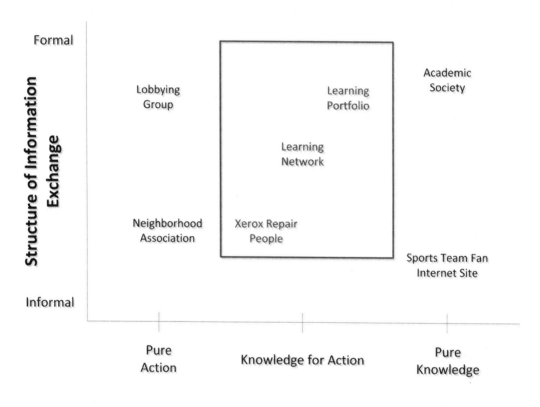

Main Focus of Network

Figure 7.4 | *Principal types of learning networks. Learning is influenced, as depicted here by the purpose of knowledge. At the endpoints of the horizontal axis, learning is applied directly to action, or, as in the case of basic science, learning occurs for the sake of learning. Structures that influence learning vary from informal, such as in a neighborhood association or collective of sports fans to more formal learning programs, such as provided in schools. The learning organizations vary from simple technical information exchange (such as a group of Xerox copy machine repairmen), to a learning network where more knowledge is created intentionally, to learning portfolios where participants follow formal protocols for experimenting, analyzing, and sharing information to improve knowledge-in-action.*

Communities of Practice

"Communities of practice," according to Wenger (2000), "are groups of people who share a concern or a passion for something they do and learn how to do it better as they interact regularly." They have three crucial characteristics:

1. Identity is defined by shared **domain** of interest, therefore shared competence that distinguishes members from others.

2. **Community** members voluntarily engage in joint activities and discussions. The key here are relationships more than infrastructure.

3. **The practice,** members are practitioners who develop shared repertoire of resources: experiences, stories, tools, ways of addressing recurring problems—in short, a shared practice. In Kuhn's terms (1962), they develop and reinforce their practice's paradigm together.

Learning Networks

Learning occurs in three domains: formal, where people learn through courses offered by academic institutions as a part of a degree program; nonformal, where people learn through educational activities organized outside of the formal classroom for specific audiences, with specific learning objectives (e.g., events such as training workshops or conferences); and informal, where people learn via a lifelong process from daily experiences and the people and resources in their environment (e.g., observing others, reading publications).

According to Brown and Salafsky (2004), there are three kinds of learning networks (Figure 7.3):

- **Type I. Information Exchange Networks**—Here, learning is primarily guided by participants' requests for information, although the network may also have some learning questions, such as a community of practice (Wenger 2000). Their membership process is usually open, and they can be any size. They usually require very little commitment from members and rely primarily on informal incentives for participation. In terms of coordination and communication, they typically have a paid coordinator and a fishing net communications structure. Information exchange networks can include virtual networks and tend to be relatively cheaper to implement.

Outside the Box 7 | *Implementing a High Reliability Organization to Fight Forest Fires and Save Firefighter Lives*

Things that never happened before, happen all the time!

—Karl Weick (2011)

Fire crew leader Lathan Johnson recalls the Little Venus Fire that trapped and nearly killed him and his nine crew members in July 2006 in Shoshone National Forest, Wyoming. What made this incident so different was that the firefighters had not even engaged the fire, but were traveling to relieve another fire crew when the fire overtook them.

When Johnson's crew arrived at the meeting point to hike in to relieve the other crew, the gear packer and his mules had not packed up the gear and did not have an operating radio. After a late start, the crew suffered poor radio communication with the incident command post and was unaware how close the fire had come. When finally Johnson recognized it was time to turn around, the packer in front turned back toward the crew and lost control of his mules. Johnson tells the tale:

> As the mules passed, they began to panic, spreading into the woods going every direction. There were mules going in every direction, crew members chasing mules, and a packer screaming obscenities. The fire continued to progress towards us. And in the confusion, one of the crew members split off, crossed the river, and nobody saw her do this.… We all began to sprint down the trail and cross the river. We could hear the fire right on our heels, the wind was howling, and there was the noise of the crown fire coming up behind us…

The crew had no escape so they found a "survivable" site to deploy their fire shelters next to a rock outcrop. Shelters look like oversized metallic-colored sleeping bags made of heat resistant materials and are designed to create a seal with the ground, protecting firefighters from the intense heat of an overpassing fire.

> We did a head count and realized that we were missing one crew member, and this was the hardest feeling that I have ever had to deal with in my entire career. There wasn't time to go back out and look … so we decided to deploy there and this was our best option for survival … As I was shaking out my shelter, I remember hearing trees snapping off … We had only one or two minutes at the most before the fire front hit us.

All nine firefighters deployed their shelters and although some suffered minor burns thanks to rips in the shelters, all survived and after forty-five minutes emerged from their fire-resistant cocoons.

> As the helicopters came in closer, we were able to start talking to them on air to ground. And during this conversation the missing crew member's voice came across the air to ground frequency. And we all let out a huge scream of relief.

When danger passed the crew located Monica Zajanc who had deployed her shelter to weather the firestorm, alone.

That national forest was already participating with the Wildland Fire Lessons Learned Center to implement High Reliability Organizing, so an immediate evaluation of the incident ensued by a peer review team (USFS 2006). But instead of assigning blame as would a conventional bureaucratic agency, the US Forest Service turned the occasion into a learning opportunity. It noted in its report that multiple factors combined to produce this near fatal miss: poor communication, late start for the hike, inability to see the fire, packer had no operating radio, ripped shelters, separated crew member, etc. Johnson concludes in a video about the incident (Wildland Fire LCC 2012), "My big goal of this presentation is that hopefully someday people learn from this and help keep some firefighters from having to pull that fire shelter and lay face down in the dirt, waiting for the unknown."

Dave Christenson, former assistant center manager and cofounder of the Wildland Fire Lessons Learned Center (LLC), an interagency body designed to generate and disseminate lessons learned about wildland firefighting in North America, said the Little Venus Fire was a turning point for the adoption of High Reliability Organizing (HRO) in the forest fire–fighting community (2014). HRO was developed by Weick and Sutcliffe (2007) based on a study of operations with small margins of human error: firefighting, nuclear reactors, aircraft carriers, oil rigs. How do these teams avoid major accidents in a world that constantly puts human error in newspaper headlines?

The book presents five principles of HRO:

1. Preoccupation with Failure. A wary and persistent attention to detecting and quickly responding to all errors and failures. Treating all errors and failures as weak signals of possible larger failures, and a signal of possible weakness in other parts of the operation or organization.

2. Reluctance to Simplify. Resisting the common tendency to oversimplify explanations of events and to steer away from evidence that disconfirms management direction or suggests the presence of unexpected problems.

3. Sensitivity to Operations. Maintaining situational awareness and the big picture of current operations. Sensitivity to operations permits early problem identification, permitting action before problems become too substantial.

4. Commitment to Resilience. Recognizing, understanding, and accepting that human error and unexpected events are both persistent and omnipresent ... developing capacity to respond to, contain, cope with, and bounce back from undesirable change swiftly and effectively.

5. Deference to Expertise. The loosening of hierarchical restraints and enabling the organization to empower expert people closest to a problem, often lower level personnel, when operational decisions must be made quickly and accurately.

Christenson coordinated the writing of a series of HRO case studies including ones about Sequoia and Kings Canyon National Parks (SEKI) and Shoshone National Forest (all available at www.wildfirelessons.net). SEKI has adopted HRO by creating a learning culture and annual learning cycle. One of the building blocks of HRO is the After Action Review (AAR) tool, originally developed by the US Army to evaluate every incident. Operational groups conduct AARs by asking themselves what they had planned to do, what they did, why there was a difference, and what would they do differently next time. To answer these, the organization first must develop an open culture where people can safely and freely speak their minds without fear of punishment. The culture also regards errors as learning opportunities rather than opportunities to name-blame-shame. SEKI developed a systematic process that incorporated results of specific AARs into an analysis of root causes and generates lessons learned that make their way into formal training and procedures to reduce that those errors repeat themselves. Figure 7.4 shows how SEKI has operationalized learning throughout the year. DeGrosky and Parry (2011) discuss the larger Action Review Cycle in which the AARs and Before Action Reviews (BARs) play vital roles in implementing lessons learned.

SEKI's case study says that to achieve a desired safety culture, first it had to create four subcultures:

1. *Reporting Culture* where people can safely repot their mistakes.

2. *Just Culture* where blame and punishment is replaced by learning from mistakes.

3. *Flexible Culture* adapts to changing demands by allowing decisions to migrate to expertise during high tempo operations.

4. *Learning Culture* captures and spreads knowledge and applies learning so that its personnel may understand events and improve performance.

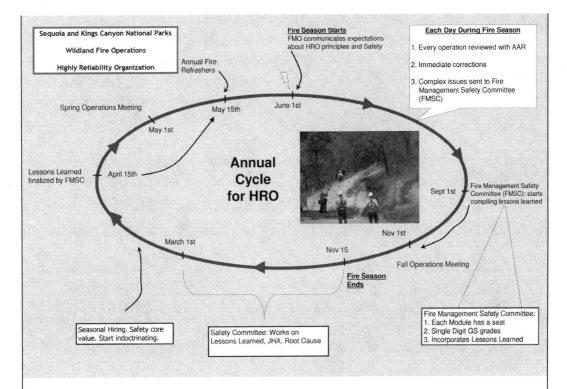

Figure 7.5 | *The Annual Wildland Fire High Reliability Organizing (HRO) Learning Cycle at Sequoia and King's Canyon National Parks (Wildland Fire Lessons Learned Center). This graphic shows how seasonal lessons learned based on experience become documented and available for application during the following fire season.*

With wildland fires increasing in North America and around the world, HRO will become increasingly desired. And not just for fires—other heritage functions will also need to act consistently in search of weak signals before bad things happen whether law enforcement, conflict resolution with communities, or wildlife management.

But even with organizations already practicing HRO, risk always lurks only a step away, as it did for firefighter Monica Zajanc who died in a helicopter crash on 13 August, less than a month after she survived the Little Venus Fire.

- **Type II. Best Practice Networks**—In these networks, participants define specific learning questions and collaborate to document, validate, and disseminate best practices. Best practice networks have learning questions and sometimes have a formal learning framework. They have a membership approval process and tend to be medium in size. They require a formal or informal commitment from participants, but they tend to rely on informal incentives for sharing information. They have paid coordinators and a bicycle wheel or spiderweb communications structure, with varying levels of participation in decision making. They usually rely on face-to-face communication and rarely include virtual networks. See Outside the Box 7.1.

- **Type III. Research Networks**—In these networks, learning centers around a formal framework designed to answer specific research questions. They tend to be small or medium in size. The process for joining the network can be entirely closed (by invitation only) or regulated by an approval process. They require a formal commitment and often offer formal incentives for sharing information. They have a paid coordinator and usually have a bicycle wheel communications structure with a strong center. Participation in decision making varies. To communicate, they rely on meeting together for at least part of their member interaction.

Learning Infrastructure

This refers to structures within organizations (LR) that promote learning. For example, infrastructure, even more than databases, computer projectors, and high-tech classrooms, includes people and offices in charge of documenting and studying innovations inside and outside the organization. These would be the people responsible for benchmarking and studying best practices and then reporting back to their own organizations. Their job spreads innovations within an organization and lobbies for the establishment or improvement of environments and processes conducive to learning. At Royal Dutch/Shell Group, for example, when management was convinced of the value of scenario planning, instead of obligating everyone to take a scenario planning course, it redesigned the planning structure so that management teams would provide different budgets that correspond to different scenarios. "Planning as learning" became the motto reflected in various structural policies (Senge 1996). Other organizations have specific positions in charge of learning, such as learning managers or in some cases chief learning officers.

Safe Spaces

Innovations and new ideas can quickly activate an organization's immune system very much like our own body isolates and destroys foreign organisms. Thus, champions of new ideas need safe spaces or practice fields in which to operate and incubate their ideas safe from defensive senior bureaucratic leaders. In this space, champions seek like-minded positive deviants, organize them, set up learning infrastructure (which may also include secret laboratories and untrackable funds, to use Hollywood examples), develop prototypes, test, and experiment.

Seligman (2005, pp. 8–9) identifies the following guidelines for setting up systems thinking at Ford Motor Company.

- *"Understand your history.* There is no ideal, perfect, or correct plan or template for rolling out systems thinking in an organization. Every situation is unique and can best be understood as the aggregate of all the history and conditions that came before.

- *"Respect and appreciate the current state of the people in the organization.* People love change, but they hate to be changed. Base your strategy on what the likely response will be to each part of the program, and do not try to overcome resistance. Appreciate the resistance and give people a chance to do more of what they find satisfying and nonthreatening.

- *"Create conditions for self-reflection inside a safe practice field.* Building a safe and collegial environment multiplies the chances of people examining and shifting their own mental models a hundredfold, which will immeasurably increase the impact of the work on both individuals and the organization.

- *"Take the deep structures into account.* The larger, older, and more traditional the organization, the more you will discover deep structures that produce patterns of behavior that explain the resistance to change you will encounter. Do not fight deep structures unless they are in your circle of control. Understand them, however, and you will know how to create micro-changes that over time can and will reach a critical mass that will impact and shift the structures.

- *"Look for similar or parallel successes in the organization, and seek to leverage them.* Spend more time studying successes than failures. Failures are enlightening in telling you which paths are likely to be blocked. Successes indicate which paths may be open to you.

- *"Concentrate on building capacity rather than achieving results or completing projects.* In one of our projects, the participants did not draw a causal loop diagram [basic systems thinking tool] until practically the last day, but this group has produced some of the most committed systems thinkers to come from any group. To be overly focused on the product and not the process will inevitably produce bad results and fail to teach the core lessons of systems thinking.

- *"Create a "pull" program by concentrating on small groups of early adopters.* Large cascaded programs invite the immune system to go into defensive overdrive. Start quietly, with people who are interested and willing to commit, and do not be in a hurry. Remember that immune system!"

A safe space may or may not protect learning from a performance paradox inherent in learning. The paradox is that when people attempt to learn new processes or systems and must leave old ones behind, performance can actually drop during this transition (Keating et al. 1999). This drop may scare senior leaders enough for them to lose confidence in the change effort and pull the plug. For example, if a heritage site tries to implement a new monitoring and evaluation system, during a time they might be confused about how to operate the computer programs, may be slow in collecting data with new tools, and unsure how to analyze data, which ends with reports not being as clear or comprehensive as they were before. A director might accuse the new innovation of wasting money simply because that person does not have patience to allow the transition to root. Thus, it is important to understand beforehand that drops in performance commonly accompany learning.

There are other reasons that learning can seem at odds with performance (Singer and Edmondson 2008):

- By focusing on one's failures and mistakes—necessary for learning—it may appear that that organization is performing worse than it is.

- Learning costs may be at times more visible than benefits. Leaders must publicize this beforehand.

- Experimentation necessarily produces failures, a prerequisite for learning.

Paid Time to Innovate, Experiment, and Practice

People need time to learn new skills. It is not enough to have a learning lab, practice field, safe space, or mandate to implement adaptive management (Inside the Box 7.1) if the responsibility of learning is simply piled onto a long list of preexisting responsibilities. Thus, when organizations create both physical space as well as time space for people to learn, their chances of building skills are greater.

Inside the Box 7 | *A Famous Adaptive Management Experiment That Failed due to Lack of Experimentation*

In the late 1980s–1990s, formidable conflict erupted in rural forest communities in the northwest United States, centered around old-growth forests, logging, and endangered species such as the northern spotted owl. President Bill Clinton wanted to resolve these conflicts with best available science to address uncertainty, by using the complex ecosystem-based approach, then becoming vogue.

So in 1994 the federal government began to implement the Northwest Forest Plan that promoted ecosystem-based management on 9.7 million hectares in California, Oregon, and Washington managed by several agencies, most notably the US Forest Service and the Bureau of Land Management. The plan also called for ten adaptive management areas (AMA) covering 6 percent of that area.

Adaptive Management (AM), due to its emphasis on experimentation, learning, and adaptive strategies, was in theory especially apt to deal with heightened uncertainty. Yet despite enthusiasm surrounding the AMAs, the experiment in adaptive management failed.

An evaluation noted that the reason that AM failed in the NW Forest Plan was principally because the government did not adapt its own culture to promote learning (Stankey et al. 2003, 2005). Such changes would have included increased transparency; horizontal, team-based decision making; greater experimentation; lower risk aversion; embracing errors as learning rather than punitive opportunities; reoriented capacity building priorities; and others.

More specifically, higher levels of agency bureaucracy did not make AM a priority, guarantee stable funding, establish incentives for AMA managers (such as training and career development), offer special training, orientation, additional support staff, and the time managers were allowed to use toward AM-related programs quickly eroded over time.

Overall both legislation (such as the Endangered Species Act) and the agencies' organizational cultures were afraid of risk. Managers' job was to minimize the possibility of harm especially to endangered species, so experimentation, inherent to AM, was often seen as too risky.

No experiment of consequence can guarantee absolutely no adverse consequences, thus making AM nearly impossible to implement. In environments of risk, instead of going in AM experimental mode, people suppress experimentation and turn on risk reduction mode. The lack of experimentation endowed people with a false sense of security that risk was being reduced even though the "no change" route was fraught with risk, provoking the president to act in the first place.

In effect, the overriding misguided and Modernist belief—that one can simply install a new tool, its worth clearly perceived, and implementation will logically follow—led to program failure as it does today with the application of any number of technical protected area tools without corresponding change in all four quadrants of the Integral Map.

Elements Necessary for the Implementation of Adaptive Management	
I • Maintain enthusiasm and morale of AM managers • Become more comfortable with uncertainty • Trust among stakeholders	**It** • Training of personnel to carry out AM
We • Organizational culture to be less risk averse • Understand the value of learning • Belief that current understandings might be wrong • Embrace error as part of the learning process • Team learning • Organizational recognition that AM represents how business is done throughout organization, not just limited AMAs • Societal dialogues to identify critical questions about endangered species and other values	**Its** • Incentives to implement AM (career development) • Legislative barriers to risk • Systems to capture learning and learning performance standards • Eliminate penalties for failure or error • Stable funding • Efforts to promote broader stakeholder participation • Continuously updated plans that are adaptable in the short term

Storytelling

Every paradigm has its stories that confer the paradigm's rules and assumptions. For example, every time a protected area wants to create another management plan, it retells the story in its mind: "First we have to find the money, then we need to hire the consultants to describe the site so that we are not criticized as inadequate scientifically..." Thus to introduce change requires new narratives to capture meaning. Often stories can be more powerful than models and analyses, as they appeal not just to rationality but also emotionality.

Manage Language and Misinformation

The use of language, information, and power intertwine. Paulo Freire (cited in Forester 1989, p. 21) says, "To deny other people's ability to communicate, to make sense, to understand and inquire both about what is and about what can yet be is tantamount to doing violence to them." Forester (1989) argues that a planner's job is also to anticipate and counteract alterable, misleading, and disabling claims and to nurture healthy and democratic discourse. Planners must ensure that communication empowers citizen action, not inhibits it, such as when management plans use a highly technical language unfamiliar to many actors. Forester continues (p. 23),

> Analysts must recognize clearly that what gets done depends heavily on what gets said, and how it is said, and to whom. By doing so, they can seize opportunities to counteract a wide range of disabling and distorting claims: exaggerated threats, needlessly obscure and confusing analyses, strategically hidden information, manipulated expectations, and so on. Working in these ways, planning analysts can expose, however subtly or partially, unwarranted exercises of power and the resulting obstacles to citizens' political action.

He offers strategies for planners to amend nonsystemic distortions, such as asking for clarifications; creating time for questions and cross-examination at hearings, reviews, or commission meetings; a sensitive chairperson can ask a speaker to speak more slowly, more directly into the microphone, less technically, and so on.

Planners must also counteract intentional misinformation with commonplace acts, according to Forester, such as checking, double-checking, testing, consulting experts, seeking third-party counsel, clarifying issues, exposing assumptions, reviewing and citing the record, appealing to precedent, invoking traditional values (democratic participation, for example), spreading questions about unexplored possibilities, spotlighting jargon and revealing meaning, negotiating

Fire Box 3| *Triple-Loop Learning: Setting Fire Free*

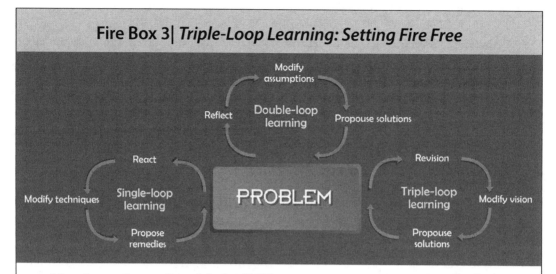

Move beyond mental models that hold us to revision or re-envision something totally different, perhaps impossible with previous mental models.

Like Houdini, triple-loop learners escape their mental model handcuffs. Once free of their previous assumptions, such people envision scenarios and worlds totally new.

Although it only takes two learning loops to add Wildland Fire Use (WFU) to the forest management approach, it takes a third to envision a world where fires burn free. "Let them burn!" Indeed, more and more people see fire as a natural part of forest ecology, and although letting fires burn without much if any interference is politically challenging, this choice to do nothing is still a forest management application. This new vision sees unhindered forest fires no longer as just another tool, but an entirely new way to manage forests according to ecological principles, rather than simply to human utilitarianism. Between 1998 and 2006, more than 579,000 hectares have burned in WFU fires on lands managed by all five federal agencies with WFU programs.

The Forest Service WFU specialist, Tim Sexton, envisions a National Forest Service—and surely all managed lands—to have the WFU option in a world where zealous fire suppression no longer persists. And it seems US policy moves in that direction. The 2001 Federal Wildland Fire Management Policy states, "Wildland fire will be used to protect, maintain, and enhance resources and, as nearly as possible, be allowed to function in its natural ecological role." Accordingly, WFU programs have been developed and expanded in many national parks and Forest Service wilderness areas.

for clearly specified outcomes and values, working through informal networks to get information, bargaining for information, holding others to public commitments, and so on.

In summary (Forester 1989, p. 41), "Progressive planners, therefore, must learn to anticipate misinformation before the fact, when something may still be done to counteract it."

As Albert Einstein said, "The world we have created is a product of our thinking; it cannot change without changing our thinking" (Fire Box 3). While thinking describes the left-hand column, in chapter 8 we visit the final quadrant of our Integral Map, where we complete the tables and model for how to apply the Integral Map to the barriers and the future of protected area planning.

> *We are in trouble just now because we do not have a good story. We are in between stories. The old story, the account of how the world came to be and how we fit into it, is no longer effective. Yet we have not learned the new story.*
>
> —*Thomas Berry*

CHAPTER 8

The Management Institutions We Build Influence Our Heritage Sites

Every nation and every man instantly surround themselves with a material apparatus which exactly corresponds to … their state of thought. Observe how every truth and every error, each a thought of some man's mind, clothes itself with societies, houses, cities, language, ceremonies, newspapers. Observe the ideas of the present day… see how timber, brick, lime, and stone have flown into conventional shape, obedient to the master idea reigning in the minds of many persons.

—Ralph Waldo Emerson

THE OTHER
SIDE OF
COMPLEXITY

EVENTS

PATTERNS

STRUCTURES

MENTAL MODELS

VISION

PURPOSE

Our Institutions, Policies, and Technologies Influence Planning

Marco Polo sheep once bounded across vast rugged mountains of Pakistan's interior. Poachers, however, eventually shot down their numbers. The Wildlife Conservation Society responded by drawing up a new national park to protect the sheep. This new park excluded local Wakhi villages, but included much of their grazing lands within its boundaries, effectively eliminating grazing. The establishment of Khunjerab National Park in 1979 brought with it an armory of Modernist tools and approaches to alpine pasture management where villagers have sustainably herded sheep, goats, and yaks for centuries.

As the Marco Polo sheep situation grew increasingly dire, IUCN conservationists formulated a management plan with the Pakistani government, creating a new governmental management authority, carrying out rapid wildlife appraisals, sending in foreign researchers, deploying paramilitary units, calculating carrying capacities, and devising local compensation schemes for domestic animals lost to wild predators. They also excluded local communities from planning and stripped their ancestral grazing rights, failing to fulfill promises, and otherwise disrespecting their personal interests and culture. The villagers struck back with a grassroots offensive to insert themselves, one way or another, into the park's management (Knudson 2009; Mir 2011; Mock n. d.).

Such situations in which well-intentioned conservation groups and government authorities develop conventional plans in response to apparent emergencies, all too frequently carry with them unforeseen and often devastating social and environmental consequences. Models of heritage management erected in one culture unlikely will work in another. Site management tools often ignore the left-hand column so much that local people's apprehension and the motivations go undetected, like silent torpedoes, until too late. Narrowly casting management as protecting natural or cultural heritage against the actions of people rather than with them, leads to both mistakes and costs. And often, we fail to ask what is a park being protected for, against what, and for whom.

Protected area planners very often frame planning as solely a biological exercise, financing buildings and plans, building roads and bridges, implementing planning and managing tools, consulting protected area categories charts (LR), or as interactions among multiple levels of government (see, for example, Togridou et al. 2006). We know now, however, that all of these reflect an incomplete understanding of what contemporary planning actually requires. For example, the GEF/UNDP-funded Strengthening the Protected Area Network (SPAN) project in Namibia summarized the main barriers to protected area stewardship in that nation as "a fragmented policy framework, weak institutional capacities, fragile human capacities for protected area operations, incomplete biogeographic coverage, and the absence of tested mechanisms for public-private-community partnerships" (Republic of Namibia and UNDP 2010). The program focused solely on the right-hand column and did not consider potential barriers from the other side.

How planners define a problem also leads to which interventions they will prescribe, and thus SPAN, which ended in 2013 emphasized (1) strengthening systemic capacity, namely the enabling legal/policy environment and financial mechanisms for protected area management; (2) strengthening the institutional capacity for protected area management; and (3) demonstrating new ways and means of protected area management, including partnerships with other government agencies, local communities, and the private sector. LR. LR. LR.

This bending toward the right side does not afflict only heritage managers but also the entire development field in which heritage management is embedded. Even cutting-edge Postmodern thinking that addresses an ailing unsustainable world follows this line. Barrett Brown, director of the Integral Sustainability Center, studied eight major sustainability books to learn which perspectives they most used (Brown 2007). Brown analyzed each sentence of each book and documented which quadrant seemed to be its focus. He added up all the lines per quadrant, divided by the total number of lines in the book to arrive at a percentage.[20] He concluded (p. 25):

> The utter dominance of the Lower-Right quadrant in these [data] has numerous implications and likely causes. First of all, it suggests that when it comes to looking at sustainability, the authors predominantly focused the attention of their readers on the systems aspects of sustainability. Sentence after sentence, book after book, the authors' lenses consistently privilege one-quarter of reality. Pollution permits, illiteracy rates, economic factors, technological advances, computer modeling to track resource usage, organizational structures, the resource base, and complementary currencies are all examples from the books.

Were I to only see sustainability as presented by many of these authors, one of my "lenses" on the world would bulge out of proportion, yet it would feel natural to me. As I faced our global challenges, I would see LR problems and prescribe LR solutions. And potentially, my interventions would fail, or at least not be as effective as they could, precisely because of my prejudiced focus on the world.

Winston Churchill alluded to the collective quadrants even before AQAL existed when he said, "We shape our buildings, and then our buildings shape us." As we have argued earlier, all quadrants interact, the LL in particular supplies collective ideas on which we clothe our society's institutions. This book is an example of multiquadrant interaction. We, the authors, felt frustration (UL) with the current state of heritage site planning. This led to our behavior of researching and writing this book (UR), drawing on our level of consciousness (UL) and the paradigm of consciousness itself (LL) to produce a book (LR) that aims to help change the paradigm of site planning (LL), and serve as the backbone to foment heritage site management institutions to rise up the other side of the iceberg (LR).

We point out this strong LR orientation in development to indicate the overwhelming role of LR in site planning. In fact, plans themselves are the incarnation of many collective LL ideas about participation, planning, organizations, forms of knowing, management, and power. The collective thoughts and hands of people throughout the ages forge plan technology.

Plans do not have to rely solely on PLUS-based Rational Comprehensive Planning or even DICE-based planning; they can also reflect Holistic Planning in their aspirations to shape the future. No matter which paradigm flows through their pages, plans as well as other collective entities emerge from LR. Table 8.1 shows the main forces from all four perspectives that influence planning, completing our survey of forces that concurrently and holistically emerge to hinder or promote planning and implementation.

Table 8.1	*Forces That Influence Planning Implementation*	
I	**It**
Perceptions, Values, and Attitudes	**Physical Health and Well-Being**
• Sense of self, level of consciousness (egocentric to worldcentric)	• Health and energy level supports or inhibits participation in plan implementation. These levels are affected not only by above factors, but also by nutrition, medical care, financial state, political culture at local and national levels
• Sense of responsibility, loyalty, and affect toward planning agency, its mission, constituent community, and managed resources	**Behavior**
• Sense of trust, transparency, and fairness within agency and stakeholder community	• Actions and behaviors promote or inhibit plan tasks, especially working with other stakeholders (opposite sex, local community members, tour

- Sense of trust, transparency, and fairness within agency and stakeholder community

- Attitude toward participation and rights of other participants in planning process (levels: none, EIS, collaborative, DNA)

- Affect toward people who inspire and guide (priest, respected site manager, president who asks for the plan, foreign donors, friends)

- Perceived behavioral control to act (such as plan), also known as perceived locus of control

- Role of self in planning (planner, facilitator, core member, peon, other stakeholder) and power to influence planning decisions

- Feeling of recognition

- Visions and dreams of the future

Skills

- Past experience in similar processes or stakeholders

- Anticipated costs of participating in planning process (time, money, risks such as disappointment or loss of face or power)

- Alternative planning approaches known

- Mental model held about the nature of transformation or change (role of science, God, individuals, systems, intuition, luck, destiny, revelation, incremental or big jumps, etc.)

- Collaborative experience held to achieve common or joint objectives (i.e., Dialogues)

tour operators, people of different status, religions, ethnicity, formality of roles in management, etc.)

- Responses to rules and stimuli from management organizations, both incentives and disincentives

- Behavior and welfare affected by the built environments, degrees of Biophilia, and structure of meeting spaces

Skills

- Skills and capabilities permit or inhibit stakeholder participation, planning, and implementation

• Purpose of plan (bureaucratic requirement, just for funding, prestige, or to change world) **Intentions** • Individual goals, interests, and motivation to participate in planning process (see Dialogues) • Intentions to implement plan and related attitudes **Cognitive Capacities** • Emotional or interpersonal intelligence to work with others in processes • Capacities to analyze data, understand issues, generate conclusions, focus attention, develop personal vision, maintain discipline • Personal mastery includes rapport with subconscious, integrating reason and intuition, continually seeing more of our connectedness to world, compassion, commitment to the whole. • Loop learning (single, double, triple, and quadruple)	
We **Paradigms, Mental Models, Assumptions** • Physics (PLUS, DICE, interior DICE) • Relationship between humans and nature • Relationships between planning, implementation, management, power, stakeholders, engagement, research	**Its** **Institutions** • Site management agencies promote or resist citizen participation, organizational learning, power sharing, alliance building, misinformation, etc. • Academic or professional institutions that train in planning styles,

- Diversity of public interests, values, objectives, and orientations of planning

- Model of social transformation (focus on individual vs. community, etc.)

- Models of capacity building (apprenticing, memorizing, learning while doing)

- Protected area planning field's principal stories, myths, texts, language, rules, etc. (components of Kuhn's science paradigm)

- Leadership style and decision making

- Ethics of public engagement

- Role of science in planning (epistemology)

- Object of study, sources of knowledge, locus of power

- Interpretation of organizational history and meaning

- Mutual understandings of planning problems

- Organizational culture and values (horizontal or vertical, team or only individual learning, adaptive or resistant to change, shared or individual visions, aligned or conflictive members, machine vs. people as caring creative innovators)

- Perception of validity and authority of plan to influence decision making

- Shared visions, goals, consensuses

Engagement and Relationships

Solidarity, trust, transparency, mutual respect, participation, and co-creation or the contrary between people, organizations, communities, and other groups

philosophies, and related capacities (facilitation, community development, science-based tools, project management, etc.)

- Organizations, networks, and associations that offer direct technical assistance and other support materials for planners and managers

- Donors that offer financial support for planning and management

- Local institutions whether farming cooperatives, tour operator associations, or other civil society constituency organizations that participate in planning process

- Formal partnerships/alliances between planning stakeholders (vs. relationships, LL)

- Private enterprises that offer products related to planning (reference materials, consulting, training packages, planning software, research tools, etc.)

Policies

- Incentives or disincentives for planning styles, financial, political, professional, or others

- Land management agency guidelines, manuals, protocols for planning and plan development

- Laws, mandates, directives, rules, and policies that support or inhibit heritage conservation, learning, science, technology, management, participation, power distribution, etc.

- Budgets and how they are used (plan/process, consultants/staff, training/outsourcing, etc.)

Communication and Collective Learning	**Technologies**
• Communication and information sharing within stakeholder community (includes heritage agency) • Organizational learning • Collective intelligence **Collective Consciousness** This field unites us all and serves as the source for collective wisdom, social movements, and self-organizing systems. It includes the Internet to create a collective brain.	• Plan format, structure, language, and design that promotes or inhibits implementation (for example, printed vs. virtual) • Printing, publishing, communication, and distribution technologies • Research technologies applied before and during planning • Milestone vs. activity planning • Planning aids such as standardized online planning wizards, adaptive management software, etc. • Group facilitation and participation methods and tools (SWOT, ToP, workshops, open space, After Action Reviews, etc.) • Measures of success (indicators, standards, project conceptualization tools, etc.)

Forces Affecting the LR

Institutions

Although the literature overflows with definitions of institution, all definitions, whether they include an informal handshake or overly formal government bureaucracies (Inside the Box 8.1) represent the external manifestation of a collective agreement. As such, we prefer, as a useful definition, "normative patterns embedded in and enforced by laws and mores (informal customs and practices)" (Bellah et al. 1992, p. 11). Institutions, then, follow the wishes and paradigms of the collective that endows them. Nevertheless, institutions can also exhibit cultures and behaviors beyond anything that their component members might have imagined. While these emergent and synergistic properties may not trace directly to the wisdom of a particular paradigm, their increasing richness, differentiation, complexity, and even consciousness only indicate more advanced forms of institutions described by the LR.[21]

Inside the Box 8 | *Bureaucracy: Once the Most Efficient Form of Government ... Then What Happened?*

Bureaucracy literally means "governance from the desk." It is not a kind of government like democracy, plutocracy, or aristocracy but rather is a means by which any of those forms operates. While bureaucracy has existed since ancient Egypt and Rome, in the modern era, bureaucracy has taken on a whole new sheen. Sociologist Max Weber (1992) shows that bureaucracies offer a large advantage over organizations that do not systematically manage, study, and implement rules. Think about a professional bureaucratic army with rigid rank-and-file, sophisticated war planning, logistics planning, and control over all aspects compared to a loose band of tribes, with lots of individual free wills, such as soldier-farmers. They stand no chance as the Romans demonstrated time and again. Anyone who has experienced the opening scene of *The Gladiator* can easily witness the difference.

This applies equally to corporations, government planning agencies, universities, or the Vatican. It is no coincidence that bureaucracy has spread to nearly every major institution in the world. For a long time it was the most efficient way to control large numbers of people and resources.

To accomplish this, bureaucracy places high value on rationality, control, and obedience.

Thus, according to Weber, the ideal bureaucracy uses elaborate hierarchical division of labor directed by explicit rules impersonally applied, staffed by full-time, lifetime professionals. These bureaucrats do not in any sense own the tools of their labor (computers, desks, machines, weapons), their jobs, or the sources of their funds, and live off a salary, not from income derived directly from the performance of their job. All these strategies promote order.

To be efficient, bureaucracies need all the professional, specialized niches (departments, offices, divisions, regiments, teams) to work in clocklike synchronicity, eliminating redundancy. Each official must receive information in the correct format at the correct moment in order to process efficiently and send modified information and inputs to the next office.

As a result of these traits, Yaffee (1997) identifies five behavioral biases of government agencies.

1. *They prefer short-term rationality over long-term rationality*. Agencies seek to minimize energy to respond to a situation while maximizing control and predictability. This promotes convenience and planning for immediate results.

2. *They prefer competition over cooperation and to protect power and not share it.* If they share some, they will lose exactly this much power in a zero sum game. This bias inhibits sharing information; promotes biases and misinformation as well as turf protection even within agency; and leads to stalemates, low morale, and low legitimacy in eyes of the public. The "bias in favor of government control" causes all negative outcomes to be attributed to the lack of government control and consequently leads to a felt need to increase regulation: the possibility that poorly designed government policies could be the cause is not entertained.

3. *They fragment interests and values.*

4. *They fragment responsibilities and authorities.*

5. *They fragment information and knowledge.*

A bureaucracy requires stability, predictability, linearity, and a professional and reductionist division of labor to function efficiently. To do this, it relies heavily on Technical Rationality tools such as diagnostic research, protocols, templates, formulas, blueprints, recipes, external consultant expertise, and other rational, comprehensive planning and decision-making processes.

For a long time the world more or less provided the conditions necessary for these requirements. Now, though, with the uncertainty and complexity of the DICE World rapidly distancing itself from its PLUS forebears, bureaucracy's demands to be efficient instead have grown inefficient. Its reliance on stability instead of producing efficiency increasingly produces inefficiency, erodes resilience, reduces its ability to problem solve, and smothers its ability to learn, adapt, keep up with surprises, and change rapidly enough to maintain pace with accelerating change in a DICE World.[1]

1. *This article taken with modifications and permission from Kohl (2010).*

Policies

Policies are collective decisions enforced by laws and mores. Even policies handed down by brutal dictators such as Saddam Hussein reflect the will, even if co-opted, of his subordinates and family members, otherwise these policies could never be implemented. Policies can be written or unwritten, formal or informal, fleeting or enduring. In all cases, they express a collective will that influences in some manner planning and managing.[22]

Technologies

Technologies represent the means to achieve policies and desired outcomes that arise from collective concepts of a problem, other predecessor technologies, and solutions that draw upon multiple authors. Given a general definition, technologies transcend mere mechanical means to include abstract combinations of solutions such as plans, methodologies, research techniques, or indicators of success.

In chapter 9, we take these forces another step by answering the question: "Now that we have identified the forces that affect planning and implementation, what do we do with them to improve implementation and management?" The Integral Map serves us poorly if it does not help practitioners understand planning and implementation problems and how to transcend them.

Conventional Planning Generates Various Institution-Based Barriers

In chapter 2, we shared the pre-Integral implementation barrier model used in the CATIE study (Figure 2.1). It attempted to explain from where implementation barriers appear and outline strategies for their removal. While the model proved a large step beyond arbitrary and often anecdotal lists of innumerable barriers, it still lacked the insights that Integral Theory can share.

Figure 8.1 now completes the updated model that we have been building with AQAL during the second half of this book. We might say that the earlier model conveyed the message, "Rational Comprehensive Planning generates conditions that result in planning implementation barriers, accompanied by a couple additional categories of barriers (poor planning practice and institutional). Also the reader should be able to infer the strategies to remove them."

The Integral-based model updates that message: "Forces arise from four concurrent, interacting, fundamental perspectives. When managers ignore those forces, they inadvertently sabotage their own planning. No forces are excluded from this framework; solutions arise from the simultaneous management of these forces that lead to plan implementation and more effective management."

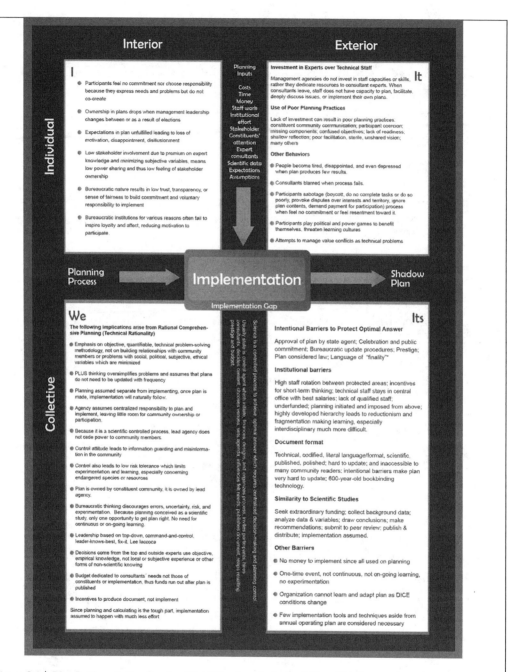

Figure 8.1 | *Plan Implementation Barriers Model Based on the Integral Map. This figure updates the earlier model presented in chapter 2 by applying the Integral Map and assigning barriers to their corresponding quadrants.*

The two models do share some elements. They both show planning inputs, a somewhat linear planning process, the existence of an implementation gap, and a shadow plan. A *shadow plan* is the plan hidden away in managers' minds that truly reflects their implementation intentions. A shadow plan actually runs the show when a formal plan either remains unimplemented due to barriers or does not exist at all, leaving no other alternative but an unwritten mental plan to implement. The CATIE study presented evidence that Costa Rica's annual national park work plans often corresponded poorly with management plans, indicating that managers derived their ideas of what needed to be done from some mysterious plane of existence beyond their management plans—that is, they invoked their shadow plans. In fact, the closer a shadow plan corresponds to a formal plan, the greater implementation should be. In other words, the closer managers' heartfelt implementation intentions overlap their written implementation goals, the narrower the implementation gap, all else being equal. Those who cannot jump the gap find their sites mired in management malaise.

Unlike the old model, the new illuminates the four fundamental perspectives and integrates development and evolution as driving forces in each quadrant. In chapter 9, we investigate pauses in the development flow—in our case, why planning does not proceed in a way that leads to implementation of plans that protect heritage values—and what we can do to free this flow by working in all four quadrants. One might visualize heritage site management like a leaf dropped in a stream. The leaf floats (management) and then gets caught on a stick (pausing an evolving development). Instead of replacing the leaf (with new kind of management) or pulling out the stick (overpower the pause with brute force), we simply free the leaf to continue its journey.

The new model is not just interesting, most of all it is eminently practical.

Lower-Right Strategies Involve Lower-Right Forces

Table 8.2 shares interventions to involve LR forces. Unlike earlier versions of this table in chapters 5 through 7, however, these interventions come from the same quadrant as the forces they intend to involve.

Table 8.2 | *Strategies to Involve the Lower-Right Quadrant (Its)*

Its

Institutions

- Strategies that promote flexible, adaptive, learning, evolving, interdisciplinary, horizontal, team-based, power-sharing, community-based institutions
- Offer facilitation and technical assistance rather than imposing plans and planning
- Train in planning conducive to implementation
- Safe spaces for real dialogue and consensus decision making
- Consulting firms that serve as guides, facilitators, trainers, and mentors to planning process
- Donors that support the above

Policies

- Promotion of adaptive comanagement, organizational learning, high levels of citizen participation, community building, continuous planning
- Incentives to do any of the above
- Policies that remove intentional barriers such as plan approval processes, expiration dates, prestige, language of finality, publication of plan, celebration of completion
- Identification and removal of misinformation
- Budget for community strengthening, participant training, internal planning facilitation, and implementation
- Recruitment and support of champions, prototypes, experimentation, risk taking
- Multiple forms of knowledge (empirical, intuitive, traditional, spiritual, collective, etc.)
- Punish corruption, misinformation, political and power games, manipulation, deception

Technologies

Plan format
- Web-based periodic releases (interactive, nonlinear, nontechnical, wiki-collective approach, multiple releases, graphical but not overly technical, online, printable and offline-capable, multimedia, interlinkable, and collaborative)

Institutions

In an integrated world, institutions that cling to bureaucratic values, whether Pakistan's national park agency or National Park Service trainers, must learn to work in all quadrants in a DICE World. Many characteristics describe these institutions, including flexible, adaptive, learning, evolving, interdisciplinary, horizontal, team-based, power sharing, and community based.

Changing conventional organizations in ways that enhance both the LR and the other three quadrants will be difficult, but it will be necessary for enhanced staff performance in decision making. For example, to build up enough staff confidence to face complex and threatening situations, organizations need to delegate to them the power to work with constituencies as well as the power to implement decisions. To do this will require the organization, according to Stankey, Bormann, and others (2003), to allow more decision making on the front lines. Such organizations must work across boundaries—jurisdictional as well as disciplinary—with a staff enriched by complementary skills and disciplines.

Examples include the Arví Corporation, which manages the Arví Regional Ecotourism Park in Medellin or Parques de Sintra, Monte da Lua, which manages the World Heritage Sintra Cultural Landscape just outside of Lisbon, Portugal. Because these state companies have shareholders who are also principal stakeholders, they must be more inclusive in their decision making. Because in theory they operate with businesslike agility and instincts (with corresponding limitations such as short-term returns thinking and more emphasis on market than mission), they typically mobilize funds much more efficiently, train personnel to be more productive, mount more effective marketing and promotional efforts, offer quality services such as interpretive guiding, respond better to market feedback, and form alliances without much of the bureaucratic rigmarole of conventional government management approaches. Sintra, for instance, has accomplished inspiring fetes of restoration of its publicly owned national palaces, such as King Ferdinand II's Chalet da Condessa, earning acclaim from other management agencies. Another option to complement governmental capacities is to enlist nonprofit friends and volunteer groups (Toolbox 8).

Toolbox 8 | *Looking for Friends to Widen Heritage Site Capacity*

Expanding Management Capacity

As budgets dwindle and the number of voices increases in democratic societies, heritage areas find themselves with too few resources to accomplish the ever-increasing public demands (Lehmann Strobel n.d.). One response to widen heritage management capacity, whether a governmental protected area such as a historical park or a nonprofit such as a museum, is the creation of friends groups, sometimes called associations, membership groups, or foundations. The United States, which enjoys a long, deep culture of philanthropy and volunteering has many thousands of such groups often with very important roles nationally, such as the National Parks Foundation chartered by the US Congress to support America's national parks and heritage, and locally, such as the Friends of Valle de Oro National Wildlife Refuge in Albuquerque, New Mexico, which formed before the refuge was even declared to lobby for its existence in their community and then serve it with volunteers and public programming. Similarly, in Panama, the nonprofit Chagres National Park Foundation was created to implement debt-for-nature swap money coming from the United States. The foundation has evolved to carry out a suite of community development programs and raises money for the park.

Nonprofit friends groups principally channel money and volunteers to organizations that lack sufficient resources or suffer from governmental systems that do not allow either speedy resource management or retention of donated or fund-raised resources. Most Latin America countries, for example, require that all park-generated revenue go to the national treasury where bureaucrats allocate funds over the entire park system. In the case of Panama, for example, a national park does not even have a mechanism to accept pocket-change donations.

Fortunately, examples and guidelines exist for protected areas that want to create friends groups. Both the US National Park Service (www.nps.gov/partnerships/friends_groups.htm) and Fish & Wildlife Service (www.fws.gov/refuges/friends/startingGroup.html) offer guidelines for setting up friends groups among their many protected areas. Furthermore the World Federation of Friends of Museums published a code of ethics for friends groups and volunteers (http://museumsfriends.com/en/code-of-ethics), and The Center for Park Management (2005) found seven elements for successful partnerships: (1) a shared mission and goals, (2) trust, (3) mutual contributions, (4) clear communication, (5) commitment to a long-term relationship, (6) a culture of sharing and collaboration, and (7) mutual respect.

Bridge to More Holistic Heritage Management

Although friends groups have been around a long time in the United States, for many in the heritage management community, this approach is innovative, explained by AQAL. A friends group is an institutional arrangement (LR), informed by shared community values about heritage (LL), that increases a site's capacity (UR), based on personal affinities and reinforces understanding and positive attitudes among visiting audiences (UL). As the management paradigm evolves along with society, that is, integrating civil society more in heritage management (rather than the traditional, centralized government management), friends groups serve as a bridge to yet more inclusive, Integral arrangements that not only respond to deficiencies in management resources but also widen the vision of heritage ownership and responsibility throughout society.

Policies

Policy options are endlessly diverse. Guiding statements and existing policies can influence planning and can take many forms, whether formal or informal, individual or collective, from the top or even bottom of a hierarchy, expressed by a living leader or a dead one (consider the ageless influence of Confucius, Gandhi, or even WWF's Miguel Cifuentes's posthumous promotion of touristic carrying capacity in Latin American protected areas). The policy could be a decision to pursue a new approach such as adaptive comanagement (Outside the Box 8.1), organizational learning, true power-sharing participation, continuous planning, or stroll the easier trail in the highlands of Technical Rationality.

Some policies are incentives. The private sector knows these well. For example, 3M allocates up to 15 percent of paid employee time to innovate. Nokia inducts engineers with at least ten patents into its "Club 10," recognizing them each year in an awards ceremony hosted by the CEO.

Consider some private sector innovation policies and how they might apply to heritage management (McGregor et al. 2006):

- Some companies have learned to reroute their reporting lines so different people in different units can work together. They also move around budgets to allow them to coordinate and collaborate across department boundaries. In heritage sites, often disciplinary and administrative boundaries, for example archaeologists involved in structural restoration, do not talk with biologists involved in wildlife management, or tourism division employees do not speak to overall site managers.

- Companies often establish physical spaces for project team members to come and work together. Every time BMW creates a new project, it brings people together from scattered units at its Research and Innovation Center for up to three years to speed up communication and hold face-to-face meetings to prevent future conflicts—between, for instance, marketing and engineering. In 2004, these teams began meeting in the center's Project House that allows them to work a short walk from the company's 8,000 researchers and developers and alongside life-size clay prototypes of the car under development. While most heritage sites cannot fund a three-year change of schedule, bringing people together from different units does apply to almost any site.

- Companies create secret or low-key safe places to innovate. These places are protected from normal budgetary constraints, reporting lines, and organizational immune systems that hunt down foreign ideas seen as disrupting the "stable" organizational body. Google X is Google's innovation laboratory that even some employees did not know about until *The New York Times* ran a story (Cain Miller and Bilton 2011, p. A1). Similar spaces allow project teams to discuss undiscussable paradigms, including the safe space established within Ford Motor Company where people talked about applied systems thinking and learning, topics forbidden by the dominant culture. Once this cabal of learners generated some successes, they enticed other like-minded systems-thinking souls out of the closet, previously too afraid to share their true desires. As one participant in this group said, "We all went underground. There are more systems thinkers here [at Ford] than you know about, but they are not willing to come out of their caves yet" (Seligman 2005).

- Companies identify people in charge of innovation, looking for new methods and ways to adapt them to their company. Through alliances with academic institutions, for instance, a protected area might search out new management techniques.

- Shell Oil integrated scenario planning into the main budget so that planners are obliged to experiment (and learn) with various possibilities.

- Getting good consumer insight is a major obstacle to innovation. Blogs and online communities now make it easier to know what visitors think. Hiring designers and ethnographers who observe customers using products helps, too.

Sites can better learn about their visitors too through

◊ Research on markets and customer behavior.

◊ Feedback boxes. Blogs and online comments as well as on-site surveys can generate data, or even just talking with visitors, getting staff to ask similar questions and report answers in a semisystematic manner.

◊ Learning trips. Bring or send staff on trips as visitors to see through a visitor's perspective and come back and share and apply insights to improve service or planning, as the case might be. There are various programs in the United States that bring managers from other countries to share ideas, such as the International Seminar on Protected Area Management sponsored by the US Forest Service and the University of Montana.

Some protected areas do offer innovation incentives. Namibia had a Park Innovation Grant that was a small grant for field staff that came up with ideas to increase management efficiencies. It had a series of other recognitions as well, for example, for bravery in the field. The Singapore National Parks Board (2011) offers incentives to apply new (for the parks) energy efficient technologies such as green roofs in its member sites.

Other policies that can improve implementation include budgets for implementation (Naughton 2007) and constituency capacity building, rather than just financing consultants and finely crafted plans; use of consultants as facilitators, mentors, and coaches, rather than doers and interveners; attempts to overcome institutional barriers by not requiring formal document publishing (see virtual plan discussion, below); celebrations for commencing implementation rather than for completing the writing of the plan. This is similar to the US university practice of celebrating student commencement rather than graduation. Sites can reward managers for implementing plans, not developing them; eliminate or modify conventional plan approval procedures; eliminate expiration dates by switching to continuous planning (see below in plan format); use "reference class forecasting" to make more realistic budget and schedule predictions based on similar past projects rather than suffer optimism bias (Pinto 2013); use forms of knowledge beyond empirical such as traditional, intuitive, experiential, spiritual, and collective; and punish corruption, misinformation, game playing, deception, and information withholding.

Technologies

The LR includes technologies that influence planning, learning, and participation. Obviously, there is or should be considerable overlap between these areas, but we divide them for the sake of comprehension.

Plan Format

Plans are actually complex technologies that combine many tools for communicating, interacting, organizing ideas, diagnosing, publishing, and others. Most readers already understand the technological bundle prescribed by RCP. Indeed, without ever taking a course, the system quietly teaches planners to plan in conventional terms, as described in chapter 2. This section describes how plans may look in the future from a LR perspective. We begin with some propositions that underlie the future of planning and constructing plans that can be implemented:

- Planning is a means of arriving, not a final destination.

- Plans record commitments, not just recommendations (see Gebhardt and Eagles 2014 as an example of how fundamental recommendations are seen as components of conventional planning). This is because a recommendation results from planners with no power to commit to action, such as when consultants write plans and then finish their contracts. An implementable plan captures or documents collective constituent commitments, or at least their best intentions.

- Thus implementable plans are not studies (as studies collect data, analyze them, and offer recommendations), rather they are tools that mobilize resources toward a desired future.

- Plans are collective, not individual works, in order to catalyze constituent community commitments and implementation.

- Plans consider all forms of knowing and do not lean only toward knowledge produced by empirical scientists and technicians to the exclusion of everyone else's.

- Plans use many media to convey ideas and scenarios, such as narrative, art, metaphor, stories, anecdotes, photos, and videos and are not biased only toward those used by scientists, such as impersonal text, empirical charts and graphs, and GIS-rendered maps.

These propositions influence in numerous ways plan format and technologies. For example, if a plan records commitments rather than recommendations, we might ask: Who actually does the planning and writing? What role would consultants have, if any? What constitutes proof of commitment? What does a constituency have to pledge to make it a commitment? How do we reframe the process of planning so that it produces commitments rather than recommendations? Would the work plan then have to disclose names instead of institutions or generic job positions?

The answers to these questions imply technologies as well as consensus and culture. Conventional planning delivers us plans still rendered in a 600-year-old publishing paradigm, made famous by Gutenberg when he built a printing press to produce high-quality Bibles. Gutenberg harbored no illusions about the lack of need to update the Bible, so he invested in all kinds of fancy decorations and designs that would have greatly impeded any attempt to update the book. Our conventional plans today, while not of Gutenberg Bible rank, still assume that no updating is necessary anytime soon and thus employ perfect binding, nice covers, continuous pagination from 1 to 100-plus, and limited press runs.

Furthermore, conventional planning sees planning as a linear, methodical protocol of steps that organize, analyze, and present information in a consistent way, apt for a docile PLUS World. In fact, an entire service industry has emerged to help conventional planners do just this. Third-party service providers offer online management planning software with templates and tables, send out planning alerts to participants as well as checklists, training videos, budgeting aids, tactical reporting formats, monitoring and performance indicators, and other logical frameworks. These largely conventional strategies can be effective insofar as the technical aspect of planning is concerned but can spell disaster when only the technical aspect of planning is concerned. They can also be useful if users actually think through tough questions, rather than unconsciously fill out planning forms and preformatted spreadsheets.

Ironically, some services laud the age of online planning because plans can be developed online and distributed as PDFs. Most of these approaches, however, barely touch the upcoming concept of virtual plans. Replacing downloadable printable plans (such as a PDF) with virtual plans is the difference between hard-copy books and e-books. A truly virtual plan has a format that is

- interactive
- easily updated (note that this quality refers to physically updating the plan; it does not refer to the ease with which a decision to make a change occurs)
- nonlinear
- multimedia
- printable (where no computers are available)
- offline capable (when no Internet connection is available)
- interconnected with other virtual communities and references

- inexpensive

- near universally accessible via web browsers

- available with a much wider pool of know-how already existent in the general population.

We refer to plans whose entire existence may well be virtual and never printed out or, where necessary, only with a printed executive summary. To date, very few such plans exist (that we know of). For example, http://winnipesaukeegateway.org/lake-management/plan-1-meredith-paugus-and-saunders-bay/introduction/.

The Internet has already dispensed with the notion of "final drafts." Websites are never final; neither are software programs. Developers constantly update them through a process of continuous updates—a paradigm completely applicable to strategic planning—called Agile Software Development. As Helmuth von Moltke the Elder, once chief of staff of the Prussian Army said, "No battle plan survives contact with the enemy." Indeed, no strategic plan survives first contact with reality. Thus, plans must adapt to survive to implementation in a DICE World.

So how do software developers develop software? Since software must respond to changing markets, technologies, competition, and ideas, they understand that software constantly goes through cycles of conceptualization, testing, releasing, and then over again. They have beta versions for testing and minor and major releases, implying the scale of change and the degree of stability and readiness for the market. In fact, the paradigm even has its own Agile Manifesto (www.agilemanifesto.org).

Plans can do the same thing to finally dispense with expiration dates and expensive planning phases followed by five- or ten-year lapses in planning. Consider the normal planning start-up, participatory or not, that involves a year or two of work assembling constituencies, hiring consultants, and writing what conventional managers call the "final draft" of a management plan. In a virtual, adaptive planning world, participants would produce version 1.0 of their plan. Users would rightfully hold some suspicion of a version 1.0 as being somewhat untested and with little real-world experience, especially in a DICE World—the same justified suspicion with which they might confront a new software package. Unlike conventional published plans, though, they would be reassured that as time passes, planners would make minor releases, perhaps monthly: 1.1, 1.2, 1.3 ... which they add to their Web-based plan, thus increasing confidence in the plan. After a year, they might go through a more intensive yearly evaluation that results in version 2.0. (See, for example, *Plan B 4.0: Mobilizing to Save Civilization* [Brown 2009a].)

They might even have 1.11 and so on to reflect more frequent After Action Reviews (chapter 7). The official version of the plan would always be on the web, and an e-mail/SMS would automatically alert the community to changes or proposed changes denominated by beta versions such as 1.11b1.

Outside the Box 8.1 | *Kruger National Park Uses Strategic Adaptive Management to Respond to the DICE World*

South Africa's iconic wildlife park, Kruger National Park, found itself caught in turmoil and change surrounding the country's bumpy transition to democracy in 1994. Already confronted by several difficult challenges—elephant management, poaching, fire management, water quality issues—democracy above all tipped the park toward greater inclusion and relevance to the people of South Africa.

The 20,000 km^2 park sits downstream of a population of about 2 million mostly poor people in the lowveld landscape of eastern South Africa. Despite the park's fence (see Inside the Box 4.1), marauding elephants frequently break through to trample maize fields, followed by leopards and lions that prey on livestock. The park attracts 1.4 million visitors per year, and the entrance and conservation fees provide about 80 percent of the revenue to operate the nineteen-unit South African National Park system.

Managers and scientists eventually came to realize that they needed a new way to manage, and even more importantly, a new way to think about managing. Roux and Foxcroft (2011) note that this need came from the realization of "(1) the existence of ecological complexity and social complexity and hence social-ecological complexity and (2) the existence of multiple stakeholders with diverse (and often divergent) perceptions, values and expectations." This kind of thinking demanded that the South African National Parks agency, now called SANParks, re-create itself, particularly with respect to neighboring populations (Swemmer and Taljaard 2011).

In the late 1990s, Kruger shifted its management approach to Strategic Adaptive Management (SAM) that should provide a flexible, responsive means to implement, reflect on, and learn about park management (Freitag et al. 2014). SAM first emerged from the freshwater management arena because of uncertainty that "conservation measures may not effectively maintain and protect the array of biodiversity that they were designed to conserve" (Kingsford and Biggs 2012). Because wildlife populations as well as the tourism industry required high-quality rivers, this concern rang especially loud in Kruger. And from the very beginning, planners worried about building a program that institutions would embrace, not just scientists.

The beginning point of SAM involves a series of value-based strategic statements, developed collaboratively among scientists, managers, and constituent communities. These statements have to secure consensus about park purposes. For example, in KNP, the "people" objective states:

> To provide human benefits and build a strong constituency in support of SANParks conservation endeavors, preserving as far as possible the wilderness qualities and cultural resources associated with South African National Parks.

This objective further divides into two more specific objectives, one dealing with benefit-sharing and one on building park constituencies. The latter states: "To build an effective constituency at all levels in South Africa and abroad, which fosters and enhances sustainable public support for SANParks' objectives and actions and for the conservation cause in general." This objective then subdivides again into four even more specific objectives, such as, "To ameliorate any negative effects experienced by people as a result of national parks, e.g., damage-causing animals, restricted access to ecosystem services, human and livestock health risks as a result of the wildlife/livestock/human disease interface."

More specific goals follow that give managers explicit endpoints, termed Thresholds of Potential Concern (TPC). TPCs mark the higher and lower limits of acceptable change given the strategic intent. These thresholds have not been articulated for the people area, but have been for other areas. For example, for woody vegetation, the TPC states:

> Inside any one of four elephant management zones making up Kruger, woody cover should not drop below 80% of its highest ever value, the mean drop parkwide should not exceed 30%.

When monitoring, SAM's third component, alerts that conditions are approaching the TPC, then managers must implement appropriate action or they could challenge the TPC itself, particularly in "data poor" environments that characterize the DICE World.

Several advantages of SAM: it makes explicit goals, objectives, indicators, and management actions that are normally only implicit; it traces a clear trail of logic to understand which actions are proposed and why; it focuses on learning in order to better understand the social-ecological system and its sustainability; and it interfaces not only with local communities but larger scale governance in South Africa.

SAM is spreading beyond Kruger National Park and influencing other conservation policies and practices. Whether SAM continues to spread to other regions as well depends largely on people's willingness to dive into the waters of the DICE World.

Learning Technologies

While learning takes place internally, whether individually (UL) or collectively (LL), the tools of learning emerge externally in the LR. Many such tools people already know well, including libraries, networks, websites, training software, workshops, classes, mentoring, coaching, simulators, games, and on-the-job practicums and internships. There also exist combinations of infrastructures and technologies with which people may be less familiar. For example, the Wildland Fire Lessons Learned Center (Outside the Box 7.1), an intergovernmental entity consisting of five federal land management agencies, uses technologies to promote better fire management practice among thousands of federal, state, county, city, and volunteer wildland firefighters in the United States. Aside from hosting an online information resource, the center also conducts workshops and courses; and it supports online forums and face-to-face dialogues, rapid online community-contributed rapid-fire lessons sharing center and research; and it backstops individuals trying to promote a learning culture necessary for high-resilience organizations within the fire management community. It is the integration of these tools to support an entire community that makes the idea of a lessons learned center or process valuable (Weber et al. 2000). The Department of Energy, US Coast Guard, and US Army also maintain lessons learned centers.

Other technologies include self-analysis tools such as participatory rural appraisals that allow communities to discover, articulate, and appreciate their own knowledge and patterns. The Center for Whole Communities' Whole Measures tool provides a framework for planning more holistically the futures communities desire (Center for Whole Communities 2007). There are systems thinking tools, adaptive management tools (see Toolbox 3).

Jared Diamond (1997) observes that societies can transmit knowledge by a variety of means, some more efficient than others. He argues that the least efficient is "idea diffusion" through which communicators relay little more than a basic idea, leaving for the learners the task to reinvent the details, to answer the multitudinous "how to" questions to make that idea work. Examples of idea diffusion include conference presentations, papers, and even books just like this one. The most efficient form is blueprint copying, when learners copy or modify an available detailed blueprint for developing a social process or engineering product. For example, Diamond cites ancient civilizations that used language blueprints from other cultures that saved those civilizations thousands of years of basic innovation work by not having to invent a language—and answer all the how-tos—from scratch.

Idea diffusion remains one of the most common forms of teaching/learning used. The Ashoka Foundation, an organization that supports social entrepreneurs the world over, is figuring how to systematically use blueprint copying to accelerate the spread of social innovations in the world. Bornstein documents Ashoka's work (2007) in social entrepreneurship.

The heritage site management field is filled with training manuals, modules, courses, and so on, that diffuse ideas but all too frequently leave the evasive how-to details to the imagination of practitioners. One blueprint effort is that developed by the PUP Global Heritage Consortium, which, since 1999, has attempted in great detail to guide and mentor heritage site managers and their organizations toward planning through adaptation of the generic but detailed blueprint to local conditions rather than blind replication, like a recipe.

Participatory Technologies

Most participatory technologies are really about social learning required for consensus and societal action (LL changes). Many approaches have emerged over the years across a variety of subfields, including the Dialogue Movement, human potential, intentional communities, popular education, grassroots development, and, of course, learning organization and systems thinking. We already saw dialogue and facilitation in action through WWF's Dialogues (Outside the Box 5.1). Other major players include the World Café, Open Space Technology, Technology of Participation (Toolbox 7), Mutual Gains Negotiation, and so on (see Table 7.2 on strategies that involve the LL). One might read any of Lawrence Susskind's books on public participation (for example, Susskind et al. 1996, 1999).

There are tools that promote democratic processes, such as Ralph Nader's Concord Principles, the Nominal Group Technique, and many other citizen tools (see The Co-Intelligence Institute, www.co-intelligence.org/CI_compilations.html, for an excellent compilation of such tools and processes). The Coffee Party USA has emerged with the purpose of reestablishing a civil, open, deliberative process into politics and democracy in America.

Certainly, no planning effort could ever be successful without institutions, policies, and technologies, but few planning efforts in the DICE World likely could be successful by only focusing on these aspects of reality to the exclusion of other quadrants.

Outside the Box 8.2 | *Integral Development Applied in the Buffer Zone of Manu National Park, Perú*

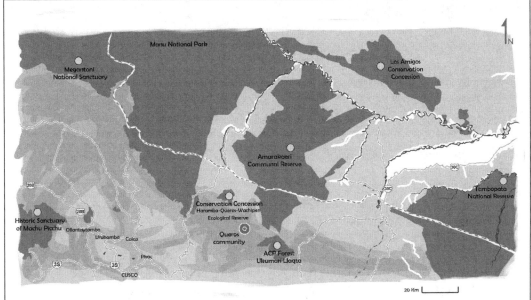

Figure 8.2 | *Map of Manu National Park in the Peruvian Amazon.*

The success that the Asociación para la Conservación de la Cuenca Amazónica (ACCA) enjoyed in establishing Perú's first conservation concession would not carry over to its second and third attempts farther south in Cusco Province. In 2001, ACCA earned the management rights to Los Amigos, a 360,000-hectare reserve in the Peruvian Amazon (ICFC n.d.) (see map). In 2006, ACCA wanted to inscribe in its own name a second reserve in the Pilcopata Municipality. But unlike the northern concession, sparsely populated and loosely organized, Pilcopata was not only more organized but in an election year. Because ACCA had not studied the local sentiment, when the organization posted its intention to acquire a concession, "all hell broke loose," according to César Moran-Cusac (pers. comm. 2014), at that time conservation director and later executive director. The community interpreted the attempt as "an American NGO asking for lands to manage and control water." Moran-Cusac continues, "This event happened in an election year where mayors where going to be elected and, for ACCA´s bad luck, it was used by one candidate as his battle horse, he proposed the motto to kick ACCA out of the region."

ACCA abandoned that site and went to work with the Andean highland Queros tribe to create a concession this time in their name in the local cloud forest. This attempt quickly turned sour as the Queros were divided, easily manipulated by outsiders, and did not want a concession in the cloud forest since they did not live in that kind of forest. ACCA had not taken the social and political conditions into account.

This grave situation greeted the Canadian NGO, One Sky, which arrived in 2007 to help ACCA improve its conservation efficacy. During one of the first meetings, recalls Gail Hochachka of One Sky (2014a), the Canadians laid out an AQAL grid on a boardroom table with the executive director, the conservation director, and other staff, explaining a four-quadrant approach to capacity enhancement for environmental conservation. After describing what kinds of capacity development were included in each of the quadrants, they asked ACCA: "Where do you see the greatest need in developing your own organizational capacity at this present time?"

Almost immediately, fingers fell on the Lower Left, the quadrant referring to capacity developing for engaging culture. ACCA staff recognized its need for learning more "social methodologies" and more participatory approaches for engaging communities, and knew that its traditional approach to conservation that it had used elsewhere was being construed as a "land grab" in this region. Without more effective cultural engagement, this previous approach had little hopes of working with the Queros indigenous community.

Now with Cusac-Moran as executive director, ACCA carried out social mapping of the area within the context of a grant that One Sky had won, and this allowed ACCA to work with the lowland Queros to establish a conservation concession in their name.

So One Sky designed an Integral capacity development program knowing that the principal quadrant that held back organizational and conservation development was the Lower Left (see also Outside the Box 6.2). While an Integral approach to capacity development has to align all four quadrants for development to stick, often an organization using this approach will do an Integral needs assessment and prioritize which quadrant needs the most attention, as well as identifying what is actually needed where. In this case, the Lower Left required special attention, some focus was also needed in the Upper Left (developing the self), as well as the Lower Right (influencing systems, particularly around strategic planning) (see following table).

Generic Integral Capacity Development Contents	
I Self and experience (spiritual assets, psychological health, consciousness) Capacity development as "developing the self"	**It** Physical health and actions (physiology, land-use practices, behaviors) Capacity development as "building skills"
We Culture and worldview (social norms, values, shared worldviews, assumptions) Capacity development as "engaging cultures"	**We** Systems (political, economic, judicial, social, and ecological systems) Capacity development as "influencing systems"

Over the next two years One Sky unrolled its capacity development project, some activities planned from the get go (such as training) and others emerged during the project. Both One Sky and ACCA worked in all four quadrants (see following table), although their donor, the Canadian International Development Agency, required a Modernist quantitative planning and evaluation system. Their wider qualitative analysis, nonetheless, identified success that transcended even the original indicators (Hochachka 2009b).

Integral Capacity Development Project with ACCA				
Quad	One Sky Activities	Training Contents	ACCA Actions	Results on the ground
UL	Trust building	Better understanding of worldviews and engaging interior changes (such as awareness, attitudes, empowerment, sense of ownership, knowledge, values, and motivation) Engender great trust and improve ACCA's image with communities and public.	Trust building, convince community to assume concession, self-esteem building of guides	Higher morale and satisfaction of ACCA employees Greater trust of communities

UR	Integral Training	Improve capacity for strategic planning	Training in concession management, training guides	Shifted approach from conservation science only to community engagement, hiring social skills to diversify ACCA's skill set
LL	Involved in local community, festivities, etc.	Improve internal organizational dynamics, internal communication, and reflective processes within ACCA Strengthen participation with communities and other actors, learning new social methodologies Develop gender awareness, and build capacity for gender mainstreaming across the organization and in programming with communities and the public	Community engagement, integral community assessments	Improved community relationships, improved organizational culture
LR	Strategic plan, construction of a canopy walkway, brought volunteers from Canada, financing of community promoters	Improve capacity for networking with other organizations (locally, regionally, internationally) Improve capacity to engage in municipal national and international policy dialogues	Gender equality policies, innovate with the conservation concession for native communities, canopy built, community promoter program operating	Earn first native community conservation concession, construction of canopy walkway, development and use of social diagnostic tools

Aside from the training, the One Sky team integrated with the local indigenous communities in the surrounding area by participating in community activities and also participating centrally in one of the religious festivals two years in a role, a first for any foreigner (LL and UL). They brought a class of graduate students to stay in the community and also placed a youth intern to work in the community for several months (UR). They contributed Integral contents to a guide training program that complemented the construction of a canopy walkway in the concession (UL and UR for the guides). They worked with a Canadian company to work with local community members to construct the cloud forest canopy walkway (LR).

In any event, in little more than a year after one community was about to red card ACCA, the organization had shifted its approach to community engagement where it respected the community's agenda as much as its own ecology-driven one. It endeavored to understand their level of consciousness, culture, and values—in other words, to meet people where they are (see Value Translation for one example of meeting people where they are, Toolbox 4). Instead of signing the second conservation concession in its own name, in 2008 it helped the Queros sign Peru's first conservation concession (6,975 ha) inscribed under the name of a native community, which elected to call the property, adjacent to their own territory, the Haramba-Queros-Wachiperi Ecological Reserve.

For this work ACCA earned much positive press (for example, AFP 2008; Andina 2008) and even a national environmental award for indigenous community engagement. Also One Sky's grant funded community promoters who worked in the concession for the first two years.

One Sky and ultimately ACCA consciously applied the theory and began to see results within one to two years by unblocking their LL to engage and understand community perspectives and objectives. Had they not worked in all four quadrants, both outsiders and ACCA itself, the situation on the ground near Queros could have ended in expulsion, rather than conservation.

To see a short documentary on this project, see Simpson (2010).

By Any Other Name, Planning Is about Power

In the late 1990s, Chabris and Simons (1999) ran one of the most famous experiments in psychology. They made a video of two small teams, one wearing black and one white. Each simultaneously passed a basketball among its members. They asked Harvard students to pick one team or the other and count the passes. Halfway through the one-minute video, a person dressed in a full-body gorilla suit walked into the center of the ball passing, turned to the camera, waved, and then walked out of view. After the video, researchers asked viewers if they saw anything else in the video aside from ball-passing teams. Fifty percent never saw the gorilla, even though it stood clearly and waved right before their very eyes. The experiment has been repeated under many different conditions, and the result is always the same. Apparently, when people focus on specific objects, they are unable to see others within full view, a phenomenon called inattentional blindness.

Power is, in fact, the invisible gorilla that planners often do not see, although it manifests in all four quadrants, all the time. Planners often talk about democracy, participation, analysis, and citizen engagement—but what about power? If power is the capacity to change things (and many definitions of power fall under this broad umbrella, e.g., seminal pieces by Foucault 1982; Habermas 1981; Lukes 2004), then planning has everything to do with power (Hoch 1994; Bryson and Crosby 1992). Although power can create galaxies and overturn patrol cars on icy park roads, the power that most concerns planners centers on relationships among community actors. Thus, here, at the end of chapter 8, after the reader has seen how all quadrants influence planning, is the ideal place to yank the cloak of invisibility off the gorilla.

As we have seen in previous chapters, rational comprehensive planners see their role as technical analysts whose prescriptions require the power of others to implement. It is not their job to implement, they think, for they do not wield that kind of power. Little surprise then that so many such planners suffer disappointment that their plans do not get implemented, that politicians invoke political rather than technical criteria for making decisions (Altshuler 1965). As a result, planners grow depressed due to their perceived powerlessness to guide their intangible calculations into tangible reality.

As Forester argues, then, planning is all about power. Planners manage power in different forms, even though they may not even recognize the power in their hands. Forester writes in his book, *Planning in the Face of Power* (1989, p. 27): "If planners ignore those in power, they assure their own powerlessness. Alternatively, if planners understand how relations of power shape the planning process, they can improve the quality of their analyses and empower citizen and community action." He says that power manifests through three modes: decision making, agenda setting, and shaping others' felt needs. In fact, many democratic participation tools distribute power through these modes.[23] Planners may be actively involved in all three modes and yet never realize their influence. The power that perhaps most applies to planning, especially planning in a DICE World, is network power.

Network power accrues when many actors influence their environment in a coherent and coordinated manner (Booher and Innes 2002). It is not unlike (as Bohm pointed out earlier) when through dialogue people focus their thoughts with the same intention, essentially making incoherent thoughts coherent and permitting coordinated actions that before were impossible. These are examples of network power, as was the French Revolution that cut off Queen Marie Antoinette's head, Gandhi's efforts to kick the British out of India, or the Occupy Wall Street protests that swept the United States in 2013 to bring attention to inequality. Network power operates in any case where the alignment of many micro-efforts can together transform into macro-effects.

For planning, network power occurs when through authentic dialogue, constituent groups work together in pursuit of higher common interests, combining their small forces to make something happen, such as implement a plan, that otherwise would never have occurred.

Network power grows increasingly relevant in a DICE World where traditional sources of power—individual wealth, charisma, inherited position—are losing ground. With globalization and interconnectivity, change accelerates as political opinion and buying preferences evolve with changing technologies and stages of consciousness. Those who can adapt to and manage information flows and public opinion garner the potential of networked power (Castells 1997).

Networked power, moreover, foments change demanded by those typically who have not swiveled in the chairs of formal power. If the planning we advocate in chapter 9 does anything, it redistributes political power—a power in heritage planning that has been historically controlled by those with technical expertise.

In the heritage area planning realm, this diversification of power has manifested in a split. In decades past, management agencies had the power both to plan and implement plans. Now, while agencies still retain the power to plan, authorized by national laws, they often no longer hold the political power to implement those plans. That power has slipped through their fingers like sand, now being caught by many constituent hands. That power has diversified into many forms. Today, laws can authorize plans but cannot obligate implementation in an increasingly politicized world. For example:

- Agencies face the indigenous Penan fighting to keep territorial land rights by blockading roads to a dam construction site in Sarawak, Malaysia (Hance 2012).

- The business sector lobbies the government to allow construction permits for hotels within Saint Lucia's World Heritage Pitons Management Area (Bishop 2012).

- Ranchers threaten to brand politicians if they support wolf reintroduction in Yellowstone (Fischer 2003).

- Tomb raiders take advantage of political chaos in Iraq to disperse Persian heritage throughout the global black market (Breitkopf 2007).

By building networks of partnerships (McCool 2009) and social capital among the heritage site's constituencies, planners or planning teams create ownership of plan and process. That is,

Fire Box 4 | *Quadruple-Loop Learning: Sacred Fire*

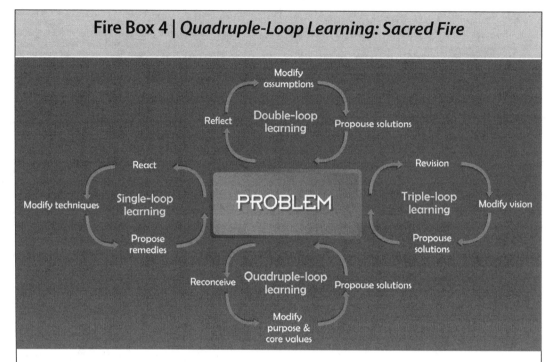

Reconceive the very nature of forest fires and forest fire management to generate new core values or purpose.

Quadruple-loop learners, rare though they may be, not only change their assumptions, their vision of the entity in question, but can reconceive that entity's very purpose or core values. In the case of forest fires, this reconceiving is not policy but rather a life perspective. They see fire as an integral function of forests, as natural and necessary as floods to rivers, and which have their own natural right to exist. Intentional fires also flash through hundreds of Native American generations, who used intentional burns to alter landscapes and species to benefit them. Deep ecologists and indigenous peoples among others see fire as a cultural, historical, and spiritual phenomenon.

As with all the learning loops discussed in this book, people capable of processing feedback and generating solutions at these deeper levels enjoy more leverage to change the system in which they find themselves

Jonathan Merritt, editor of *Sacred Fire Magazine*, which promotes healing and sacred wisdom tied to the land, recounts in an editorial, "I dream a little, gazing at the small flame, and in my dreaming I hear the land. The land says, 'All this arises from me and belongs to me. Everything is born and spun from me, grows and lives on me and will return to me to be reformed and reborn. With Wind and Fire and Rain I call everything into Life. Listen, Life is speaking to you in ten thousand ways."'

For additional reading on the evolution of forest fire policy toward quadruple-loop learning see Wuerthner (2006) and Zimmerman and Sexton (2010).

ownership occurs in the process and outcome and is distributed across the community, which can mobilize ideas and resources that before were out of reach to the management agency (Lachapelle and McCool 2005).

As mammals emerged to rule when dinosaurs ceded their kingdom or grasses took over when loggers chopped down Brazilian rain forests, so too dominant heritage management agencies find themselves unwillingly yielding to a new source of distributed power, one that can be harnessed by the principles of Holistic Planning.

Chapter 9 concludes our journey by both demonstrating how Integral Theory helped us create Holistic Planning and showing heritage site managers how to use the Integral approach to design their plans and their management. Ultimately, we will discover on the far side of the iceberg that Holistic Planning really is not about planning at all (Fire Box 4).

The world we have created is a product of our thinking; it cannot change without changing our thinking.

—*Albert Einstein*

Toward Holistic Planning

You can never change things by fighting the existing reality. To change something, build a new model that makes the existing model obsolete.

—*F. Buckminster Fuller*

THE OTHER
SIDE OF
COMPLEXITY

EVENTS

PATTERNS

STRUCTURES

MENTAL MODELS

VISION

PURPOSE

We Are on a U-Shaped Journey to the Depths of the Iceberg and Back up Again toward a New Understanding of Planning and Implementation

U-Shaped Journey Around the Iceberg

Since opening the front cover, we have embarked on a journey down the side of an iceberg. In chapter 1, where the journey began, we witnessed at the surface how so many conventional plans shipwreck on the shoals of the underlying assumptions of the PLUS World, leading to failed plans, unhappy constituents, and frustrated planners. Then we dived. We saw how these isolated shipwreck events of planning failures aligned into patterns of repeating shipwrecks. As we descended deeper, we realized that those shoals were in fact outdated or unrealistic assumptions about planning against which planners continuously crashed.

Down into chapter 2, the cold water darkened, requiring new navigational equipment. So, we invoked Thomas Kuhn and his thoughts about how paradigms change and how double-loop learning is needed to make out assumptions underlying the continual destruction of heritage plans. We then saw how Rational Comprehensive Planning was based on PLUS World assumptions and recognized that those assumptions did not describe how the world really behaves. Chapter 3 uncovered a new mental model—which we termed the DICE World—that demanded a new kind of planning in order to build better plans that would be supported and could be implemented.

Chapter 4 introduced a new theory and practice to survive in the DICE World, Integral Theory. With chapters 5 through 8, we learned about the four fundamental perspectives embodied by the Integral Map and how forces that arise from different quadrants can sink our projects or breathe life into them. We then directed the Integral lens to see formerly unseen barriers and innovative strategies to overcome them.

With each successive chapter, you probably sensed that we were heading somewhere, some future for planning not yet revealed, but were unsure how it could look or how to get there. We knew from the introduction's quote by Oliver Wendell Holmes, Jr. that simplicity lay on the other side of the iceberg after we reach its deepest point. Thereafter, we ascend into the light. The light of what, you may ask? We have termed this light Holistic Planning (HP), and you may legitimately ask, What would Holistic Planning look like?

You may also have noticed that the iceberg metaphor works in another way. We talked about increasing pressure and darkness, elements that resisted our descent. You may have felt some resistance to the ideas in this book. Perhaps, you felt that these ideas were too "New Age" or unconventional for practical use. Perhaps you felt confounded by the attack on conventional planning, even though scholars have been challenging conventional planning for decades. You might have experienced profound disappointment knowing that you have worked your career seeing through only one or maybe two quadrants. It is not that you, or we, were wrong, we were simply partial in our understanding of how to plan in a DICE World. Could people's feelings really prove as consequential to our desired outcomes as heritage resource assessments and biodiversity gap analyses?

That you have reached this final chapter means you may have dealt with these feelings. Many choose not to confront them at all. Many have built entire careers, professional reputations, and self-identify on PLUS-based approaches and will never let go.

Your journey around the iceberg traces a U shape. This trip actually follows U Theory, a transformation process for individuals and groups popularized by Scharmer and colleagues (2008). Although originally conceived in 1968, the views of psychologists such as Jung and Freud and others more recently have been transformed in an Integral light.

Basically, you entered this book's U in the upper-left corner by becoming aware of the vexing planning problem. This self-inquiry, in general, pulls a person or group down the left side of the U. Along the way they encounter blocks or shadow material that stand in the way of individual and collective psychological growth. Only by throwing light at these shadows can a person identify them, deal with them, re-own them, and ultimately progress beyond them. Shadows include fears, superstitions, habits, contradictory objectives, or other blocks buried deep in our psyche, hidden from consciousness, often because the pain of thinking about them would be too great. By hiding them, they fester into neurotic symptoms, fears, irrational and counterproductive behaviors, and depression.

The Modern world teaches us planners that if we are not technical experts, then we are not planners, so we resist threats to our expertise. Some people believe they have no power to change the massive system about them, for example the Fiji culture of silence (Madraiwiwi 2014) or any community that has become dependent on external charity.

Whatever shadows lurk, we require courage and strong intent to overcome them. We do this by converting what was formerly subject (part of our self-identity) into object (something no longer part of us that we can now see, evaluate, and reject or re-own). Thus, as we proceed to the bottom of the U (deepest tip of the berg), we dissociate ourselves from old habits, beliefs, or fears by calving them off like glaciers falling into the sea. Then we proceed up the right side where we prototype new beliefs and practices, rehearse them, and make them permanent without falling back into the arms of seductive old habits. To do that requires discipline, a support network, and awareness of where shadows draw their strength.

Many tools (Toolbox 9) exist along the U (Figure 9.1). To transcend resistance to facing shadows, the person or group generally needs a guide or a strong reflective dialogue group to talk and walk their way through the shadow … and dispel it.

Toolbox 9 | *Immunity to Change Maps Help You Travel the U to Transformation*

As Figure 9.1 shows, numerous tools help us travel around the U. One of the more well-known tools is the Immunity to Change Map based on Kegan and Lahey's book, *Immunity to Change: How to Overcome It and Unlock Potential in Yourself and Your Organization* (2009). The book and tool start with the observation that so often we want to change some behavior (bottom of U or UR), maybe make an earnest effort (going up right side), but just fall back into old habits (left side). The book cites the ever-common case of weight loss, where people try time and again to meet their goal of permanent weight loss by targeting their undesirable habits but to no avail. For example, they target eating too much with a diet and then find out that within a few short years, the vast majority gain back 107 percent of the weight they had before going on the diet.

Kegan and Lahey say that happens because we are not just pursuing one set of goals (lose weight) but two sets of goals where the second hides in our shadows. That second set actually motivates the undesirable behaviors to control what would otherwise be a chronic source of anxiety, also known as a social trap. These behaviors are in effect part of a psychological immune system to protect our psychological well-being, but it comes at the cost of behaviors that consciously we deem undesirable (eating too much).

Once people can reel in their hidden commitments to the surface, pulling them from the shadows, turning subject into object, then they can target those commitments and the big assumptions that give them life in order to change undesirable behaviors. This does not require additional willpower for most people, simply a change in mindset and practicing new behavior. Which is not so simple. With these elements, the authors created the Immunity to Change Map. Consider a map for weight loss that describes many people.

My visible or stated goal	Behaviors that go against my stated goal	My hidden competing commitments
I am committed to losing weight.	I eat too much.	Person A: I am committed to not being bored, to feeling stimulated and energized.
	I eat even when I'm not hungry.	I am committed to not feeling empty.
	I eat food with too much fat.	Person B: I am committed to feeling well connected to my people, to receiving love when it is offered to me.
	I eat food with too much carbohydrate.	Person C: I am committed to not being seen, and related to, as a sexual object. I am committed to not feeling overwhelmed and enraged.

This map shows that different people have very different hidden or shadow commitments that motivate the same undesirable behaviors. These behaviors respond to their hidden goals in column 3. Thus targeting the behaviors in column 2 to fulfill the commitment in column 1 very often fails because the person in effect needs those behaviors to achieve the hidden goals. But when the person can identify the hidden commitments and pull them from the shadows, they can study and adopt new beliefs through experimentation that supplant the old goals and make changing the undesirable behaviors much easier.

In the full Immunity to Change Map, Kegan and Lahey add a fourth column about the big assumptions behind hidden commitments. Consider this example from the heritage planning world based on the worksheet found at the authors' website www.mindsatwork.com.

Improvement goal	Behaviors that go against my goal	Hidden competing commitments	Big assumptions
I want to be more participatory in my planning, bringing in community members so that they feel ownership in what we create and will participate in the plan's implementation.	I tend to invite friends and like-minded people to join the planning sessions. I always hire expert outsiders to make sure that the decisions do not go against good conservation science. I prefer to edit the documents with a few trusted colleagues and the hired expert consultant.	I worry about my reputation and the future of my protected area.	Local community members are technically unqualified to contribute to technical determinations. If I cede power to the community, I will lose a corresponding amount of power in a zero sum game. If I lose power in my protected area, I lose credibility among my peers.
What I would like to do differently: Remove obstacles so that anyone in the community can attend planning sessions. Allow participants to make important planning decisions based on community consensus. Have community members themselves help to write up the plan.		I need to create management plans of high technical quality so that donors will fund my projects. I need to create management plans of high technical quality in order to properly conserve heritage. I need to create management plans of high technical quality in order to earn the respectability that I crave among my technical peers. I want my vision reflected in the protected area because I know best.	

We can see that if a manager digs into his or her technical shadows and finds these big assumptions and makes them objects, then he or she can begin to find evidence and test these assumptions and perhaps learn that maybe they are incorrect. When the beliefs that anchor these assumptions change, necessarily the hidden commitments will change, then the undesirable behaviors, finally permitting the manager to carry out the stated, desired goals.

When this process works its way through, the manager will in effect increase his or her mental complexity, increase the sphere in which the mind thinks. This process may also drive an increase in consciousness as the manager comes to understand more deeply the value of participation and to value community contributions, thus paving the way from a Modernist perspective (which characterizes the above map) to a Postmodernist one.

So this book has guided you first to see the once-hidden mental model of Rational Comprehensive Planning (RCP) and its PLUS assumptions, then to bring it to the surface where it becomes easier to evaluate, and eventually cast off the old beliefs and associated habits that have caused our plans time and again to shipwreck. We have motivated you through the resistance by offering glimpses of Holistic Planning from the introduction onward, hoping that your desire to discover a new way to plan that leads to implementation would inspire you to transcend experiences, reward systems, professional literature, and all those structures that keep antiquated habits alive. It is an entire system entrenched in all four quadrants, not just in your mind (UL) and practice (UR), but in university studies and global institutions (LR) that defend a way of thinking (LL) about heritage management.

We hope by now that you have objectified RCP and cut it loose to melt in warmer waters, and now we can look up to the light of new prototypes and models. Now we must know what Holistic Planning could look like and chart a course to get there in order to make this journey worth the effort.

Inside the Box 9 | *Avoiding the Shadows of Nonimplementation*

Jean Peur was a site manager in a French-speaking country. He had participated in many planning processes throughout his long career that ended with shelved plans. For years this professional with a degree in heritage management and specialization in planning blamed the Big Five Lacks for the failure to implement: lack of money (Gebhardt and Eagles 2014), time, personnel, information, and political will.

It was a convenient argument because these deficiencies always seem to originate from outside his system of control. Lack of budget was the fault of his superiors, lack of political will the fault of politicians. Sometimes the lack of good technical staff assigned to him by others limited plan quality. Since the blame lay outside his control, then his approach to planning may still be the best possible option. So with every failed plan he simply planned to plan again, the next time with more of the resources he lacked.

He didn't realize, however, that his blaming these external factors allowed him to wash his hands of responsibility. It allowed him to avoid what he had intuited for many years but refused to confront: that maybe the way he planned was actually where the deficiency could be found. In his shadows lurked a deeper fear that the approach he had studied in school, practiced in the field, and for which he had been rewarded time and again at conferences, with promotions and publications, and slaps on the back from colleagues might be the real cause of plan nonimplementation.

To question his lifelong investment in conventional planning would be to call into question everything he had done professionally in planning—to change approaches now would render meaningless all his experience! His subconscious self, his ego, thus decided it was better to tell himself a false story about exterior deficiencies and hide the true fear in his interior shadows, out of sight, but not out of mind.

Definition and Principles of Holistic Planning

We recognize that the 21st Century DICE World needs a new form of planning, which we term "Holistic Planning." We define HP as *a facilitated, continuous dialogue with heritage area constituencies designed eventually to construct a consensus about a desired evolving future.* To accomplish this, Holistic Planning

- recognizes emerging phenomena and interprets them through interior and exterior perspectives,

- redistributes political power by integrating different forms of knowledge and implementing democratic reforms,

- transforms constituency visions into reality through authentic conversation that defines many facets of vision, and

- cultivates constituent communities and strengthens their social capital, cohesion, and trust to learn from and implement management decisions, with sufficient adaptability to protect heritage values and share them with the wider public over the long term.

This definition includes society's evolutionary nature, considering for example, just as the information society is the next stage of human organization that has evolved from industrial society, HP is the next stage evolved from Postmodern planning that has evolved from RCP. In each case, later levels transcend and include the previous. HP does not discard RCP, rather it preserves many healthy, adaptive, and useful aspects of both RCP and Postmodern planning (while letting other unadaptive features go, such as the lack of interiority and the worship of empirical science). For example, HP still uses rationality, the scientific method, quantitative analysis, methodical tools, democracy, and international finance mechanisms—all valuable innovations of Modernism. It still uses public participation, community development, multicultural inclusion, and consensus building—all contributions from Postmodernism. It uses these contributions in a new light and the recognition that different levels of consciousness exist and thrive under different life conditions.

Thus as each level of consciousness evolves, people do not just see the world differently, they, as Wilber (1996) argues, literally re-create the world through new eyes. For example, with the rise of Modernism, came the nation-state, abolition of slavery, global organizations, and professional sports. Each level of consciousness drives major interior and exterior changes. This evolving perspective drives changes in planning (and the larger arena of organizational management), ideas, skills, and systems in all four quadrants (Table 9.1). HP, in good evolutionary fashion and through its principles (below), builds on all the levels that have come before.

Table 9.1 | *Holistic Planning as AQAL Processes*	
I	**It**
Chapter 5: A process that cares for stakeholders, mediates conflicts, establishes conditions where they can trust, and feel they have power. It responds to their needs, fears, concerns, values, and consciousness, turns them into both inputs and outputs of the planning process.	*Chapter 6:* A process that trains people to take part in the conversation, arms them with enough knowledge that they understand and appreciate different components, allows them to transcend conflicts, and attends to their physical well-being so that they can participate without distraction of basic necessities.

We	**Its**
Chapter 7: A process that in effect is a facilitated conversation that not only strengthens a constituencies' social capital and cohesion to act together even in the face of conflicting values, but also allows a common vision to emerge and evolve as the process continues. Through this process the community develops trust, sense of fairness, power redistribution, transparency, and a new worldview about managing heritage and operating as a community.	*Chapter 8:* A process that creates a plan that holds temporary consensus-driven commitments and establishes a procedure, space, and institution so that dialogue is ongoing and even intensifies when change accelerates. It creates institutions that provide feedback for and strengthen an Integral planning by creating incentives for organizational learning, conflict management, etc., that validates the interior necessities of development, creates governmental institutions more capable of resilience and adaptation especially in times of crisis, and introduces new tools and protocols designed to take advantage of a culture based on learning, adaptation, and systemic thinking, such as LAC, ROS, mind mapping, and others profiled in preceding chapters.

Now that we have seen the problem that motivates HP, its component theories and tools, and its definition, we share principles that define its application and lay out concrete examples. By the end of this section, you should have not only a theoretical and practical grasp of HP but also a mental image of its shape and behavior.

Ensure Constituencies Are Ready and Aligned for Planning

Aside from the obvious institutional distractions of political or financial crises, volcanic eruptions, military invasions, or forest fires that might impede launching a new planning process, planners must consider another deeper level of readiness that inhabits the darker corners of the UL and LL.

Constituencies must enjoy a minimal level of trust and experience working together in order for planning to achieve any reasonable level of implementation (Lachapelle and McCool 2011). They must also share at least a common objective to plan. Consider these examples of readiness and alignment for planning:

- A conservation agency earns the trust of a tour operator by stating how private business can contribute to the protection of irreplaceable endangered species or fragile rock art. So the operator elects to participate in the strategic planning.

- When a park agency returns land to indigenous groups or at least makes the effort to honor its sacred ancestral lands, as the US National Park Service tried to do with the Oglala Sioux tribe in Badlands National Park (Tupper 2015), it reduces a long-simmering conflict in order that the indigenous tribes participate in the planning process.

- Planners prior to planning convene representatives from a herding community in the cold mountains of the biosphere reserve and those of a hot and humid coastal fishing village in the same reserve to share perspectives and objectives so that they might be more willing to work together to plan the reserve's common future.

- Planners work with groups and individuals who have suffered through tiring and ultimately shelved planning processes to earn their trust that this planning process will be different from those of the past and is worth their renewed faith.

- Planners earn pledges from high agency officials to try HP in order to reassure staff who fear bureaucratic punishment for sharing too much control with the public.

In general, planners might have to mediate land tenancy conflicts before critical partners come to the table. Planners might have to speak with different groups individually for weeks, months, or more about a new kind of planning process, about visions that include other groups, before they can even bring the groups together in the same room. In all these cases, planners would have to work with constituent groups to ready them, align their objectives, and build minimal trust in order to jointly create and eventually implement the plan.

The notion that a site can simply invite all groups together suddenly under the same roof and have a professional facilitator work through the problems and generate consensus smacks of children's fantasy. Groups might come physically together, but constructing a group composed of different constituencies to work together requires a foundation of trust that itself must be built.

In short, planners invest in developing social capital. That is social networks, norms of reciprocity, mutual assistance, and trustworthiness. Planners help build relational capital. When people know each other, crime rates drop (Putnam et al. 2004). When people understand each other, they empathize. When people trust each other, they discuss questions previously off-limits. Elinor Ostrom won the 2008 Nobel Prize in Economics in part on her research (Ostrom and Nagendra 2006) that showed that local communities implement forest protection plans such as monitoring and enforcement when they enjoy levels of trust and feel the planning process is legitimate.

Planners first measure readiness through integrated, participatory site analyses. Conventional site assessments can be highly technical ventures where consultants mine information for technical planning purposes. Naturally, like all planning processes, site assessments can be more or less sensitive to interior issues. Through dialogue, for example, the PUP Global Heritage Consortium learns about people's thinking, from which level of consciousness they operate, and needs that motivate them.

Such an advanced application of the Integral lens to site assessment occurred in 2007 in the World Heritage City of Bosra, Syria. There, within the context of a larger European Union project called Sustainable Human Activities in Mediterranean Systems (SHAMS), organizers[25] carried out a Strategic Environmental Assessment (SEA) using an Integral perspective to set up a guiding framework for more in-depth urban planning in a World Heritage site (pre-civil war). Bosra had 27,000 inhabitants, largely semi-desertic farmers, living within and on spectacular archaeological ruins dating back 3,500 years to times of the Nabateans, Canaanites, Byzantines, Romans, Arabs, and others, without understanding why Westerners got so excited about them. Yet their traditional values "no longer provide the answers to arising economic, social and environmental tensions, problems and requirements, as the local population is ever more exposed to tourist demands, its own youth, opening global markets, and the internet" (Caspari n.d., p. 1).

The European Union mandates SEAs for all natural resource- and sustainability-related planning as a preliminary and participatory step to ensure that environmental and social aspects are integrated into planning (Partidário 2012). The facilitators in this case overlaid an Integral lens to a more traditional SEA and identified the following objectives:

- Consolidate notions of "strategic planning," "sustainability," SEA, and adaptation of concepts to local realities and value systems as a foundation for strategic planning.

- Create a "value-system landscape" of people involved in the project to better target communications.

- Inform stakeholder groups about project aims.

- Exchange information with stakeholder groups on main issues, problems, and goals.

- Determine the scope (topics, geographical area, etc.) of the strategic plan with the administration and stakeholder committee.

- Identify tasks for various stakeholders.

Elza Maalouf, a team member and founder of the Center for Human Emergence Middle East (n. d.), explains that the objective of the Integral SEA was to determine HOW does WHO lead/teach/train WHOM to do WHAT? And WHERE? The first step was to define the job and its requirements (WHAT) and in which value systems (WHERE). Second, which value systems need to be activated to get this job done (WHOM). Third, find the people with the right capacities for the various jobs (WHO). Fourth, decide on management procedures, motivational techniques, teaching styles—in other words, the appropriate systems (HOW).

The first round of AQAL analysis showed a significant misfit between Postmodern values of European outside experts and Traditional and Modernist values of locals and the national administration. For example,

- Some local entrepreneurs demanded quick fixes (UR), such as the restoration of single houses along with expropriations and removal of locals from the heritage area in order to make a guest house ("instant gratification" characteristic of the Warrior level).

- Locals needed instant tangible results rather than an abstract plan created by well-meaning European projects based in Modernist and Postmodern values. Locals had no direct understanding of concepts such as sustainability. At the Tribal/Warrior level there is no strategic thinking evolved yet; they still see time cycles as seasonal harvest cycles, festivals, and holy days.

- The local and national administrations (LR) were trying to protect sites without a real planning strategy and were totally overwhelmed by the sheer quantity (170 hectare archaeological sites) and quality of artifacts and monuments.

- National laws (LR) tried to protect heritage sites from destructive attitudes (Tribal, Warrior, LL) opposed to artifacts and statues of non-Islamic origin.

- A common disregard (LL) of poorer locals existed for the heritage values of the archaeological sites in which they still lived.

- Little problem awareness and absence of an overall strategy to manage regional water problems (LL, Tribal) or (worldcentric) concerns for climate change impacts made development more challenging. For locals there was no water problem, as the reservoir has been dry in recent years.

Maalouf notes (p. 4),

> So a project that is prepared by the EU at the [Modernist/Postmodern] levels (*development of Bosra, SEA process, etc.*) is being applied in a [Tribal/Warrior] culture and life conditions (such as *the level of poverty, schools with very little funds, scarcity of water and poor economy*). Most engineers involved in the project are capable of [Modernist] thinking, but are also eager to get paid and to show the city that they are providing good services.

After this scoping exercise had finished, SHAMS continued with a more informed SEA. Similarly, Maalouf offered special trainings about Integral Theory for interested locals, the stakeholder committee in charge of the project, and the Bosra mayor, all to improve communications. Soon participants began to see patterns of behavior and started to reference different levels of consciousness, becoming more sensitive to diverse values.

Create Balanced Relationships of Power and Heartfelt Needs

Much conventional planning descends from above, where donors, governments, and even high-powered specialists dictate what gets planned, how, and where. As a result, coercive measures (the big three are money, politics, and technical expertise) often result when sites participate out of compliance rather than heartfelt need or self-commitment. When community members feel they must surrender their needs and vision to those of bureaucratic agents, their participation often ends when the money stream dries up. When people must comply with the required, they will not commit to the process and thus will not own it. When they comply, they do the minimum necessary. Sometimes they cross the line into resistance—they do not show for meetings, do not complete the assigned task, defame the organizers with gossip[26]—and when coercion ends, their efforts cease and the plan lies down on the shelf to die.

When planners can create more balanced relationships that share power and responsibility (Block 2000), opportunity emerges for all participants to publicly express their heartfelt needs and visions. If they can design the planning process to meet those needs, then participants are more likely to commit rather than simply comply.

We do not of course assume that HP or any planning approach can eliminate power inequalities completely. Some actors will always wield more power than others so planners can take some measures to compensate for power imbalances: give resources to disempowered groups to educate themselves and hire professional help to allow them to discuss technical issues with technical experts. When weaker constituents participate in consensus, then their opinion has much more weight than in voting where more power stakeholders can earn votes. Sometimes, in fact, a planning process may even choose to exploit different sources of power in order to achieve implementation. The important point, though, is to openly acknowledge where the power lies and how best to manage it for the heritage area community.

Establishing equity and building projects founded on intrinsic motivation rather than motivations imposed by donors, politicians, and others outside the heritage community is not easy. This is why the PUP Global Heritage Consortium carries out its very first site visit—the exploratory trip—ideally before a major donor enters the scene. It occurs when a site and the PUP Consortium have shown interest in working with each other because they think that a relationship might meet their organizational and community felt needs, before money and politics distort motivations, before bureaucratic interests supplant felt needs.

So the PUP Consortium insists that each side—the site and the Consortium—contribute to trip costs. Typically, one local PUP facilitator and one international representative donate time to visit and cover country-of-origin travel expenses, and the site pays for one international ticket and local destination expenses. Both sides must invest and in a sense sacrifice their own resources (not those of a donor), something they would do only if they truly believe a project could meet core interests. It also sows seeds for cooperation and partnership rather than seeds for a typical relationship in which the heritage site and donor pay the consultant and everything else. When both sides commit resources, both can demand of the other fair response and cooperation. Both sides buy and sell.

Unlike conventional consultant-driven site assessments where outside experts collect mountains of data through interviews, document reviews, and field measurements, an exploratory trip investigates potential relationships—a relationship assessment—between PUP Consortium and the site's community of actors. It involves conversations with them to learn about their needs, problems, current relationships, and objectives. PUP also makes short presentations to explain its needs and methodology. It asks questions such as:

- Why are we here today? Why did the site host the PUP Consortium?

- What do you want a public use plan to do? What do you really want to create at your site that does not currently exist?

- What is the role of the community in determining the site's future?

- Are you willing to do all facilitation, planning, and writing yourselves rather than ask consultants to do it for you?

- What are you willing to let die in order to create a new process that leads to implementation? Or what must we destroy in order to build something new?

- What are deeper reasons plans have failed to be implemented in the past—beyond simply a lack of resources (time, money, personnel, information, or political will)?

Build Consensus

Recognizing the proliferation of political actors makes the DICE World so different from the PLUS, where politics is assumed not to matter. Democratic principles encourage actors to vie for power and assert their perspectives, often in complex situations. Addressing conflict, however, requires that sides agree on a desired future and a pathway to get there. As Innes (1996) explains, consensus is "a way to address complex controversial public issues where multiple interests are at stake."

What is consensus, and how do we achieve it? Often practitioners confuse consensus with unanimity where a full slate of "yeahs" and no "nays" herald a consensus. In the facilitation field, however, consensus means much more.

Consensus hinges on process. When facilitators create conditions in which participants can share doubts and interests and thoroughly discuss alternative courses of action that make every effort to accommodate their interests, then participants often feel that the process is fair. They feel that the group did its best to find creative solutions acceptable to every participant, and there exists a joint desire to do what is best for the entire group or community, not just to enrich individual agendas.

When facilitators can create this space, participants may agree to implement the group's decision, even if they do not personally favor the decision, but can live with it. Some consensus approaches do, however, allow an individual to block the entire group's decision, sometimes it requires two blocks, and other forms promote reaching an overwhelming agreement (Susskind et al. 1999). Nevertheless, it is often said that while consensus building takes more time up front, it saves much more time later on because participants do not resist implementation.

Participants then do not uncover consensus; rather, they carefully build it brick by brick through dialogue, learning, trust, and mutual respect. McCool et al. (2000) identify the following conditions for consensus to occur:

- Participants share the problem definition. Whether a general management plan or a specific issue, participants jointly construct and hold ownership in the problem description. Problem resolution requires that participants address the same topic.

- Constituencies involved must agree that the issue can be resolved through public engagement. If the issue is purely technical, then it makes no sense trying to get a consensus as it requires a technical solution, such as the restoration techniques used in stabilizing a historic building. Of course, what would be subject to consensus building in this situation is agreeing on the objective to be sought.

- A decision must affect at least two constituencies. If there is only one, then consensus makes no sense. Holistic planners must practice due diligence to identify all impacted interests. Consensus also does not apply to a situation where an interest holds an actual legal right, such as a Native American tribe holding a legal right to hunt on lands ceded to the American government as a result of a treaty. Rights holders are not constituencies in the same sense as we have used elsewhere in this book, as rights identified by treaty or other means are by definition not subject to consensus. The US Constitution says I have a right to practice my religion. That is nonnegotiable.

- The public must hold some knowledge about the issue, conflict, value, or belief. If the public has no knowledge, then a legitimate consensus cannot be developed. For example, a European pharmaceutical company with the help of an indigenous group discovers a plant with curative powers in a forest reserve. The market is huge. If the indigenous group enjoys little or no knowledge about markets, how can the company forge a consensus with them about managing the plant? This condition also implies that if low levels of knowledge exist, then the holistic planner works to fortify that knowledge.

- The process includes all affected interests. "Consensus building processes that exclude legitimate affected interests and values are fraudulent, will lead to increased distrust—particularly about 'hidden agendas'—and create additional conflict" (McCool et al. 2000, p. 3). Susskind and Field (1996) offer several cases of poorly handled negotiation, including the *Exxon Valdez* oil spill and the Bhopal disaster with Union Carbide.

- Consensus-building processes emphasize cooperation over competition that may mean that they build value for participants through willingness to negotiate, focus on interests rather than positions, and work toward goals held in common.

- Participants engage other participants on equal footing, including heritage site managers and scientists. Planners facilitate understanding of technical or specialized information where participants may not hold such knowledge beforehand.

- The heritage management agency must have "permission to act." While the agency may hold legal authority to implement a plan, it must have political credibility to act. Permission to act is based on both the agency's credibility and its perceived capacity to carry out planned actions.

Consensus involves more than a multilateral agreement. Processes of dialogue, learning, negotiating, and reflecting lead to new responses and innovations, shared understandings, redefinitions of the planning problem, and enhanced social, political, and relational capital (Innes 2004; Nkhata et al. 2010). Consensus-building processes may also redistribute power since they require that all participants be equally informed. Such redistribution requires candid and open dialogue, transparent agendas, trust, and mutual respect. The motivating force behind a consensus-building process is the participants' belief that their interests are better served through participating rather than "going it alone."

We should note, nonetheless, that consensus as described here is a Postmodern value that does not necessarily apply to communities with other centers of gravity. In the cases, for example, of Traditional and Warrior groups, people often prefer authoritative leaders to tell them what to do. The notion of consensus would make no sense and would have no reference point in their culture.

Wilber (2007a), however, suggests an Integral approach to consensus building. That is, through value translation (Toolbox 4) different levels can agree to a single decision, although their reasons for supporting that decision may be completely different. Wilber calls this a "conveyor belt," a way to build cohesion that can then convey people toward higher values related to that decision. For example, both Postmodern and Traditional people could align to protect heritage because of their own values, and over time Traditional folk could come to appreciate values of other members of the coalition.

Integrate Multiple Forms of Knowledge

Looking through the eyes of just one kind of knower can hurt a heritage manager in two ways. First, one lens only reveals a partial reality, sentencing the rest to unhidden forces that can topple even the most meticulously designed plans (Caron 2014). Second, preference for just one form of knowledge excludes holders of other forms from contributing to and owning the planning process. Now we will look at both in more detail.

Multiple channels exist by which to know the world and consequently generate new knowledge. Aside from the empirical-scientific method that only considers real that which can be measured and verified, other sources include tradition, collective interaction, personal experience, a priori reflection, intuition, spiritual experience, and probably others.

In Western society, people tend to think of scientists, engineers, and inventors when they consider sources of knowledge. In reality, we accumulate knowledge most of all through informal interactions with friends and colleagues and from rituals, norms, and behaviors passed down through the ages. In dealing with complex systems that envelop protected areas, most knowledge actually comes from people around us. Bohm said that no one ever has an original idea as all ideas come from a collective awareness (2004). US wildland fire managers had little direct experience with fuel accumulation, for example, but relied on measures of accumulation by others and on theories of plant succession formulated by still others. Many heritage sites, whether natural or cultural, simply lack the ability to generate scientific knowledge and out of necessity depend on experiential knowledge, such as knowing where and when polar bears wander in Auyuittuq National Park in the Canadian Arctic, or knowing how Mayans cultivated crops and constructed roads in Mexico and Central America.

In addition to scientific knowledge, there has been increased interest in traditional knowledge in managing complex social-ecological systems. Berkes et al. (2000, p.1252) define indigenous knowledge (although "traditional" knowledge is broader than "indigenous") "as a cumulative body of knowledge, practice, and belief, evolving by adaptive processes and handed down through generations by cultural transmission, about the relationship of living beings (including humans) with one another and with their environment." Such traditional knowledge can often complement or even supplant scientific knowledge in some management situations.

All these sources nevertheless do share several aspects. Knowledge, as Ackoff (1999) explains, is know-how, or knowing how systems function, what works and what does not. And such knowledge spans all four quadrants. Know-how is not restricted to scientists, either. If it were, then how did humans survive millennia prior to the birth of the first scientist?

In conventional planning, scientific knowledge dominates. Such knowledge is heavily oriented toward data, useful for knowing what things are. A baobab tree in the savanna of eastern Africa, for example, has an average height and crown diameter. It is a savanna keystone species as well as water source for elephants. Knowing what things are will not make a heritage plan.

Knowing how things work is another aspect. Technical experts often have good ideas, such as how baobab trees reproduce in the savanna, but they have more difficulty in the lowveld of South Africa. Knowledge about protected areas concerning how organizational culture affects implementation, how to deal with stubborn constituencies, or even how to build an effective interpretive display is often held by people with personal experience as much as those with technical certifications.

Knowing why things work is essential to design heritage planning processes because such knowledge helps planners to engage constituencies, identify innovative solutions during a consensus-building process, or even design an interpretive program that links people with heritage. Knowing why the baobab tree prefers savanna environments helps protected area planners develop effective planting programs or knowing why people say and do things they do may help planning participants understand how to communicate better.

With respect to the second point, when planners rely on only one kind of knowledge, this preference creates what Friedmann (1973) called a "gap in knowing," often so broad that planners and constituencies can no longer communicate across it. Consider the invitation of farmers to a management planning meeting. Because they know little about zoning or the tourism market, they sit quietly in the back of the room sipping their sodas while at the front of the room those with university degrees debate the future. This happens even while the farmers' traditional knowledge could have informed the placement of zones and the characterization of the very attractions being positioned for the international market.

Whatever managers think they know and choose to do today in their heritage areas will almost certainly be replaced as the DICE World spins. To understand the world and its dynamics, managers need to consciously tap different sources of complementary knowledge, even if they already do so haphazardly and unconsciously. In so doing, they not only strengthen their grasp of reality, but they allow other kinds of knowledge experts to contribute to the management conversation. As Arthur Koestler (1964, p. 252) wrote,

> Einstein's space is no closer to reality than Van Gogh's sky. The glory of science is not in a truth more absolute than the truth of Bach or Tolstoy, but in the act of creation itself. The scientist's discoveries impose his own order on chaos, as the composer or painter imposes his; an order that always refers to limited aspects of reality, and is based on the observer's frame of reference, which differs from period to period as a Rembrandt nude differs from a nude by Manet.

Facilitate Community-Based Heritage Interpretation

Heritage is nothing more than the meanings that a community ascribes to it. In return, heritage shapes a community's identity and sense of place. Director-general of UNESCO Irina Bokova, in announcing the Emergency Red List for Syrian Cultural Objects at Risk noted (UNESCO 2013, p. 1):

> At UNESCO, we believe there is no choice to make between saving lives and saving cultural heritage. Protecting heritage is inseparable from protecting populations, because heritage enshrines people's identities. Heritage gives people strength and confidence to look to the future—it is a force for social cohesion and recovery. This is why protection of heritage must be an integral part of all humanitarian efforts.

The obvious centerpiece of a heritage area is the heritage itself. A local community's self-esteem, self-identity, pride, sense of place, place attachment, and even market potential all depend on meanings that people assign to the place. Just as the coherence of light can turn a lightbulb into a laser, the coherence of thought and meaning turns mental noise into a force that mobilizes action and development in that community. Often community members may have perceived only a shadowy notion of their site's worth or its central story and have never joined together with thoughts of fellow members in a facilitated, consensus-building conversation. Where meanings conflict, wars can erupt, such as between Israelis and Palestinians (Silberman 2013); where meanings cohere, communities enjoy a positive identity, pride, and market attraction, such as the Big Apple, New York City, or the Little Apple, Manhattan, Kansas.

Thus, Holistic Planning sees the LL essence of heritage and its importance for the psychological and even physical health of the community. Unfortunately, most mechanical and technical plans spend little or no time describing heritage meanings and even less time making the connection between community health and the role of heritage. Holistic Planning, however, engages in community or participatory heritage interpretation where the larger constituent community articulates its meanings that contribute to its sense of place. This process can generate passion for the place, a passion that infuses the rest of the planning process. As the study of heritage tells a story of the past and lays the groundwork for the future, it also embodies the story behind a plan.

The Interpretive Framework (Kohl 2014) is a tool that uses a consensus approach to generate a series of hierarchical meanings (themes, universal processes, and essence) that appeal to community actors of different levels of consciousness and different aspects of heritage at a particular site. This framework then provides a context in which people can tell their stories and understand their attractions.

It can also provide the raw material for marketing a site based on its real story and attributes rather than PR firm–concocted slogans that ultimately and cleverly say nothing.

Design Planning to Manage Technical Problems and Build Social Capital

Holistic Planning is dual-purpose planning. It recognizes that the capacity to implement arises from the very process creating the plan. As community constituencies converse about management problems and solutions, they also build their social cohesion and capital—that is, their relationships amongst each other. Constituencies learn many things in this process: constructing consensus, building new forms of dialogue, developing trust and reciprocity, sharing mental models, and becoming better colleagues and forming new friendships.

The DICE World demands that multiple community constituencies contribute resources and ideas to plan implementation. It also requires that constituencies continuously rework their plans and vision as the world changes, sometimes violently, around them.

As participants discuss zoning, for instance, they will be learning together, knowing each other through dialogue, being trained together in the use of the tool, and deepening their appreciation for power redistribution and organizational learning. It is not unlike the reason parents put their kids on sports teams: to learn to play the sport but, even more important, to learn to work as a team, to submit one's interests to those of the whole, interpersonal skills, sportsmanship, and a host of other developmental skills that have little relation to the actual sports skills and nothing at all to do with who wins the game.

The planning process then, if well designed, develops a sense of community across all four quadrants, evolving it toward greater creativity, self-organization, technical capacity to manage, and resilience to flow with surprise and change.

Facilitate Development of Others, but Don't Do Their Work for Them

Because the development field has so long favored technical expertise that most local communities do not possess, agencies have felt compelled to bring experts to work on projects in communities and sites where their only interest is the consulting fees they charge. While faraway experts do produce high-quality technical plans, those plans come at great cost. Not only are locals largely excluded from preparing these plans and thus feel little or no ownership for them, but the very act of using external experts in this way deprives local practitioners of opportunities to learn and grow. This effectively degrades the local ability to plan. This also means that when experts leave, locals are even worse equipped to implement technical plans left behind (see chapter 6 for this "shifting the burden" phenomenon). Furthermore, locals often feel little ownership or motivation to implement plans that other people created. Conrad Lanza, historian of Napoleon Bonaparte, said, "No plan originated by another will be as sympathetically handled as one's own plan."

For Holistic Planning, then, experts that come from beyond the community must guide, facilitate, and mentor community members to do their own work for themselves and grow for themselves. This proves difficult oftentimes for bureaucratic organizations who may only offer short-term funding cycles (say, one year at a time) for an inherently multiyear development process. They also find it much easier to manage detailed and inflexible program development calendars despite the fact that development does not move forward at a constant, predictable pace. Rather, it takes a couple steps forward and another step back as local problems emerge and locals struggle with new values and skills.

Holistic Planning and its kindred holistic training (Kohl 2007b; Horton et al. 2003) prefer long-term learning rather than one-off trainings (a quick training where trainers abandon trainees to figure it all out for themselves), building relationships of several years with or without necessary startup funds. Kegan and Lahey (2009) make the distinction between shorter-term technical learning (new skills and knowledge) and longer-term adaptive learning (see "Learn Continuously," below), where the mental capacity of people actually increases.

To avoid hypocrisy and improve their own effectiveness, facilitators, whose true interests include the development of the people and places where they work, must also pursue their own personal development (see "Self as Instrument," below). Experiencing a development process personally also makes them better technical assistants. As U Theory indicates, when someone practices a new behavior or tries to establish a new habit on the right side of the U (kicking a diet soda addiction or adopting Holistic Planning), the individual or team faces the ominous risk of falling back into old patterns of thought and habit. As Pablo Picasso said, "Every act of creation is first an act of destruction." To slay the dragon of old requires more than a single fated arrow such as the one that killed Tolkien's Smaug. It requires a series of repeated thrusts over a prolonged period. In fact, it may take as many as five years to fully replace an old worldview, if conditions are right (Kegan 1983). Thus, the assumption that new practices necessary for implementation will simply begin after a plan is completed shows disregard for the human development process.

This is why an Integral technical assistance program works with a heritage site to move up the U's right side, supports the site, urges the site, and creates a social support network for the site to avoid falling back. Also, technical assistance would aim to help align quadrants for the site (Table 9.2).

Table 9.2 | *AQAL Alignment for Adoption of Holistic Planning (TA=Technical Assistance)*	
I TA helps constituencies to achieve healthy frame of mind and motivation to change to new practice and beliefs. TA helps further expose shadow elements that keep them anchored in RCP. TA connects them to a network of respected social actors who already adopted or support adoption. TA creates space to dialogue with actors about how they feel during the adoption process and how to transcend counterproductive feelings.	**It** TA teaches actors to carry out new practices such as weekly evaluation meetings, periodic updates of an online plan, and periodic releases of incremental plan versions to heritage site constituencies. TA accompanies actors while they practice new skills and habits, reflecting on their mistakes and turning them into learning and improved practice. TA defends the new behavior from attacks originating in the old bureaucratic establishment.
We TA promotes reflection among actors to internalize new culture of adaptive learning and paradigm of Holistic Planning. TA facilitates that actors replace belief that planning is merely a technical-scientific process based on relatively stable conditions that only needs to be redone every five years. TA helps planning team develop pride and common vision of their pioneering work in this area so that they support each and persevere through the early adoption phase and its risks of falling back into old habits.	**Its** TA helps site managers lobby higher levels of government to permit virtual plans that use the Agile Software Development approach, as well as softening rigid plan approval procedures. TA creates extrinsic incentives to allow time for the new habit to take hold such as having a public celebration or eligibility for additional training or financing when planners reach six months of continuous planning. TA develops and adapts planning tools to fit site's social conditions. TA accompanies site in the use of a monitoring system to measure adoption progress.

If any quadrant falters, then adoption goes down. True development in any quadrant means that the system evolves of itself, without the need for external force. For example, a site might plan continuously because some external paid consultants are pushing, but once they leave, if the practice has not embedded in the LL and the LR, it will fail. All four quadrants together must learn to reproduce desirable results, for eventually external money, assistance, or political interest will run dry. Often, when participants taste the possible during a funded project but then collapse into old habits when the project ends, they become depressed—and grow worse than if no intervention had been tried at all.

Build Holistic Planning Teams

In the PLUS World, the basic consideration for planning team composition involves getting the right mix of disciplines—say a protected area planner, biologist, hydrologist, landscape architect, tourism specialist, and so forth. Similarly, a team filled with people chosen only to represent their organizations or disciplines can become an impediment to creative and collective thinking. Meanwhile, an effective HP core team will establish a culture of learning, engagement, and consensus building, bridging interior and exterior perspectives, and forging common visions that motivate people to choose responsibility in this process and thus own it.

In an HP world, however, a planning team would be characterized by:

1. *Multi-perspectives.* The participatory research field (such as Participatory Rural Appraisals) has emphasized that teams come with many biases (Chambers 1997). The most effective way to address bias is for the planning team to represent a diversity of perspectives, not just those of each member's professional discipline. Other variables include gender, age, geographical origin, level of consciousness, and experience. A planning team would contain a diversity of perspectives without having too many people on the team. A team can also use advisors and thematic committees to widen perspective and keep the core small.

2. *Legitimacy among constituencies.* Teams must be regarded by their constituencies as legitimate and trustworthy as they cannot normally include representatives of every constituency. This general sentiment arises from the need for the process to be both transparent and fair. Participants would be respected members of their corresponding constituency. Similarly, project partners must feel represented. Again, teams as well as their advisors, related committees, and even volunteers all contribute to a team's public image.

3. *Enthusiastic and capable of implementing holistic solutions.* Team members must be more than bureaucratically appointed individuals who would rather be somewhere else doing something else besides serving the team. Members should be enthusiastic in effort and capable in judgment. See below for how to select team members capable of implementing an integral perspective, even when none may be at the Integral level of consciousness.

4. *Contain at least one champion. Every team will have at least one champion of HP and of the values contained within the protected area.* He or she could be a formal or informal leader who can work within the management agency or come from outside it. A champion is driven from heartfelt motivation and passion to implement a new approach. They are willing to experiment, capable of mustering resources and support inside an organizational structure, capable of overcoming organizational resistance to change, and can contribute to the creation of a safe space (see chapter 7).

5. *Transdisciplinary.* Beyond multidisciplinary (having different disciplines represented) and interdisciplinary (having different disciplines interact), transdisciplinary implies people who truly listen to other voices and integrate different forms of knowledge into one, both in process and result, that transcends the perspective of any one discipline.

Ideally, the planning team will understand and implement HP principles to make both its analysis and prescriptions more effective; after all, the team will reach and integrate a community's interior perspectives. In chapter 6, we discussed how Martineau put together an integral team of nonintegral thinkers. The Integral SEA (see first principle, "Ensure Constituencies Are Ready and Aligned for Planning") similarly used other Integral criteria to form a committee from all four quadrants (leaders, experts, administration, and locals). It chose people from all the main levels, including religious leaders and tourist guides from Tribal/Warrior, administrators and entrepreneurs from Traditionalist, Modernist engineers, and Postmodern planners.

Plan and Implement Continuously

In the PLUS World, planners made final, peer-reviewed, polished, and published plans that could not easily be updated and then expired after five years or so. In a DICE World, however, such plans go out of date—sometimes within months—and fall out of use at similar speeds.

To keep up not only with a rapidly changing world but also an evolving understanding of the site and its management by the constituent community, a plan must adapt easily. That is, heritage sites must continuously plan and implement, not just once every five or ten years when extra funding becomes available, but every week, every day.

Thus, site budgets and donors must invest in a continuous planning and implementing process. Traditionally, sites would seek funding only to create a plan, assuming that implementation would follow naturally. We now know that this is not true, and any initial planning start-ups contain funding for planning as well as ongoing planning/learning/implementing, like the three sides of a coin (and yes, all coins have three sides). With such a goal, sites actually seek not a planning document but rather a planning process, which implies a learning and implementing process as well.

As this book has worked hard to demonstrate, the capacity to implement arises from the planning process itself and how the process involves constituencies, empowers them, and trains and relates to them. Asking how to implement a plan after the plan has been created is like asking how to use a ticket to a football match that has already happened.

The first big challenge in shifting from discontinuous to continuous planning is to reorient people's thinking so that the end result is process rather than plan. Here are some ways to awaken this new perspective:

1. Part of the change comes with instilling from the outset the notion that we set up a continuous planning process one time and then keep using it forever after. We do not find extraordinary funding every five years to make a plan with an expiration date. As President Dwight D. Eisenhower said (who was a World War II military general before becoming commander-in-chief of the US Armed Forces), "Plans are worthless, but planning is everything." He understood very well that the context in which plans emerge is uncertain and continuously changes, so plans and goals have to be continuous to change along with it (Dvir and Lechler 2004).

2. Another important perspective avows that a plan is only meant to store or document temporary consensus-based decisions, nothing more. It is like a closet or pantry that stores decisions rather than clothes or cans of food, both of which change dynamically and continuously within this space.

3. Funding negotiation might consider that a planning process does not end with the published document but rather includes some implementation time, at least six months or a year or more.

4. Traditionally, the big event is plan finalization or publication or termination or any kind of language that implies "the end." Rather, the big event occurs when version 1.0 of the plan is ready, and the site celebrates the commencement or launching of implementation.

5. To avoid some implementation problems, the very first negotiations of the planning process include issues related to implementation such as approval, funding, periodic meetings, electronic format of plan, and use of plan version numbers.

6. A planning process that offers skills trainings for implementation throughout helps constituent communities build expectations and capacities toward commencement. Because these skills may take months to acquire, the process begins with the outset of training.

7. The lead agency or community offers incentives for people who come up with solutions that promote implementation, such as resolving conflicts, overcoming bureaucratic impediments, and forms of social organizing and motivating that will facilitate the participation of different actors' involvement in implementation. The process also applauds actors who bring people together during the planning process rather than those who stubbornly keep to a strict schedule to finish a document.

In summary, both what we normally term "planning activity and implementation" are phases of planning. In fact, both are continuous aspects of planning. Leaders, when they deal with their constituencies, the press, donors, and so forth, constantly reiterate that the goal is implementation and continuous planning process, not a document that is peer-reviewed, polished, and published like any other scientific study.

When one considers that plans begin falling out of date within weeks or months of completion, a document that cannot be easily updated resembles more a writ of death than a map of the future. Chapter 8 describes the paradigm of Agile Software Development and how it applies to planning. Here we visualize how this technology applies to a heritage planning process.

Imagine this: A protected heritage area begins its planning process through physical and virtual workshops (especially important when constituencies number in the thousands or millions and live many kilometers apart). They may use software such as *Mindmixer* whose goal is to make planning processes more participatory through large-scale Internet crowdsourcing conversations.

After going through the processes above, the core planning team prepares its plan as a website.

This Version 1.0 the government approves as the plan simultaneously enters implementation. The site does not have to wait for a lengthy approval process because the government participated throughout the process, and there is general agreement that the plan will be updated continuously and thus can respond agilely to any concerns that come from participants, including government. In many cases, governments have checks on the process to avoid too much politicization or economic influence, such as appeals processes and environmental impact statements. Ideally, in a participatory process these checks, balances, and appeals would all be subsumed in the consensus process. But until they truly become integrated, they must exist outside the planning process, as we currently find in the approval stage.

After month one, for example, the team then does its first plan evaluation and makes minor changes. They designate their online plan, Version 1.1. They notify those who signed up for updated versions. Planners also send a README file that explains updates, just like software developers do. Each month they do small evaluations, another at six months, and a big one at twelve months. When they finish the annual evaluation, they release Version 2.0, quickly approved by government. Just like software, they continuously plan using their regular budget.

But what if some users do not have an Internet connection? Send them a USB drive with each full version release, or send them a notice indicating where they can download the plan version at their next convenience. But what if some users do not use a computer? Then send them a paperbound synthesis. But what if some farmers do not read? Then no traditional plan would have worked anyway. But by its more graphical nature, a HTML-based plan with pictures rather than words could be developed!

Carry Out Every Planning Moment Holistically

Conventional planning approaches the world one piece at a time. It does not see complexity, internal phenomena, context, dynamic change, and really has a distaste for uncertainty. No wonder the PLUS World appears such an inviting and comfortable place to work. HP on the other hand integrates various perspectives necessary to more fully engage the whole of evolutionary unfolding and survive in a DICE World during all phases of planning and managing. Consider the following as ways to address every planning moment.

Fundamental Perspectives of the Quadrants

HP recognizes that forces arise from all four quadrants that can facilitate planning or sink projects. It also understands, thanks to Integral Theory, that quadrants interact and must move forward together in order to achieve change that sticks and does not regress.

Stages of Development

HP understands within every quadrant that the objects of concern evolve along lines through stages, and we as development agents unblock the flows so they continue evolving.

Context

To do the above requires a deeper understanding of context and how it changes. Universal methods are convenient and simpler, but planners have to manipulate them to fit specific situations.

Change

Change can be random, evolutionary, or somewhere in between. HP focuses attention on various change processes whether U Theory, evolution, organizational change through learning and adaptation, or paradigm change. We cannot, however, simply engineer change, buy it, or legislate it into existence.

Humility in Face of Uncertainty

Technical experts often see uncertainty as a direct threat to their skills. They often think it can be minimized through calculation, analysis, and rational planning. Yet uncertainty does not bow to human cleverness. Rather, HP confronts uncertainty with humility and understanding that we must learn to live with it, adapt to its ever-emerging threats and opportunities, and never be satisfied with the status quo or get too comfortable with what we have achieved so far.

Learn Continuously

In the DICE World, most knowledge has a shelf life: what once seemed to work no longer does. So, if heritage managers must continuously clear the shelves of expired techniques, perspectives, and understandings, likewise, they must continuously learn and restock those shelves. W. Edwards Deming commented ironically on this point: "Learning is not compulsory, neither is survival."

For holistic planners, learning must occur in all four quadrants. In the UL, we learn about ourselves—our values, priorities, strengths, and weaknesses. In the LL, we learn about our communities, culture, values, and beliefs. Clearly, in the UR we learn new skills and behaviors. And, in the LR, we learn about varying institutional and organizational arrangements; we come to understand what rules, laws, and policies may facilitate or hinder implementation.

Learning in heritage planning encompasses four basic elements. When we learn through error several things happen that enhance learning. First, we assess what happened. We also need to reflect on our assessment. Reflection considers what factors both internal to a system and "external" to it may have led to the error. We then apply modified approaches (i.e., "learning") to our new understanding in a way that is distinctly and explicitly experimental, thus managing adaptively. We test our knowledge and then assess, reflect, and apply again. In this sense, learning itself becomes a cyclical, adaptive process.

Such a process does not just happen by luck. Management occurs not only as a collaborative effort among constituencies playing different roles, but within an agency with the responsibility and mandate to protect public interests. Thus, the protected area organization must construct an environment that enables a learning culture. To this end it must avoid what Senge (1990) describes as organizational learning disabilities—behaviors and beliefs that discourage staff from engaging in assessment, reflection, and application of knowledge.

Attention to the four quadrants helps organizations assemble a structure and value system conducive to learning, recognizing that mistakes happen but in the long run can be beneficial to higher quality heritage management. McCool et al. (2015) suggest specific steps to enable organizational learning.

Monitor Management Action Implementation

In general, monitoring involves the systematic and periodic measurement of variables. Without awareness of their situation, planners cannot reflect on that situation.

Assess and Reflect

Managers then reflect on that data. If outcomes deviate from expectations, they need to identify why the deviation occurred and ways in which to correct (or accept) it that are efficient, effective, and equitable.

Develop, Adapt, and Revise System Models

New application requires that managers cast light on their mental models if mistakes and surprises occur not from operational problems but rather from deeper places. Mental models then help them more to learn than to predict (Sterman 2002).

Most learning occurs through the interaction of people. So learning organizations participate in "communities of practice." Wenger et al. (2002) define them as "groups of people informally bound together by shared expertise and passion for joint enterprise." Advancing knowledge and performance in a community of practice is facilitated by voluntary contributions, critical discourse, shared experiences, and "creative ways that foster new approaches to problems." Rather than focus on implementation and monitoring of contractual obligations, the output of a community of practice is enhanced knowledge and learning.

The commencement of implementation comes with frequent evaluation. Evaluations may come fast in the first six months, the period in which a planning process shows its mettle and survives or collects dust on the shelf. Whatever frequency, the contents of that evaluation are even more important.

We already know from where the iceberg peaks above water (chapter 2) that measuring only conformity is a recipe for failure. The DICE World will see to that. We also know that measuring performance makes more sense and has been in the planning literature for some time.

Noble (2013) argues that most development organizations use indicators from the LR, but in reality, performance indicators from all four quadrants will be selected, as quadrant alignment allows development to move forward and sustain itself through internal energy, not just external incentives and coercions. He also notes that donors and project evaluators often narrowly define success by what they can see in the LR (plan implementation or road construction), ignorant of all potential progress in other quadrants.

Besides, true development is emergent, problems are wicked, and we cannot predict what really arises unless we grasp at fruit so low hanging that we can almost guarantee delivery (an unfortunately frequent arrangement in the development world where NGOs in effect buy low level outcomes from communities through offers of assistance and sell those outcomes to donors, according to Noble [2013]).[27]

Noble argues that expanding evaluation to all quadrants promotes quadrant alignment. Wilber builds on Noble's idea of multiquadrant evaluation by saying that each major actor (site/community, donor, technical assistance) influences the outcome and thus has its own quadrant evaluation and must be monitored to gain a holistic view of progress. This leaves us with at least twelve quadrants to monitor (3 main actors x 4 quadrants). Table 9.3 shows both their baseline and progress.

Table 9.3 | *Integral Evaluation of the Three Main Actors in an Intervention*			
Actor → Quadrant ↓	Heritage Site Community	Technical Assistance	Donor
UL (I)	**Indicator** Trust in other members of community (site manager, local village leaders, tour operators, etc.) **Baseline** Low trust, local leaders do not work together except to attend meetings convened by site managers **Progress** Medium trust; stakeholders now forge consensus decisions about relatively noncontroversial topics, excluding land tenancy	**Indicator** Trust site managers **Baseline** Low trust as meetings are formal, documents are signed by multiple parties, unsure of each other's true agenda **Progress** High trust; social contracts bound by a handshake, site does not oversee technical assistance budget. Director invited technical assistant to spend night at house when on-site.	**Indicator** Trust of Holistic Planning Process **Baseline** Agrees with technical aspects but fearful that participation will get out of hand and use up budget unnecessarily **Progress** Donor has appropriated additional funds to extend participatory process beyond what project originally solicited in its proposal
UR (It)	**Indicator** Participatory meeting facilitation skills **Baseline** Site manager accustomed to stand at front of room and talk to participants seated in school-like rows; largely uni-directional communication **Progress** Site manager learned and applies Technology of Participation consensus workshop methods	**Indicator** Improvements to planning methodology **Baseline** Planning methodological manual **Progress** Project report requested revamping the entire community cultivation chapter to include considerations of strict centralized planning culture	**Indicator** Project evaluation **Baseline** SMART objectives (specific, measurable, attainable, relevant, and time-bound) **Progress** SMART objectives with openness to emergent benefits as well
LL (We)	**Indicator** Role in heritage site decision making	**Indicator** Conception of participatory planning	**Indicator** Role in development process

	Baseline Local community felt it had little or no role, that it was responsibility of manager almost exclusively **Progress** Local community believes it has a direct and inalienable right to support and contradict formal authority of site manager	**Baseline** Believed it to be a sequential, time-bound series of workshops leading up to a plan **Progress** Planning is seen as an ongoing facilitated conversation that never ends	**Baseline** To set the ball in motion and then step back **Progress** Active participant in conversation wary of its own power to influence conversation
LR (Its)	**Indicator** Employment in tourism services industry **Baseline** Ten people were employed in tourism services industry in local community **Progress** Twenty-three additional jobs added to tourism service industry in local community	**Indicator** Degree of continuous, virtual planning present at site **Baseline** No continuous virtual plans exist at site (or ever existed) **Progress** Plan version 1.0 is posted to manager website as a PDF with intention to design web-based version later	**Indicator** Plan is approved by national government agency **Baseline** No approved plan currently in use **Progress** Plan version 1.0 approved simultaneously with the launch of plan implementation

One final aspect of Holistic Planning recognizes that learning can be technical or adaptive. Technical learning adds knowledge and skills but does not help the mind to evolve in terms of developing new cognitive abilities, while adaptive learning actually evolves and transforms the mind through stages. According to Kegan and Lahey (2009, p. 310), most training programs ignore the transformational aspect of training:

> While the language of "growth" and "development" is widespread, the actual practices we see tend to be grounded in a transmission model (rather than transformational model) of learning, with a goal of transferring knowledge from one person (typically an expert) to the learner. The expectation is that the learner will "add" more to his mind rather than reconstructing it to achieve greater mental complexity: more files and applications for the operating system; no significant enhancements to the operating system itself.

To underline this useful metaphor: technical learning is like adding new programs to a computer while adaptive learning is like upgrading the operating system itself.

Meet People Where They Are

Every person and community has its center of gravity, that level of consciousness that most influences thought and behavior. Although we have built Holistic Planning largely on values of consensus, trust, community building, and ownership, these values are not universal and will not work or at least be understood the same way in all cases, especially when working with levels prior to Postmodernism. An Integral perspective then works with communities at their center of gravity, respecting who and where they are. For example, Modernism may understand and perhaps even prefer a more democratic approach. Traditional people prefer a clear black-and-white top-down application of law and punishment. While no one wants to be punished, the clarity of rules and consequences appeals to that level. The Warrior level as well responds to strong leaders, even without rules, while Tribalism uses a decision-making process whereby venerable elders make decisions in the best interests of the group.

When planners apply solutions, language, or define problems from one level without translating adequately to another (Toolbox 4), failure often results. Consider how the United States tried to impose democracy (Modernist tool) in Iraq, whose center of gravity is Traditional. The majority of people do not have Modernist values but are rather a mix of Modernist, Traditional, and even Warrior groups (Wilpert 2003). The conflict in this region will burn for years (McIntosh 2007). Similarly, several Latin American countries, including Venezuela and Nicaragua, have used democracy to elect former military leaders (with the authority similar to a Traditional ruler with top-down control), which more closely matches a Traditional center of gravity and a desire to have a strong leader who tells people what to do.

When planners work with different levels through an Integral perspective, they understand that problem definitions and solutions from any level may be the most appropriate depending on the conditions and center of gravity of the people around a heritage area (recall the earlier example of Bosra, Syria).

"Meeting people where they are" means to respect, talk, and negotiate at the level where they are. If someone is Traditional, as much as we might like them to be Postmodern, they have a right to be who they are. Besides, it would take far longer for them to transform to a higher level than any typical planning process would allow. As spiritual teacher Iyanla Vanzant says, "You have to meet people where they are, and sometimes you have to leave them there."

Managers Can Head down the Holistic Planning Path

Now you have seen Holistic Planning tools and principles, the theoretical framework that guides them, and moments when they can be applied. While this book alone is insufficient to cause someone to deeply internalize Holistic Planning, you have probably decided at this stage if you want to continue up the U on the other side. You have several ways to ascend.

Set Up Your Planning Process with a Holistic Planning Approach

Cultural historian Morris Berman said, "An idea is something you have; an ideology is something that has you." Similarly, change is something an organization does or change is something that undoes an organization. Assess your site's readiness to embark on something new. How much resistance will the culture throw against a new approach? You must also keep this determination in perspective as a change process does not require that a site fully understand all theory at the outset. People can begin a relatively nonthreatening process and over time evolve their perspective when they feel the power of a participatory process, when they overcome formerly intractable challenges, or when they can see change occurring in themselves individually and as teams.

Make sure, however, if you look for external funding that you obtain funding not just to create a document. The expectations of creating only a plan will generate impatience if you try anything more. A budget almost always includes

- money to work with the community,
- training of community constituents,
- plan creation, and
- at least as much time for implementation as for planning.

Both SMART objectives that precisely define what you want to create and at the same time are open to results you never anticipated are needed. These emergent results are a regular part of reality and their documentation appears alongside formal results.

Additional Resources Related to Integral Theory

We already cited many fine organizations and efforts related to quadrant-based approaches. Here we share some organizations that specifically use Integral Theory and can be resources for managers who want to learn more and also desire outside support.

- The Center for Human Emergence in the Middle East
- The Center for Human Emergence in the United States
- Integral Life
- Meta-Integral
- Integral Without Borders
- PUP Global Heritage Consortium

Develop Yourself as Instrument

The Integral community talks a lot about "self-as-instrument." Ironically, many who work as conventional consultants or for donors and governmental agencies greatly concern themselves with developing others yet do so little to develop themselves, despite the human mind having so much potential (Outside the Box 9.1). Such an attitude, despite being widespread and lucrative, smacks of hypocrisy. For development work, multiple benefits emerge by improving one's own consciousness.

- The better you know yourself, the more you can help others by transcending your own ego and its inner-focused interests and idiosyncrasies.

- By experiencing transformation, you can better guide others who go through the same process. "Knowing (and feeling) what the journey is like from the inside can only enhance your capacity to lead in a setting where others can successfully and safely unlock their own potential as well" (Kegan and Lahey 2009, p. 323).

- The more you widen your zone of caring and your sphere of connection from egocentrism → sociocentrism → worldcentrism, the more reality you perceive in designing development interventions and the more caring and love you direct toward others.

- Greater consciousness allows for greater depth of perception and intuition into both problems and solutions. It also allows a much more complete and deep embrace and use of Holistic Planning and the Integral lens.

Developing one's spiritual side is inseparable from Integral practice due to its focus on interiority and consciousness. There is a wide field of spiritual practice from which to choose for all levels of consciousness (well, possibly not for Modernism) (Outside the Box 9.1).

Outside the Box 9.1 | *Can Meditation Reduce Crime? Well, Perhaps*

Can Meditation Reduce Crime? Well, Perhaps

In 1993, 4,000 practitioners of Transcendental Meditation assembled in Washington, D.C., for seven weeks to carry out a truly outside-the-box experiment. Project designers predicted before the meditators began that their meditation would lower violent crime substantially in the city. They hypothesized this effect would result because the increase in the group's coherence would reduce stress in the field of collective consciousness around the District. The project gradually increased the number of meditators over the time period noting the corresponding change in crime activity.

The project assembled a twenty-seven-member review panel of independent scientists and leading citizens who approved project protocol and monitoring procedures. District police reported weekly crime data. Researchers carried out statistical analyses to determine the effect of weather, daylight, historical trends, and annual patterns in the District as well as in neighboring cities. After controlling for temperature, crime rates dropped significantly and inversely correlated with the number of meditators present. Analysis further concluded that the drop could not be accounted for by additional police staffing. The results were robust and persisted even after the demonstration study ended. The study did not examine any other possible effects of the experiment besides crime.

This study (Hagelin 1987; Hagelin et al. 1999) and others like it have been cited and reviewed many times. The primary investigator is an acclaimed quantum theory physicist who uses quantum mechanics to explain that the collective consciousness field operates much like, if it is not in fact, a unified quantum field.[1] The transcendental explanation, moreover, says that a society is characterized by the quality of its collective consciousness. If there is much stress in society, that stress reflects in consciousness and then influences behavior manifesting in crime rates, violence, and other social problems. But if coherence and harmony can be increased in the population and thus the field, quality of life can improve too.

Any partially open-minded reader should see the implications for managing visitors in a protected area using a collective consciousness approach; in fact, for seven weeks this approach improved the protection of Washington, D.C. For an extensive review of both research and the quantum physics explanation of paranormal phenomena (group and individual), see Radin's *Entangled Minds: Extrasensory Experiences in a Quantum Reality* (2006).

---

1. *Hagelin has worked at the European Center for Particle Physics and the Stanford Linear Accelerator Center who helped to develop the Grand Unified Field Theory based on superstrings. Dr. Hagelin is founding director of the Institute of Science, Technology and Public Policy, a leading science and technology think tank, and International Director of the Global Union of Scientists for Peace, an organization of leading scientists throughout the world dedicated to ending nuclear proliferation and establishing lasting world peace. See www.hagelin.org/about.html. Also Maharishi Mahesh Yogi (1978).*

Integral Theory is broad and deep and, as we showed in previous chapters, can include most tools and frameworks. On one hand, you do not need much theory to use AQAL. On the other hand, Integral Theory is rigorous, and if you are interested in learning more there are many informal outlets such as Facebook and LinkedIn groups on various Integral topics, as well as organizations such as the PUP Global Heritage Consortium and Integral Without Borders, a nonprofit network of development practitioners who apply Integral Theory to their work. You can take online and in-person meditation courses at The Integral Center in Boulder, Colorado, USA, or even get a masters of arts in Integral Theory at the John F. Kennedy University.

There are also many books and articles on Integral Theory. Wilber himself has written more than thirty books, one of which defines all the basic terms: *The Integral Vision: A Very Short Introduction to the Revolutionary Integral Approach to Life, God, the Universe, and Everything* (2007b), and another that discusses the basic philosophical issues, *A Brief History of Everything* (1996).

Guest Essay | *Planning from Now*

By Michael Simpson
Co-founder
Integral Without Borders

Nowhere is the modern mind more thoroughly stabbed by the arrow of time than when it plans. Our concept of the future, while it never actually happens and which has other plans, is rife with variables that so often dash the sentiments of planners, particularly when their sentiments nostalgically cling to the past. A past that, despite the greatest clarity of hindsight, never actually occurred the way we now see it. For example, if someone declared "let's plan to punish the savages" 500 years ago and they did something, but now ideas of punishing and savages are completely different so the past eludes our current perspective. In retrospect, too many unseen variables blurred the predictions, and so the planner finds him- or herself caught witnessing time as both a past and a future, only able to act right now, in this very instant. As inhabitants of now, planners must do the impossible: decipher value from what has gone and was never fully understood to create something that is coming and cannot fully be predicted.

Yet this very moment seems to depend on the foundation of the past, which appears to grow more complex as it projects toward what seems like a future; in Integral terms each moment is grasping to understand the previous and laying the framework for the next. The planner is enmeshed in this exquisite unfolding hierarchy of time trying to preserve the best of what has been laid down by previous generations in pursuit of the highest potential of what has yet to happen. The plan itself, however flawed, is a touching statement about our species, about our desire to bridge what we valued in our heritage with what we desire.

An Integrally influenced holistic approach to planning allows us to understand how perspectives can differ on this intention, how a particular worldview can orient from the personal or from the collective or from an interior or exterior orientation. A single opinion on planning is likely limited by only one of these four orientations or quadrants. Conversely when these partial views combine and a plan reflects an all-quadrant approach we come that much closer to understanding our past and effectively steering our future. An all-quadrant approach forces us to be more objective about our unavoidable subjectivity.

Of course, our challenge is to create the conditions that invite this simultaneous all-quadrant development in planning. A single-quadrant worldview infrequently leaves room for a different opinion. An all-quadrant worldview, by its very definition, allows for truth but admits it is only partial. An Integral way of understanding planning rarely chooses to throw ideas completely out and vastly prefers building a more complex understanding of what the seeds of these ideas could sprout. There is room for empirical methodologies, for dreamers, and thoughts moved by spirit. There is enough space in the planning room for doubt and conviction, for new ideas and old ones. By admitting partiality, we admit we never quite understood the past and the future is simply a preference.

While time seems to have a direction, evolution appears to have an intention. An Integrally informed planner understands this creative urge or drive toward complexity from matter to life to mind to spirit. Just as each moment builds toward grasping the next, our understanding of what is good planning will depend on where we are right now in our own personal and collective evolution. At no point in history has the need for holistic, all-quadrant planning that brings this self-awareness of an evolving sense of self been more apparent than right now. What this book has so clearly pointed out is that an all-quadrant Integral approach to planning provides a better, holistic understanding of what was good and worth preserving and what will be good and worth pursuing for future generations, whose subjective worldview we will never truly know: a responsibility that can only be approached with humility.

Finally, We Ascend the U into the Light on the Other Side of Complexity

Our journey here is all but done. We now head toward simplicity on the other side of complexity. Along the way, we have deconstructed RCP and replaced it with a new model. However, this model will not last long if we do not practice and build a support network to sustain it. We must find the discipline to act while the idea remains fresh. We, Steve and Jon, cannot complete the journey with you beyond this point. We are still on our own journey, and all books have their limits. Even the greatest of holy books, whether the Bible, Koran, or Upanishads, require strong support to implement. They enjoy a hierarchy of clergy, congregations, fellowships of followers, and of course the inspiration of a higher power to make it all work. You must step forward to avoid tumbling back into old habits after you close the back cover. Do not go alone. Learning and evolving is a social process.

Table 9.4 | *Holistic vs. Conventional Planning*

Trait	Holistic Planning	Conventional Planning
Worldview	Assumes the DICE World	Assumes the PLUS World
Forms of knowing	Integrates a variety of kinds of knowing to understand the world (scientific, intuitive, collective, traditional, spiritual, experiential, others)	Accepts only scientific knowledge and none other to know the world
Dimensions of reality	Works with interior subjective part of each person (feelings, worries, vision, etc.) as well as groups (culture, paradigms, relations) as much as the material exterior part of the world	Accepts only scientific knowledge and none other to know the world
Participants	Includes all community actors to forge a consensus about what to do	Works only with the material, objective, physical, and measurable part of the world (scientific materialism)
Power	Distributes power among many actors	Centralizes power among those legally constituted management authorities

Planner's role	Planners are facilitators of social processes	Planners do all the technical work
Endgame	The endgame is a community with the capacity to adapt and plan and manage continuously	The endgame is to produce an approved, technical document
Implemenation	Assumes that implementation begins with the emergence of the first idea to create a plan	Assumes that implementation follows automatically after plan approval
Responsibility to plan	Assumes the responsibility to plan and manage rests in the constituent community	Assumes that the responsibility to plan and manage rests with the government or its legal delegate
Role of science	The role of science is to inform decision makers	The role of science is to determine which actions to take
Planning frequency	Strategic planning is a continuous process	Strategic planning is a punctuated or cyclical process done every five or ten years
Community involvement	Cultivates and aligns the constituent community prior to planning so they are ready to work together	Since community actors only offer ideas to the planners, they do not need any special preparation prior to planning
Metaphor for planning	Visualizes planning as a facilitated conversation	Visualizes planning as a scientific study
Planning investment	Planning resources are invested in community strengthening, planning, and implementing	Planning resources are invested only in the process to produce a document
Document format	The document format can be virtual and informal, with accessible language for many audiences, and easy to update mechanically once a decision to update has been made	The document format is polished, bound, formal, with scientific language, and difficult to update mechanically once a decision to update has been made

None of us can be sure what Holistic Planning will look like on the other side. Just like Integral consciousness, Holistic Planning is still taking shape. New paradigms always demand a few pioneers to stake out boundaries of the new level. Kuhn said this about science paradigms, and Wilber repeated the same about consciousness. Fortunately, a young community already exists to help nurture the emergence of this new level. Every one of us who seeks a new way participates in writing the story of this level. Every new effort to plan beyond the limits of convention represents a new chapter in this story.

Planning is, after all, a conversation that helps the subject (community of actors at a heritage site) move closer and understand more deeply the object (our natural and cultural heritage that we manage) by illuminating previously invisible connections, by guiding people to create new meaning and, with new meaning, take ownership. In so doing, as subject and object grow closer and closer through increasingly tighter connections, they become, in effect, one. We have all felt the power and love of a strong sense of place that contributes to us as we contribute to it, whether that place is set in natural or cultural heritage. In this way, planning as conversation encourages spiritual development in the same way that all great spiritual and meditation schools seek to create nondual union, where objects melt into a single communion of subjects, a single unity, and a single song of the universe.

We know the future has other plans, and we can choose to be part of those plans if we truly desire—but to participate in the Integral future requires that we integrate all aspects of our being: interior and exterior, individual and collective. This way, we will be better development agents, and better people.

With that, then, we let you go . . . and hope to see you on the other side.

*One of the first steps toward an integral postmodernity is the development
and establishment of a genuine environmental ethics, or a moral
and ethical stance to nonhuman holons.*

—Ken Wilber

Heritage Management Field Evolves Inevitably toward a Tipping Point

That is our larger destiny: to allow the Earth to organize in a new way, in a manner impossible all the billions of years prior to humanity.

—*Brian Swimme*

Ken Wilber argues that all evolution, whether from atoms to molecules, mice to men, or agrarian to industrial societies evolve when quadrants align. If they do not align, the emergent experimental form or the proposed theory will perish. Indeed, science shows us that most experiments in nature and in human society ultimately fail.

Before AQAL forces of selection decide the experiment's fate, incremental change in one quadrant or another contributes to growing tension, whether gradual environmental change (global warming), an accumulation of scientific data about an anomaly, or, in the case of planning, worsening conditions and new technologies that stress out the RCP worldview. This pressure often builds from change in the LR because material changes much easier and faster (spears to guns, snail mail to e-mail, tourism carrying capacity to Limits of Acceptable Change) than does consciousness (LL and UL).

At first tension builds slowly—almost incrementally—and then exponentially until reaching a crescendo tipping point and the system jumps. This change might be an assassination, rupturing of a dam, revolution in scientific paradigms, collapse of a civilization, or the arrival of the Arab Spring.

The governments of Tunisia, Libya, Egypt, Yemen, and Syria all had Traditional-based authoritarian regimes that held citizen freedoms in check to differing degrees (LR). Nevertheless, the region's youth sopped up the Internet, enjoyed increasing levels of education, Western democracy and culture, and in short became budding Modernists (LL). So an LR authoritarian block fed a tension between LL and LR, and eventually the lid burst off in country after country as the region literally fights for AQAL alignment.

Blocks can occur in any quadrant. They can be outdated cultural norms (LL) against women, anguish caused by war (UL), poor health (UR), or government structures such as dictatorships (LR). This is why Hochachka (2008) argues that rather than reengineer systems for development (i.e., the Green Revolution), those who work in Integral development should instead work more modestly to unblock natural development flows that lead to AQAL alignment at the next level.

In our heritage management world, we can feel quadrants that develop together as well as growing tension of quadrants out of sync. In the LR we have new tools that require higher levels of consciousness to operate, including Limits of Acceptable Change, Appreciative Inquiry, and Recreation Opportunity Spectrum, in a world increasingly Postmodern, which diverts more power to indigenous and local communities, endowing protected areas with new values (ethical, spiritual, democratic, ecosystem services). Even large bureaucratic institutions such as the UN continually issue new conventions and declarations saturated with Postmodern values (e.g., UN Convention on the Rights of Persons with Disabilities). Yet Modernists still largely dominate the heritage management worldview along with a strong dose of Technical Rationality, probably driven by historic leadership of scientific professionals such as biologists, foresters, and archaeologists.

This tension, then, between LL and LR (tools and institutions) manifests by adoption of Postmodern ideals (participation, indigenous rights, local involvement, fair trade coffee) as well as Postmodern tools without a corresponding increase in consciousness necessary to properly use participatory and interior-focused tools and techniques. Organizations such as the PUP Global Heritage Consortium and Integral Without Borders respond as well to this tension by focusing their energy on accelerating the transition. Eventually a tipping point will be reached—whether a transition marked by leading organizations such as IUCN, UNESCO, or ICOMOS, for instance, issuing new guidelines focused on human interiority alongside, not in the dark shadow of, science-driven decision making about exteriors or an internal revolution of one or more of these organizations.

The same forces have compelled change in other fields. This is why the PUP Consortium imports into our field leading-edge ideas, tools, and approaches from all quadrants representing many fields, whether organizational learning, Resilience Theory, adaptive comanagement, systems thinking, Mutual Gains Approach, or Integral Theory. Heritage management, too, flows toward AQAL alignment, but will it reach through a guided transition or through a jolting revolution?

As practitioners and theorists, we can remain stalwart guardians of a transcended worldview that shipwrecks plans on the shoals of outdated assumptions, or we can cut a path toward this transition toward the leading edge of evolution.

> *What could change the direction of today's civilization? It is my deep conviction that the only option is a change in the sphere of the spirit, in the sphere of human conscience. It's not enough to invent new machines, new regulations, new institutions. We must develop a new understanding of the true purpose of our existence on this Earth. Only by making such a fundamental shift will we be able to create new models of behavior and a new set of values for the planet.*

> —*Václav Havel*

Notes

1. See for instance, Frampton (1983), Moore (2007), Waldheim (2005), and Mohsen and Doherty (2010).

2. See for instance, Bandarin and van Oers (2012).

3. Other fields suffer similar problems. Consider, Dibb et al. (2008) for marketing; in the education field, see Buzhardt et al. (2007).

4. While having skilled planners and facilitators would seem a prerequisite to successful planning no matter what planning theory or framework you use, the lack of these skills often directly results from RCP assumptions, where managers place a premium on expert knowledge, often hiring consultants to plan and write plans. Not only does the use of consultants rob a site's own staff of the opportunity to practice and learn, but it also often diverts staff training budgets to their compensation packages. The underlying assumption is why invest in my own technical staff if my money is better spent hiring outside experts who are best equipped to produce the most technically superior plan my money can buy? In terms of institutional barriers, we find that the assumptions of Technical Rationality go to the very heart of what bureaucracies are. Bureaucracies basically look to apply technical criteria to create a highly efficient machine to achieve their ends. Many institutional barriers then derive from values that come out of the Enlightenment, Modernism, Positivism, and Technical Rationality (choose your favorite). For example, bureaucracies are designed with a hierarchy in which each person is a technical specialist charged with fulfilling his singular function (accountant, engineer, salesperson, security guard, PR person, manager). These people receive orders from the top, execute exactly to protocol, receive information and materials in a standard format at a specific moment, and must pass on information and materials likewise to other technical specialists. You should be able to see some problems that emerge with the standard bureaucratic format. In terms of greater forces, it is true that many events are beyond anyone's control, but the perspective of seeing the world only as events and patterns and not deeper systems leads organizations to be reactive rather than proactive; reductionist rather than holistic, and fragile, rather than resilient when these events occur.

5. Ayn Rand (1957, p. 946) takes the point to criticism: "All work is creative work if done by a thinking mind, and no work is creative if done by a blank who repeats in uncritical stupor a routine he has learned from others." At least one study shows that when people are faced with financial decisions, those with expert advice shut down parts of their brain responsible for decision making, while those without such advice show activation of those brain regions. For the study, see, Engelmann et al. (2009). For a popular rendition of the study, see Keim (2009).

6. Demographers often ignore feedbacks when making linear projections of human population growth—feedbacks such as disease, water scarcity, food scarcity, etc. See Engelman (2011).

7. Allen and Gould (1986). This is the initial, if brief, statement on the lack of stopping rules in natural resources and the complexity of decisions in this area.

8. For discussion of population dynamics of Easter Island, see page 125–127 in Sterman (2000) and Chapter 2 of Diamond (2005).

9. Hilborn (2004): "The butterfly effect has become a popular metaphor for sensitive dependence on initial conditions— the hallmark of chaotic behavior. I describe how, where, and when this term was conceived in the 1970s. Surprisingly, the butterfly metaphor was predated by more than 70 years by the grasshopper effect."

10. In all fairness, many metaphysicians argue that consciousness is a characteristic of energy, and that all objects, not just organisms, have a degree of consciousness. Wilber argues that even a rock reacts to gravity, heat, force, and other stimuli in its world-space. While that may be, we will stick to organisms for the purposes of understanding planning.

11. For a great online introduction to Integral Theory which goes into more detail than this chapter can, visit https:// www.dailyevolver.com/theory/

12. In other fields, professional quality might be measured by more objective standards, such as in public health where a program's ability to reduce indices of a health threat may convey professional competence. Publications mark academic success; goals work well for soccer players. In conservation, however, some argue there are no consensus criteria for success. This concern has unleashed efforts by groups such as Foundations of Success, the Conservation Measures Partnership, and the Center for Evidence-Based Conservation to create standardized, science-based criteria with which to measure achievement of all conservation efforts.

13. This movement encompasses many tools and approaches, all based on the premise that dialogue is fundamental to human development. Some examples include the Dialogue Society, Coffee Party USA, World Café, Panos Network, National Coalition for Dialogue and Deliberation, and Dialogue Institute.

14. One of the leading thinkers in development and UL has been Robert Chambers (1997). He traces the history of such research and all the errors in development to developers' construction of reality not usually matching that of the people they are ostensibly trying to assist. In other words, they do not understand the left-hand column. Or often do not even try.

15. For a classic application of this idea to agricultural development, see Bunch (1982).

16. After Wilson's book, Kellert and Wilson edited a book of essays (1995) to develop the theory and application. Later still Kellert et al. edited the landmark Biophilic Design: The Theory, Science, and Practice of Bringing Buildings to Life *(2008). The contributed volume covers much of the research that supports biophilic design as well as current practice and desired future.*

17. In order to be used, LAC, for instance, requires that its users have sufficient awareness of group social processes and inherent variability rather than stability in a DICE World, which demands continual experimentation, both more characteristic of Postmodern worldviews than Modernist, even though the methodology along with adaptive management were born during Modernism. The Recreation Opportunity Spectrum or any product development tool that depends on experience planning requires that its planners are conscious of the UL enough to understand visitor experiences. In other words, to train people to use such tools requires adaptive learning, which leads to greater mental capacity, not just transmission of knowledge and skills (Kegan and Lahey 2009).

18. Freire also set off the ecopedagogy movement. Following Freire, ecopedagogy's mission is to develop a robust appreciation for the collective potentials of being human and to foster social justice throughout the world, but it does so as part of a future-oriented, ecological-political vision that radically opposes the globalization of ideologies such as neoliberalism and imperialism on one hand, and attempts to foment forms of critical ecoliteracy on the other. Additionally, ecopedagogy has as one of its goals the realization of culturally relevant forms of knowledge grounded in normative concepts such as sustainability, planetarity (i.e., identifying as an earthling), and biophilia (i.e., love of all life).

19. In the planning literature, there is much discussion about the transition from the design school of planning where solutions are designed and then implemented in a rational decision-making manner (RCP) to the process school, which emphasizes that people and organization often do not decide in a perfectly rational way and that participation and multiple actors are important to moving forward incrementally. For a brief overview on this transition, see Lusiana and Zan (2013).

20. In the cited text, Brown seems to confuse sentences and lines in the methodology section and also does not cite any particular content analysis methodology. Despite these points, the study is unique and revealing for purposes of our analysis.

21. It is precisely this argument that the Simultaneous Policy applies. Proponents argue that the Modernist structure of the nation-centric state has largely gone obsolete, incapable of solving problems that are increasingly global and complex. As such, human organization (LR) must continue to evolve toward global governance, which requires an increasingly Integral perspective to manage. See www.simpol.org.

22. Ironically, Hussein punished cultural heritage looters with death, and the war that ousted him brought with it massive cultural heritage destruction and looting (Breitkopf 2007).

23. http://www.planningtoolexchange.org/resource/urban-research-program-toolbox

24. Wilber (1996) defined twenty tenets that describe all of evolution, only one of which is that emergent holons transcend and include their predecessors, where a holon is an evolving whole as well as part of later holons in a natural hierarchy or holarchy. The postformal governance structure of Holacracy is modeled on holons or nested circles that distribute power among workers (Robertson 2015).

25. This description comes from internal project documents, including the mission report by Bettina Geiken and Anne Caspari for the SHAMS/Integral SEA Scoping Seminar (23–27 July 2007) and others found at www. humanemergencemiddleeast.org/meshworks-syria.php

26. Scott (1987) discusses how even poor farmers in Malaysia influenced policy through sabotage, silent noncompliance, foot-dragging, theft, character assassination, and gossip among other tactics. Often they reacted against top-down planning and policy making that excluded them. The principle holds in most planning contexts today where people resist processes that they do not own and often work against their intrinsic motivations.

27. This observation and that of Wilber in the following paragraph come from an Integral Without Borders Sangha Call facilitated by Noble, February 8, 2014. See www.integralwithoutborders.org/news/iwb-sangha-call-dynamics-emergence-local-economic-development.

REFERENCES

Academy for Educational Development. (2004). Going to SCALE: *System–Wide Collaborative Action for Livelihoods and the Environment.* Washington, DC: USAID/GreenCOM. www.fhi360.org/sites/default/files/media/documents/Going%20to%20SCALE.pdf.

Ackoff, R. L. (1999). On Learning and the Systems That Facilitate It. *Reflections* 1(1): 14–24.

———. (1974). *Redesigning the Future.* New York: John Wiley.

AFP. (2008). Grupo indígena en peligro de extinción logra un acuerdo histórico con el Estado peruano. *La Jornada.* July 14. www.jornada.unam.mx/2008/07/14/index.php?section=mundo&article=027n1mun.

Ajzen, I. (1991). The Theory of Planned Behavior. *Organizational Behavior and Human Decision Processes* 50(2): 179–211.

Alexander, E. (2000). Rationality Revisited: Planning Paradigms in a Post-Postmodern Perspective. *Journal of Planning Education and Research* 19(3): 242–256.

Alexander, E. R., and A. Faludi. (1989). Planning and Plan Implementation: Notes on Evaluation Criteria. *Environment and Planning B: Planning and Design* 16(2): 127–140.

Alexander, S. (2011). MAP Executive Director Visits Thailand Mangrove Project. *The MAP Newsletter* #254. http://mangroveactionproject.org/the-map-news-254th-ed-08-january-2011/.

Allen, G. M., and E. M. Gould Jr. (1986). Complexity, Wickedness and Public Forests. *Journal of Forestry* 88(4): 20–23.

Altshuler, A. (1965). *The City Planning Process: A Political Analysis.* Ithaca, NY: Cornell University Press.

Anderies, J. M., M. A. Janssen, and E. Ostrom. (2004). A Framework to Analyze the Robustness of Social-Ecological Systems from an Institutional Perspective. *Ecology and Society* 9(1): 18 (www.ecologyandsociety.org/vol9/iss1/art18).

Andina. (2008). Estado peruano otorga primera concesión de conservación a comunidad nativa del Cusco. Agencia Peruana de Noticias (Andina). July 2. www.andina.com.pe/agencia/noticia-estado-peruano-otorga-primera-concesion-conservacion-a-comunidad-nativa-del-cusco-182629.aspx#.U6x1jLFZjt8.

Andreasen, A. (1995). *Marketing Social Change: Changing Behavior to Promote Health, Social Development, and the Environment.* San Francisco: Jossey-Bass.

Appelo, J. (2011). Complexity Thinking. www.slideshare.net/jurgenappelo/complexity-thinking.

Arguayo, R. (1991). *Dr. Deming: The American Who Taught the Japanese about Quality.* New York: Fireside Publishing.

Arguedas, S. (2009). Personal communication. Technical director, Escuela Latinoamerica de Áreas Protegidas, San José, Costa Rica.

———. (2007). *Aspectos conceptuales para el diseño de procesos de elaboración de planes de manejo para áreas silvestres protegidas: Un aporte salido del Proyecto para la Elaboración de los Planes de Manejo de*

7 áreas protegidas de ACOSA. Research Report. Escuela Latinoamericana de Áreas Protegidas, Universidad para la Cooperación Internacional, San José, Costa Rica.

Armitage, D., F. Berkes, and N. Doubleday. (2007). *Adaptive Co-management: Collaboration, Learning, and Multi-Level Governance*. Vancouver, BC: University of British Columbia Press.

Arnold, M. (1869). *Culture and Anarchy: An Essay in Political and Social Criticism*. Oxford, UK: Oxford University Press (published as Oxford World's Classics paperback in 2009), 5–6.

Arnstein, S. R. (1969). A Ladder of Citizen Participation. *Journal of the American Institute of Planners* 35(4): 216–224.

Asimov, I. (2004). *The Foundation Trilogy*. Science Fiction Book Club.

Ball, I. R., H. P. Possingham, and M. Watts. (2009). Marxan and Relatives: Software for Spatial Conservation Prioritisation. In *Spatial Conservation Prioritisation: Quantitative Methods and Computational Tools*, ed. A. Moilanen, K. A. Wilson, and H. P. Possingham. Oxford, UK: Oxford University Press, 185–195.

Bandarin, F. (2014). Introduction: Urban Conservation and the End of Planning. In *Reconnecting the City: The Historic Urban Landscape Approach and the Future of Urban Heritage*, ed. F. Bandarin and R. van Oers. Chichester, UK: John Wiley & Sons, 1–16.

Bandarin, F., and R. van Oers, eds. (2014). *Reconnecting the City: The Historic Urban Landscape Approach and the Future of Urban Heritage*. Chichester, UK: John Wiley & Sons.

Bandarin, F., and R. van Oers. (2012). *The Historic Urban Landscape: Managing Heritage in an Urban Century*. Chichester, UK: Wiley-Blackwell.

Barborak, J. (2010). Gestión y Planificación de Áreas Protegidas: Aplicaciones del Enfoque Ecosistémico. Presentation, XIV Mesoamerican Conservation Biology Congress, San José, Costa Rica. 9 November.

———. (2009). Personal communication. Co-director, Center for Protected Area Management and Training, Fort Collins, Colorado State University.

Bardwell, L. V. (1991). Problem-Framing: A Perspective on Environmental Problem-Solving. *Environmental Management* 15(5): 603–612.

Barker, J. A. (1992). *Paradigms: The Business of Discovering the Future*. New York: HarperBusiness.

Barrett, B., and M. Taylor. (2007). Three Models for Managing Landscapes. *The Journal of Heritage Stewardship* 4(2): 50–65.

Bartunek, J. M., and J. K. Murnighan. (1984). The Nominal Group Technique: Expanding the Basic Procedure and Underlying Assumptions. *Group and Organization Management* 9(3): 417–432.

Baum, H. S. (1996). Why the Rational Paradigm Persists: Tales from the Field. *Journal of Planning Education and Research* 15(2): 127–135.

———. (1988). Planning Theory as Political Practice. *Society* 26(1): 35–42.

Beck, L., and T. T. Cable. (2011). T*he Gifts of Interpretation*, 3rd ed. Urbana, IL: Sagamore.

Bellah, R., R. Madsen, S. M. Tipton, W. M. Sullivan, and A. Swidler. (1992). *The Good Society*. New York: Vintage.

Berke, P., M. Backhurst, M. Day, N. Ericksen, L. Laurian, J. Crawford, and J. Dixon. (2006). What Makes Successful Implementation of Plans? An Evaluation of Local Plans and Implementation Practices in New Zealand. *Environment and Planning B: Planning and Design* 33(4): 581–600.

Berkes, F. (1999). *Sacred Ecology: Traditional Knowledge and Resource Managements.* Philadelphia: Taylor & Francis.

Berkes, F., J. Colding, and C. Folke. (2000). Rediscovery of traditional ecological knowledge as adaptive management. *Ecological Applications* 10(5): 1251–1262.

Biggs, D., N. Abel, A. T. Knight, A. Leitch, A. Langston, and N. C. Ban. (2011). The Implementation Crisis in Conservation Planning: Could "Mental Models" Help? *Conservation Letters* 4(3): 169–183.

Biggs, H. C., and K. H. Rogers. (2003). An Adaptive System to Link Science, Monitoring and Management in Practice. *In The Kruger Experience Ecology and Management of Savanna Heterogeneity*, ed. J. T. du Toit, K. H. Rogers, H. C. Biggs, and A. R. E. Sinclair. Washington, DC: Island Press, 59–80.

Bishop, S. (2012). PMA Status Jeopardized. The Voice SLU. June 19.

Bisina, J. (2004). Mediation in Ongoing Crisis between Ijaws and Itsekiris of Warri Delta State Nigeria. Listserv post. http://lists.openspacetech.org/pipermail/oslist-openspacetech.org/2004-January/010269.html.

Block, P. (2008). *Community: The Structure of Belonging.* San Francisco: Berrett-Koehler.

———. (2000a). Strategies for Engagement. In *Flawless Consulting: A Guide to Getting Your Expertise Used*, ed. P. Block. New York, NY, USA: Jossey-Bass/Pfeiffer, 263–280.

———. (2000b). *Flawless Consulting: A Guide to Getting Your Expertise Used*, 2nd ed. New York: Jossey-Bass/Pfeiffer.

Block, P., and J. McKnight. (2010). *The Abundant Community: Awakening the Power of Families and Neighborhoods.* San Francisco: Berrett-Koehler.

Bloom, H. (2001). *Global Brain: The Evolution of Mass Mind from the Big Bang to the 21st Century.* New York: Wiley.

Bohm, D. (2004). *On Dialogue.* London and New York: Routledge Classics.

Booher, D. E., and J. E. Innes. (2002). Network Power in Collaborative Planning. *Journal of Planning Education and Research* 21(3): 221–236.

Bornstein, D. (2007). *How to Change the World: Social Entrepreneurs and the Power of New Ideas, updated* ed. New York: Oxford University Press.

Breitkopf, S. (2007). Lost: Looting of Iraq's Antiquities. Museum News. American Association of Museums. January/February 44–51.

Brockington, D. (2002). *Fortress Conservation: The Preservation of the Mkomazi Game Reserve, Tanzania.* Bloomington: Indiana University Press.

Brody, S. (2001). *The City of Sarasota, FL 2001 Comprehensive Plan: The Role of Communicative Culture and Informal Public Participation in Plan Making.* Chapel Hill, NC: The Center for Urban and Regional Studies.

Brody, S.D., and W. E. Highfield. (2005). Does Planning Work? Testing the Implementation of Local Environmental Planning in Florida. *Journal of the American Planning Association* 71(2): 159–175.

Brown, B. C. (2007). *The Four Worlds of Sustainability: Drawing upon Four Universal Perspectives to Support Sustainability Initiatives.* Version: February 20. Integral Sustainability Center. http://nextstepinte-gral.org/wp-content/uploads/2011/04/Four-Worlds-of-Sustainability-Barrett-C-Brown.pdf.

———. (2005). Integral Communications for Sustainability. *Kosmos: An Integral Approach to Global Awakening* IV(2): 17–20.

Brown, J., D. Isaacs, and N. Margulies. (1997). *The World Café: Creating the Future, One Conversation at a Time.* Whole Systems Associates.

Brown, J., D. Isaacs, and World Café Community. (2005). T*he World Café: Shaping Our Future Through Conversations That Matter.* San Francisco: Berrett-Koehler.

Brown, L. R. (2009a). *Plan B 4.0: Mobilizing to Save Civilization*, substantially rev. ed. New York: W. W. Norton & Company.

———. (2009b). What's Needed: A Copernican Shift. Earth Policy Institute. Adapted from Chapter 1: The Economy and the Earth. *Eco-Economy: Building an Economy for the Earth.* New York: W. W. Norton & Company.

Brown, M., and N. Salafsky. (2004). Learning about Learning Networks: Results from a Cross-Disciplinary Study. Foundations of Success. www.fosonline.org/wordpress/wp-content/up-loads/2010/06/Learning_About_Networks_7_July_04.pdf.

Brown, M. (2012). It's Official: Neutrinos Cannot Beat the Speed of Light. *Wired.* June 8. www.wired.com/2012/06/neutrinos-cant-beat-light/.

Brumfiel, G. and *Nature.* (2011). Particles Found to Travel Faster Than the Speed of Light: Neutrino Results Challenge a Cornerstone of Albert Einstein's Special Theory of Relativity, Which Itself Forms the Foundation of Modern Physics. *Scientific American.* September 22. www.scientifi-camerican.com/article.cfm?id=particles-found-to-travel.

Bryson, J. M., and P. Bromiley. (1993). Critical Factors Affecting the Planning and Implementation of Major Projects. *Strategic Management Journal* 14: 319–337.

Bryson, J. M., and B. C. Crosby. (1992). *Leadership for the Common Good: Tackling Public Problems in a Shared Power World.* San Francisco: Jossey-Bass.

Bunch, R. (1982). *Two Ears of Corn: A Guide to People-Centered Agricultural Improvement.* Madison: World Neighbors and University of Wisconsin–Madison.

Bunker, B. B., and B. T. Alban. (1996). *Large Group Interventions: Engaging the Whole System for Rapid Change.* San Francisco: Jossey-Bass.

Burke, J. (2009). Rebellion in Provence at Paris Plan for National Park. *The Guardian.* July 26. www.theguardian.com/world/2009/jul/26/paris-calanques-national-park-rebellion.

Buzan, T. (1993). *Mind Maps, Radiant Thinking.* London: BBC Books.

Buzhardt, J., C. R. Greenwood, M. Abbott, and Y. Tapia. (2007). Scaling Up Class-Wide Peer Tutoring: Investigative Barriers to Wide-Scale Implementation from a Distance. *Learning Disabilities: A Contemporary Journal* 5(2): 75–96.

Cain Miller, C., and N. Bilton. (2011). Google's Lab of Wildest Dreams. *The New York Times.* November 14. www.nytimes.com/2011/11/14/technology/at-google-x-a-top-secret-lab-dreaming-up-the-future.html?pagewanted=all&_r=0.

Caldwell, L. K. (1992). *Between Two Worlds: Science, the Environmental Movement, and Policy Choice.* New York: Cambridge University Press.

Caron, F. (2014). Planning and Control: Early Engagement of Project Stakeholders. *The Journal of Modern Project Management* 2(1): 85–97.

Caspari, A. (2013). "U" Process and Development. Discussion Paper 36 of Integral Mentors. https://mindshiftintegral.files.wordpress.com/2013/01/u-and-development-paper036.pdf.

Caspari, A. (ed.). (n.d.). *Integral Strategic Environmental Assessment (iSEA).* Bosra, Syria within the EU project "SHAMS." https://mindshiftintegral.wordpress.com/shams-syria/.

Castells, M. (1997). *The Power of Identity. The Information Age: Economy, Society and Culture*, Vol. 2. Malden, MA: Blackwell.

Cazar, S. (2007). Personal communication. Ecotourism and protected areas expert, Conservational International, Quito, Ecuador.

Center for Park Management. (2005). *Best Practices in Friends Groups and National Parks.* National Parks Conservation Association. www.nps.gov/partnerships/best_practices_rpt.pdf

Center for Whole Communities. (2007). *Whole Measures: Transforming Our Vision for Success.* Version 6. http://measuresofhealth.net/pdf/WholeMeasures_6.pdf.

Chabris, C., and D. Simons. (2009). *The Invisible Gorilla: How Our Intuitions Deceive Us.* New York: Broadway Paperbacks.

Chambers, R. (1997). *Whose Reality Counts? Putting the First Last.* Bath, UK: Intermediate Technology Publications.

Chapin, M. (2004). A Challenge to Conservationists. *WorldWatch.* 17(6): 17–31. http://www.worldwatch.org/system/files/EP176A.pdf.

———. (1997). Defending Kuna Yala: The Proyecto de Estudio para el Manejo de las Áreas Silvestres de Kuna Yala (PEMASKY). Center for the Support of Native Lands.

Chaves, E. (2008). El Metrocable de Medellín, el teleférico de los pobres. *Superblog* by J. Genao. December 7. http://josegenao.wordpress.com/2008/12/07/el-metrocable-de-medellin-el-teleferico-de-los-pobres.

Chichakly, R. (2010). Shifting the Burden. Making Connections. http://blog.iseesystems.com/systems-thinking/shifting-the-burden/.

Chirikova, Y. (2010). The Battle for Khimki Forest. Open Democracy Russia. August 23. www.opendemocracy.net/od-russia/yevgenia-chirikova/battle-for-khimki-forest.

Christenson, D. (2014). Personal communication. Former assistant manager, Wildland Fire Lessons Learned Center. May 21.

Cilliers, P. (1998). *Complexity and Postmodernism: Understanding Complex Systems.* London: Routledge.

Colding, J., and C. Folke. (2001). Social Taboos: "Invisible" Systems of Local Resource Management and Biological Conservation. *Ecological Applications* 11(2): 584–600.

Commission of Inquiry into the Collapse of a Viewing Platform at Cave Creek Near Punakaiki on the West Coast. (1995). Report Presented to the House of Representatives by Command of Her Excellency the Governor-General. Wellington Department of Internal Affairs. Auckland, NZ.

Comte, A., and J. H. Bridges, trans. (1865). *A General View of Positivism.* London: Trubner and Co.

CONANP. (2007). *Programa Nacional de Áreas Protegidas 2007–2012. Comisión Nacional de Áreas Naturales Nationales. Mexico City, Mexico.* www.conanp.gob.mx/quienes_somos/pdf/pro-grama_07012.pdf.

Cooperrider, D. L., and D. Whitney. (2005). *Appreciative Inquiry: A Positive Revolution in Change.* San Francisco: Berrett-Koehler Publishers.

Crichton, M. (2005). Fear and Complexity and Environmental Management. Speech given at the Center for Complexity and Public Policy. Washington, DC. November 6. http://www.blc.arizona.edu/courses/schaffer/182h/Climate/Fear,%20Complexity,%20&%20Environmental%20Management%20in%20the%2021st%20Century.htm.

Culbert, M. L. (1997). *Medical Armageddon.* C & C Communications. San Diego, CA.

De Geus, A. P. (1988). Planning as Learning. *Harvard Business Review* 66(2): 70–74.

DeGrosky, M. T., and C. S. Parry. (2011). Beyond the AAR: The Action Review Cycle (ARC). In Proceedings of the 11th International Wildland Fire Safety Summit, April 4–8, 2011, comp. M. Robinson, J. Ziegler, M. E. Alexander, C. L. Bushey, and M. Ekstrom. Missoula, MT: International Association of Wildland Fire.

Denning, P. J. (2006). Hastily Formed Networks: Collaboration in the Absence of Authority. *Reflections* 7(1): 1–7.

Diamond, J. (2005). *Collapse: How Societies Choose to Fail or Succeed.* New York: Viking.

———. (1997). *Guns, Germs, and Steel: The Fates of Human Societies.* New York: W. W. Norton.

Dibb, S., L. Simkin, and D. Wilson. (2008). Diagnosing and Treating Operational and Implementation Barriers in Synoptic Marketing Planning. *Industrial Marketing Management* 37:539–553.

Dixon, P. (2014). Why Future of MedTech, Global Economy etc. Will Be Driven by Emotion. Futurist MedTech keynote. February 14. www.youtube.com/watch?v=ahcAFnY6iAY.

du Toit, J. T., K. H. Rogers, H. C. Biggs, and A. R. E. Sinclair, eds. (2003). *The Kruger Experience: Ecology and Management of Savanna Heterogeneity.* Washington, DC: Island Press.

Dvir. D., and T. Lechler. (2004). Plans Are Nothing, Changing Plans Is Everything: The Impact of Changes on Project Success. *Research Policy* 33(1): 1–15.

Eagles, P. F. J., J. Coburn, and B. Swartman. (2014). Plan Quality and Plan Detail of Visitor and Tourism Policies in Ontario Provincial Park Management Plans. *Journal of Outdoor Recreation and Tourism* 7–8: 44–54.

Ehler, C., and R. Douvere. (2009). *Marine Spatial Planning: A Step-by-Step Approach Toward Ecosystem-Based Management.* Intergovernmental Oceanographic Commission and Man and the Biosphere

Programme. IOC Manual and Guides No. 53, ICAM Dossier No. 6. UNESCO, Paris. www.unesco-ioc-marinesp.be.

Ellingwood, K. (2009). Tourists Weigh Mexico Drug Violence. *Los Angeles Times.* March 6. www.latimes.com/world/la-fg-mexico-travel6-2009mar06-story.html.

Ellinor, L., and G. Gerard. (1998). *Dialogue: Rediscover the Transforming Power of Conversation.* New York: Wiley.

Engelman, R. (2011). Revisiting Population Growth: The Impact of Ecological Limits. *Yale Environment 360.* October 13. http://e360.yale.edu/feature/how_environmental_limits_may_rein_in_soaring_populations/2453/.

Engelmann, J. B., C. Capra, C. Noussair, and G. S. Berns. (2009). Expert Financial Advice Neurobiologically "Offloads" Financial Decision-Making under Risk. *PLoS ONE* 4(3): e4957. doi:10.1371/journal.pone.0004957.

Enright, J. (2011). Personal communication. Asia coordinator, Mangrove Action Project. February 28.

Ferguson, J. (1994). *Anti-Politics Machine: Development, Depoliticization, and Bureaucratic Power in Lesotho.* Minneapolis: University of Minnesota Press.

Ferguson, J., and L. Lohmann. (1994). The Anti-Politics Machine: "Development" and Bureaucratic Power in Lesotho. *The Ecologist* 24(5): 176–181.

Ferse, S. C. A., M. Máñez Costa, K. Schwerdtner Máñez, D. S. Adhuri, and M. Glaser. (2010). Allies, Not Aliens: Increasing the Role of Local Communities in Marine Protected Area Implementation. *Environmental Conservation* 37(1): 23–34.

Fischer, H. (2003). *Wolf Wars: The Remarkable Inside Story of the Restoration of the Wolves in Yellowstone.* Missoula, MT: Fischer Outdoor Discoveries.

Fishbein, M., and I. Ajzen. (2009). *Predicting and Changing Behavior: The Reasoned Action Approach.* East Sussex, UK: Psychology Press.

Fisher, R., W. L. Ury, and B. Patton, eds. (1991). *Getting to Yes: Negotiating Agreement without Giving In,* 2nd ed. New York: Penguin Books.

Flyvbjerg, B. (2011). Over budget, Over Time, Over and Over Again: Managing Major Projects. In *The Oxford Handbook of Project Management,* ed. P. W. G. Morris, J. K. Pinto, and J. Soderlund. Oxford, UK: Oxford University Press, 321–344.

Forester, J. (1989). *Planning in the Face of Power.* Berkeley: University of California Press.

———. (2006). Feedback Loops. Post to listerv on February 7. http://clexchange.org/cle/k12listserve_viewpost.asp?Post=460.

Foucault, M. (1982). The Subject and Power. *Critical Inquiry* 8(4): 777–795.

Frampton, K. (1983). Towards a Critical Regionalism: Six Points for an Architecture of Resistance. In *The Anti-Aesthetic: Essays on Postmodern Culture,* ed. H. Foster. Port Townsend, Washington: Bay Press, 16–30.

Freud, S. (1930). *Das Unbehagen in der Kultur*. Internationaler Psychoanalytischer Verlag Wien. Multiple versions in English such as S. Freud and J. Strachey, trans. (1962). *Civilization and Its Discontents*. New York: W. W. Norton.

Friedmann, J. (1993). Toward a Non-Euclidian Mode of Planning. *Journal of the American Planning Association* 59(4): 482-485.

————. (1973). *Retracking America: A Theory of Transactive Planning*. New York: Anchor Press.

Friere, P., and M. Bergman Ramos, trans. (2000). *Pedagogy of the Oppressed*, 30th anniversary ed. New York: Continuum.

Frissell, S. S., D. P. Duncan. (1965). Campsite Preference and Deterioration in the Quetico-Superior Canoe Country. *Journal of Forestry* 63: 256–260.

Gallwey, T. (1999). *The Inner Game of Work*. New York: Random House.

Gardner, H. E. (2006). *Multiple Intelligences: New Horizons in Theory and Practice*. New York: Basic Books.

Gebhardt, A., and P. F. J. Eagles. (2014). Factors Leading to the Implementation of Strategic Plans for Parks and Recreation. *Managing Leisure* 19(5): 1–24. DOI: 10.1080/13606719.2014.895127.

Gelfand, M. (1979). *Growing Up in Shona Society: From Birth to Marriage*. Gweru, Zimbabwe: Mambo Press.

Gerckens, L. (1994). American Zoning and the Physical Isolation of Uses. *Planning Commissioners Journal* 15: 10.

Gerzema, J., M. D'Antonio, and P. Kotler. (2010). *Spend Shift: How the Post-Crisis Values Revolution Is Changing the Way We Buy, Sell, and Live.* San Francisco: Jossey-Bass. See also a TED video by Gerzema on this theme: www.ted.com/talks/john_gerzema_the_post_crisis_consumer.html.

Gibbs, N. (2014). Toyota Still the World's Biggest Car Manufacturer. *The Telegraph*. January 24. www.telegraph.co.uk/motoring/car-manufacturers/toyota/10594637/Toyota-still-the-worlds-biggest-car-manufacturer.html.

Gladwell, M. (2002). *The Tipping Point: How Little Things Can Make a Big Difference*. Boston: Back Bay Books.

Gold, J., and S. Watson. (2001). The Value of a Story in Organizational Learning. *Futures* 33: 507–518.

Goleman, D. (2006). *Emotional Intelligence: Why It Can Matter More Than IQ*, 10th anniversary ed. New York: Bantam.

Grand Canyon News. (2009). World-Renowned Author to Present at Grand Canyon National Park. *Grand Canyon News*. September 1. www.grandcanyonnews.com/Main.asp?SectionID=1&SubSectionID=1&ArticleID=8292.

Grewenig, M. M. (2011). Völklingen Ironworks: European Centre for Art and Industrial Culture. *World Heritage* 58: 44–49. UNESCO. http://whc.unesco.org/en/review/58/.

Grimmett, R. F., and M. P. Sullivan. (2001). U.S. Army School of the Americas: Background and Congressional Concerns. Congressional Research Service Report RL30532. www.au.af.mil/au/awc/awcgate/crs/rl30532.pdf.

Habermas, J. (1981). *The Theory of Communicative Action: Reason and the Rationalization of Society*, Vol. 1, trans. Thomas McCarthy. Boston: Beacon.

Hagelin, J. S., M. V. Rainforth, K. L. C. Cavanaugh, C. N. Alexander, S. F. Shatkin, J. L. Davies, A. O. Hughes, E. Ross, and D. W. Orme-Johnson. (1999). Effects of Group Practice of the Transcendental Meditation Program on Preventing Violent Crime in Washington, D.C.: Results of the National Demonstration Project, June–July 1993. *Social Indicators Research* 47(2): 153–201.

Hagelin, J. S. (1987). Is Consciousness the Unified Field? A Field Theorist's Perspective. *Modern Science and Vedic Science* 1(1): 28–87.

Hall-Jones, P. (2006). The Rise and Rise of NGOs. Global Policy Forum. www.globalpolicy.org/component/content/article/176/31937.html.

Ham, S. H. (2013). *Interpretation: Making a Difference on Purpose.* Golden, CO: Fulcrum Publishing.

Ham, S. H., T. J. Brown, J. Curtis, B. Weiler, M. Hughes, and M. Poll. (2009). *Promoting Persuasion in Protected Areas: A Guide for Managers Who Want to Use Strategic Communication to Influence Visitor Behaviour.* Sustainable Tourism Cooperative Research Centre.

Hamilton, C. (2004). Come Together: Can We Discover a Depth of Wisdom Far Beyond What Is Available to Individuals Alone? *What Is Enlightenment?* May–June.

http://facweb.northseattle.edu/chamilton/Come%20Together.pdf

———. (n. d.). The Next Big Bang: Awakening to Conscious Evolution. http://integralenlightenment.com/academy/the-next-big-bang-awakening-to-conscious-evolution/.

Hance, J. (2012). Indigenous Blockade Expands against Massive Dam in Sarawak. Mongabay.com. October 8. http://news.mongabay.com/2012/1008-hance-dam-blockade-penan.html#PljHY-282QdtKWYMS.99.

Hawking, S.W. (1988). *A Brief History of Time: From the Big Bang to the Black Holes.* New York: Bantam Books.

Harrison, O. (2008). *Open Space Technology: A User's Guide.* San Francisco: Berrett-Koehler Publishers.

Heath, C. (2007). *Made to Stick: Why Some Ideas Survive and Others Die.* New York: Random House.

Heinrichs, J. (2007). *Thank You for Arguing: What Aristotle, Lincoln, and Homer Simpson Can Teach Us about the Art of Persuasion.* New York: Three Rivers Press.

Hilborn, R. C. (2004). Sea Gulls, Butterflies, and Grasshoppers: A Brief History of the Butterfly Effect in Nonlinear Dynamics. *American Journal of Physics* 72(4): 425–427.

Hirt, S. (2007). The Devil Is in the Definitions: Contrasting American and German Approaches to Zoning. *American Association of Planning Journal* 73(4): 436–450.

Hoben, M. (2011). Personal communication. Director of Washington, DC, office. Consensus Building Institute. January 25.

Hoch, C. (1994). *What Planners Do: Power, Politics and Persuasion.* Chicago: Planners Press.

Hochachka, G. (2014a). Personal communication. Co-director of One Sky. June 25.

———. (2014b). Keynote on Integral Development. Integral Without Borders Retreat. Integral Center. Boulder, CO. March 1.

———. (2009a). *Developing Sustainability, Developing the Self: An Integral Approach to International and Community Development.* Vancouver, BC: Trafford Publishing. Downloadable in English and Spanish at https://integralwithoutborders.net/sites/default/files/resources/DSDS_txt%206x9.pdf.

———. (2009b). *Integral Approach to Capacity Building for Amazon Rainforest Conservation.* www.onesky.ca/images/uploads/Integral_Approach_to_Capacity_Building_for_Amazon_rainforest_conservation_June_4_2009_resized.pdf.

———. (2008). Case Studies in Integral Approaches in International Development: An Integral Research Project. *Journal of Integral Theory and Practice* 3(2): 58–108. https://integralwithoutborders.net/sites/default/files/resources/IIDBook_Overview.pdf.

———. (2005). Integrating interiority in community development. *World Futures: Journal of General Evolution,* 61(1–2): 110–126.

Holling, C. S. (1978). *Adaptive Environmental Assessment and Management.* International Series on Applied Systems Analysis. Caldwell, NJ: The Blackburn Press.

Horton, D., A. Alexaki, S. Bennett-Larty, K. Noele Brice, D. Campilan, F. Carden, J. de Souza Silva, L. T. Duong, I. Khadar, A. Maestrey Boza, I. K. Muniruzzaman, J. Perez, M. S. Chang, R. Vernooy, and J. Watts. (2003). *Evaluating Capacity Development: Experiences from Research and Development Organizations around the World.* The International Development Research Centre. Ottawa, Canada: IDRC. http://idl-bnc.idrc.ca/dspace/bitstream/10625/33404/19/IDL-33404.pdf.

Hostovsky, C. (2006). The Paradox of the Rational Comprehensive Model of Planning: Tales from Waste Management Planning in Ontario, Canada. *Journal of Planning Education and Research* 25(4): 382–395.

Hubbard, J. D. (n. d.). Promotional video for work in El Mirador Basin produced for the Global Heritage Fund and Foundation for Anthropological Research and Environmental Studies. See related press release (April 30, 2003) at http://globalheritagefund.org/in_the_news/press_releases/global_heritage_fund_and_fares_are_establishing_a_break-through_525820-acre.

Hudson, B. M. (1979). Comparison of Current Theories: Counterparts and Contradictions. *APA Journal* 45(4): 387–398.

Human Emergence Middle East. (n. d.). MeshWORKS in Syria: A Cultural Vision: Introducing Integral Thinking, Design and Application to Syria. www.humanemergencemiddleeast.org/meshworks-syria.php.

Hungerford, H. R., W. J. Bluhm, T. L. Volk, and J. M. Ramsey. (2001). *Essential Readings in Environmental Education.* The Center for Instruction, Staff Development and Evaluation. Champaign, IL: Stipes Publishing.

Huston, T. (2006). Enabling Adaptability and Innovation through Hastily Formed Networks. *Reflections* 7(1): 9–27.

Hvistendahl, M. (2008). China's Three Gorges Dam: An Environmental Catastrophe? *Scientific American.* March 25. www.scientificamerican.com/article/chinas-three-gorges-dam-disaster/.

ICFC. (n. d.). Los Amigos Conservation Concession: Lasting Protection through a Conservation Trust Fund. International Conservation Fund of Canada. http://icfcanada.org/lacc.shtml.

Igoe, J. (2004). Fortress Conservation: A Social History of National Parks. In Conservation and *Globalization: A Study of National Parks and Indigenous Communities from East Africa to South Dakota*, ed. J. A. Young. Belmont, CA: Wadsworth/Thompson Learning. 66–102.

INDECON, UNWTO, OMT, and IOHBTO. (n. d). *Community Involvement Plan: Tourism Development Supporting Biodiversity Conservation in Pangandaran, Indonesia*. Report. http://cf.cdn. unwto.org/sites/all/files/docpdf/communityinvolvementplan.pdf.

Inkley, D., M. Price, P. Glick, T. Losoff, and B. Stein. (2013). *Nowhere to Run: Big Game Wildlife in a Warming World*. National Wildlife Federation report. www.nwf.org/~/media/PDFs/Global-Warming/Reports/NowheretoRun-BigGameWildlife-LowResFinal_110613.ashx.

Innes, J. E. (2004). Consensus Building: Clarifications for the Critics. *Planning Theory* 3(1): 5–20.

———. (1996). Planning through Consensus Building: A New View of the Comprehensive Planning Ideal. *Journal of the American Planning Association* 62(4): 460–472.

Innes, J. E., and D. E. Booher. (2010). *Planning with Complexity: An Introduction to Collaborative Rationality for Public Policy*. New York: Routledge.

Jackson, E. T., and Y. Kassam, eds. (1998). *Knowledge Shared: Participatory Evaluation in Development Cooperation*. West Hartford, CT: Kumarian Press.

Jacobs, J. (1961). *The Death and Life of Great American Cities*. New York: Random House.

Jacobson, S. K., M. D. McDuff, and M. C. Monroe. (2006). *Conservation Education and Outreach Techniques*. New York: Oxford University Press.

Jones, D. T., and J. P. Womack. (2003). *Lean Thinking: Banish Waste and Create Wealth in Your Corporation*, rev. and updated. Rockland, ME: Free Press.

Jones, N. A., H. Ross, T. Lynam, P. Perez, and A. Leitch. (2011). Mental Models: An Interdisciplinary Synthesis of Theory and Methods. *Ecology and Society* 16(1): 46.

Juffe-Bignoli, D., N. D. Burgess, H. Bingham, E. M. S. Belle, M. G. de Lima, M. Deguignet, B. Bertzky, A. N. Milam, J. Martinez-Lopez, E. Lewis, A. Eassom, S. Wicander, J. Geldmann, A. van Soesbergen, A. P. Arnell, B. O'Connor, S. Park, Y. N. Shi, F. S. Danks, B. MacSharry, and N. Kingston. (2014). *Protected Planet Report 2014*. Cambridge, UK: UNEP-WCMC.

Kahneman, D. (2011). *Thinking Fast and Slow*. New York: Farrar, Straus, Giroux.

Keating, E., R. Oliva, N. Repenning, S. Rockart, and J. Sterman. (1999). Overcoming the Improvement Paradox. *European Management Journal* 17(2): 120–134.

Kegan, R. (1994). *In Over Our Heads: The Mental Demands of Modern Life*. Cambridge, MA: Harvard University Press.

———. (1983). *The Evolving Self: Problem and Process in Human Development*. Cambridge, MA: Harvard University Press.

Kegan, R., and L. L. Lahey. (2009). *Immunity to Change: How to Overcome It and Unlock Potential in Yourself and Your Organization*. Cambridge, MA: Harvard Business Press.

Keim, B. (2009). Given "Expert" Advice, Brains Shut Down. *Wired*. March 25. http://www.wired. com/2009/03/financebrain/.

Kellert, S. R., and E. O. Wilson, eds. (1995). *The Biophilia Hypothesis*. Washington, DC: Island Press.

Kellert, S. R., J. Heerwagen, and M. Mador. (2008). *Biophilic Design: The Theory, Science, and Practice of Bringing Buildings to Life*. New York: Wiley.

Kim, D. (2005). Declaration of Interdependence. Keynote address. 15th Annual Pegasus Conference, San Francisco. November.

Kingsford, R. T., and H. C. Biggs. (2012). Strategic Adaptive Management Guidelines for Effective Conservation of Freshwater Ecosystems in and around Protected Areas of the World. IUCN WCPA Freshwater Taskforce, Australian Wetlands and Rivers Centre, Sydney.

Knowles, M. S. (1984a). *The Adult Learner: A Neglected Species*, 3rd ed. Houston, TX: Gulf Publishing.

———. (1984b). *Andragogy in Action*. San Francisco: Jossey-Bass.

Knudson, A. (1999). Conservation and Controversy in the Karakoram: Khunjerab National Park, Pakistan. *Journal of Political Ecology* 56: 1–30.

Koestler, A. (1964). *The Act of Creation*. New York: The Macmillan Company.

Kohl, J. (2014). Achieving Self-Identity and Self-Worth. *Interpretation Journal* 19(1): 24–26.

———. (2011). Public Use Planning: Managing the Tourism Flood in Central Vietnam. *World Heritage* 58: 22–27. http://whc.unesco.org/en/review/58/.

———. (2010). Bureaucracy: Once the Most Efficient Form of Government … Then What Happened? *Site Planning for Life*, Background Reading 9. PUP Global Heritage Consortium.

———. (2008). *Stories of the Reef: Report from the Field* #2. Field evaluation report. Washington, DC: Summit Foundation, Mesoamerican Reef Program.

———. (2007a). Putting the Ecotour Guide Back into Context: Using Systems Thinking to Develop Quality Guides. In *Quality Assurance and Certification in Ecotourism*, ed. R. Black and A. Crabtree. London: CAB International, 337–363.

———. (2007b). Holistic Training: Putting Trainees Back into Context. *Reflections* 8(2): 25–32.

———. (2006). Mental Models That Block Strategic Plan Implementation. *Reflections* 7(3): 30–42.

———. (2005). Converting Unseen and Unexpected Barriers to Park Plan Implementation into Manageable and Expected Challenges. *Parks* 15(1): 45–57.

Koole, S., and M. Spiker. (2000). Overcoming the Planning Fallacy through Willpower: Effects of Implementation Intentions on Actual and Predicted Task-Completion Times. *European Journal of Social Psychology* 30: 873–888.

Koolhaas, R., and B. Mau. (1995). S,M,L,XL. New York: Monacelli Press.

Kuhn, T. S. (1992). *The Copernican Revolution: Planetary Astronomy in the Development of Western Thought*. Cambridge, MA: Harvard University Press.

———. (1962). *The Structure of Scientific Revolutions*. Chicago: University of Chicago Press.

Kull, C. A. (2002). Madagascar Aflame: Landscape Burning as Peasant Protest, Resistance, or a Resource Management tool? *Political Geography* 21(7): 927–953.

Kurzweil, R. (2004). *The Law of Accelerating Returns*. www.kurzweilai.net/kurzwei-ls-law-aka-the-law-of-accelerating-returns.

Lachapelle, P. R., and S. F. McCool. (2011). The Role of Trust in Community Wildland Fire Protection Planning. *Society & Natural Resources* 25(4): 321–335.

———. (2005). Exploring the Concept of Ownership in Natural Resource Planning. *Society & Natural Resources* 18(3): 279–285.

Lachapelle, P. R., S. F. McCool, and M. E. Patterson. (2003). Barriers to Effective Natural Resource Planning in a "Messy" World. *Society & Natural Resources* 16(6): 473–490.

Lane, A. (2003). Obstacles to Implementing Strategic Plans: A Study of Honduran Protected Areas. Master's thesis. Nicholas School of the Environment and Earth Sciences, Duke University, NC.

Larson, C. (2009). China's Grand Plans for Eco-Cities Now Lie Abandoned. *Yale Environment 360*. April v. http://e360.yale.edu/content/feature.msp?id=2138.

Lasch, C. (1979). *The Culture of Narcissism: American Life in an Age of Diminishing Expectations*. New York: W. W. Norton.

Laurian, L., M. Day, M. Backhurst, P. Berke, N. Ericksen, J. Crawford, J. Dixon, and S. Chapman. (2004). What Drives Plan Implementation? Plans, Planning Agencies and Developers. *Journal of Environmental Planning and Management* 47(4): 555–577.

Laurian, L., M. Day, P. Berke, N. Ericksen, M. Backhurst, J. Crawford, and J. Dixon. (2004). Evaluating Plan Implementation: A Conformance-Based Methodology. *Journal of the American Planning Association* 70(4): 471-480.

Lax, K., trans. (2010). Forum on 21st Century Sustainability for Taiwan's National Parks. October 5. CPAMI.

Lehmann Strobel. (n.d.). Fundraising Through Friends Groups. http://lehmannstrobel.com/articles/fundraising-through-friends-groups/.

Lehrer, J. (2007). Eggheads: How Bird Brains Are Shaking up Science. *The Boston Globe,* September 16. www.boston.com/news/globe/ideas/articles/2007/09/16/eggheads.

Leverington, F., K. L. Costa, J. Courrau, H. Pavese, C. Nolte, M. Marr, L. Coad, N. Burgess, B. Bomhard, and M. Hockings. (2010). *Management Effectiveness Evaluation in Protected Areas*—a Global Study, 2nd ed. Brisbane, Australia: The University of Queensland.

Lindsay, W. K. (1988). Integrating Parks and Pastoralists: Some Lessons from Amboseli. In *Conservation in Africa: People, Policies, and Practice*, ed. D. Anderson and R. Grove. New York: Cambridge University Press.

Lingard, M., N. Raharison, E. Rabakonandrianina, J. Rakotoarisoa, and T. Elmqvist. (2003). The Role of Local Taboos in Conservation and Management of Species: The Radiated Tortoise in Southern Madagascar. *Conservation & Society* 1: 223–246.

Lovelock, J. (2000). *Gaia: A New Look at Life on Earth*. Oxford, UK: Oxford University Press.

Lukes, S. (2004). *Power: A Radical View*. Basingstoke, UK: Palgrave Macmillan.

Lundquist, C. J., J. M. Diehl, E. Harvy, and L. W. Botsford. (2002). Factors Affecting Implementation of Recovery Plans. *Ecological Applications* 12(3): 713–718.

Lundy, T. (2007). The Integral Approach: A Tool for Addressing Sustainability Change. BC Healthy Communities. *PowerPoint* presentation. www.ideal.forestry.ubc.ca/cons481/Lundy.pdf.

Lusiana, M., and L. Zan. (2013). Planning and Heritage. *Journal of Cultural Heritage Management and Sustainable Development* 3(2): 108–115.

Maalouf, E. (n. d.). Biographical Sketch. www.humanemergencemiddleeast.org/elza-maalouf-biography.php.

Madraiwiwi, J. (2014). Beyond a Culture of Silence. *Republika Magazine*. March.

Maharishi Mahesh Yogi. (1978). *Enlightenment to Every Individual, Invincibility to Every Nation.* Rheinweiler, FRG: Maharishi European Research University Press.

Majchrzak, A., D. Logan, R. McCurdy, and M. Kirchmer. (2006). Four Keys to Managing Emergence. *Sloan Management Review,* January 1. http://sloanreview.mit.edu/article/four-keys-to-managing-emergence/.

Mallari, N. A. D., N. J. Collar, P. J. K. McGowan, and S. J. Marsden. (2013). Science-Driven Management of Protected Areas: A Philippine Case Study. *Environmental Management* 51: 1236–1246.

Manfredo, M. J. (1992). *Influencing Human Behavior: Theory and Applications in Recreation and Tourism Natural Resources.* Urbana, IL: Sagamore Publishing.

Margoluis R. A., and N. Salafsky. (1998). *Measures of Success: Designing, Managing, and Monitoring Conservation and Development Projects.* Washington, DC: Island Press. Free Spanish version downloadable at www.fosonline.org/resource/medidas-de-exito.

Martin, A. P. (2010). New Paradigm Incubation Roadmap: A Conceptual Framework for Changing Mindsets on Complex Issues and Important Projects. Monograph. Cambridge, MA: The Professional Development Institute, Harvard University.

Martineau, S. (2008). Achieving Integral Solutions in a Multi-Level Stakeholder Situation. Proceedings from the Integral Theory Conference, Boulder, CO. August.

———. (2007). Humanity, Forest Ecology, and the Future in a British Columbia Valley: A Case Study. *Integral Review* 4. http://nextstepintegral.org/resources/integral-ecology-resources.

Masica, M. B., S. Pailler, R. Krithivasan, V. Roschanka, D. Burns, M. J. Mlotha, D. R. Murray, and N. Peng. (2014). Protected Area Downgrading, Downsizing, and Degazettement (PADDD) in Africa, Asia, and Latin America and the Caribbean, 1900–2010. *Biological Conservation* 169: 355–361.

Maslow, A. H., and D. C. Stephens, eds. (2000). *The Maslow Business Reader.* New York: John Wiley & Sons.

Maslow, A. H. (1943). A Theory of Human Motivation. *Psychological Review* 50(4): 370–96.

Mastop, H., and A. Faludi. (1997). Evaluation of Strategic Plans: The Performance Principle. *Environment and Planning B: Planning and Design* 24(6): 815–832.

Matsuo, P. M., and V. Boucinha. (2005). Teacher Training for Conservation of the Golden Lion Tamarin (*Leontopithecus rosalia*) and the Atlantic Forest in Brazil. *Neotropical Primates* 13(3): 41–43.

McCool, S. F. (2009). Constructing Partnerships for Protected Area Tourism Planning in an Era of Change and Messiness. *Journal of Sustainable Tourism* 17(2): 133–148.

———. (2000). Evolving Models of Public Participation in Wilderness and Protected Area Planning. In *Wilderness within the Context of Larger Systems*, Volume 2, comp. S. G. McCool, D. N. Cole, W. T. Borrie, and J. O'Loughlin. Wilderness Science in a Time of Change Conference, May 23–27, 1999. Missoula, MT. Proceedings RMRS-P-15-VOL-2. Ogden, UT: U.S. Department of Agriculture, Forest Service, Rocky Mountain Research Station, 301–304.

McCool, S. F., W. A. Freimund, and C. Breen. (2015). Benefitting from Complexity Thinking. In *Protected Area Governance and Management*, ed. G. L. Worboys, M. Lockwood, A. Kothari, S. Feary, and I. Pulsford. Canberra: Australian National University Press, 291–326.

McCool, S. F., K. Guthrie, and J. Kapler-Smith. (2000). Building Consensus: Legitimate Hope or Seductive Paradox? Res. Pap. RMRS-RP-25. Fort Collins, CO: U.S. Department of Agriculture, Forest Service, Rocky Mountain Research Station.

McCool, S. F., and K. E. Khumalo. (2015). Empowering Managers: Enhancing the Performance of Protected Area Tourism Managers in the Twenty-First Century. *Tourism Recreation Research* 40(2): 169–180. DOI: 10.1080/02508281.2015.1039333.

McCool, S. F., B. Nkhata, C. Breen, and W. A. Freimund. (2013). A Heuristic Framework for Reflecting on Protected Areas and Their Stewardship. *Journal of Outdoor Recreation and Tourism* 1(1.2): 9–17.

McGrath, M. (1998). Strategic Planning within a Postmodern Context. *Journal of Humanistic Education and Development* 37(2): 78–84.

McGregor, J., M. Arndt, R. Berner, I. Rowley, K. Hall, G. Edmondson, S. Hamm, M. Ihlwan, and A. Reinhardt. (2006). The World's Most Innovative Companies. *Bloomberg BusinessWeek Magazine*. April 23. www.businessweek.com/stories/2006-04-23/the-worlds-most-innovative-companies.

McIntosh, S. (2007). *Integral Consciousness and the Future of Evolution*. St. Paul, MN: Paragon House.

Meadows, D. (1999). Leverage Points: Places to Intervene in a System. The Sustainability Institute. www.donellameadows.org/wp-content/userfiles/Leverage_Points.pdf.

Meadows, D. (2008). *Thinking in Systems: A Primer*, ed. D. Wright. White River Junction, VT: Chelsea Green.

Medeiros, R., and G. Simas Pereira. (2011). Evolução e implementação dos planos de manejo em parques nacionais no Estado do Rio de Janeiro. *Revista Árvore, Viçosa-MG* 35(2): 279–288.

Merriam, L. C., and C. K. Smith. (1974). Visitor Impact on Newly Developed Campsites in the Boundary Waters Canoe Area. *Journal of Forestry* 72(10): 627–630.

Merritt, Jonathan. Editorial. *Sacred Fire Magazine*. Accessed 4 June 2009. http://sacredfirefoundation.org/sacred-fire-magazine.

Miller, K. (2004). Foreword. *Securing Protected Areas in the Face of Global Change: Issues and Strategies*. Gland, Switzerland: IUCN—The World Conservation Union.

———. (1989). *Planning National Parks for Ecodevelopment: Methods and Cases from Latin America*, Volumes I and II. Peace Corps, Information Collection and Exchange. (Volume II was originally published in 1978.) www.eric.ed.gov/ERICWebPortal/custom/portlets/recordDetails/detailmini.jsp?_nfpb=true&_&ERICExtSearch_SearchValue_0=ED309033&ERICExtSearch_SearchType_0=no&accno=ED309033.

Mintzberg, H. (1994). *The Rise and Fall of Strategic Planning*. New York: The Free Press.

Mir, S. (2011). Khunjerab National Park: A Failed Project. *The Express Tribune with The International New York Times*. June 27. http://tribune.com.pk/story/197118/khunjerab-national-park-a-failed-project.

Misgeld, D. (1985). Education and Cultural Invasion: Critical Social Theory, Education as Instruction, and the "Pedagogy of the Oppressed." In *Critical Theory and Public Life*, ed. J. Forester. Cambridge, MA: MIT Press, 77–118.

Mock, J. (n. d.). Mountain Protected Areas in Pakistan: The Case of the National Parks. www.mockandoneil.com/paknp.htm.

Mohsen, M., and G. Doherty, eds. (2010). *Ecological Urbanism*. Baden, Germany: Lars Muller Publishers.

Moore, S. A. (2007). Technology, Place and Non-modern Regionalism. In *Architectural Regionalism: Collected Writings on Place, Identity, Modernity and Tradition*, ed. V. Canizaro. New York: Princeton Architectural Press, 432–442.

Moran-Cahusac, C. (2014). Personal communication. Former executive director of ACCA. July 12.

Mosimane, A. W., S. McCool, P. Brown, and J. Ingrebretson. (2013). Using Mental Models in the Analysis of Human-Wildlife Conflict from the Perspective of a Social-Ecological System in Namibia. *Oryx* 48(1). doi:10.1017/S0030605312000555 (online).

Mungazi, D. A. (1989). *The Struggle for Social Change in South Africa*. New York: Taylor & Francis.

Naughton, L. (2007). Collaborative Land Use Planning: Zoning for Conservation and Development in Protected Areas. Madison, WI: USAID and Land Tenure Center/University of Wisconsin–Madison.

Nettle, D., and Z. Romaine. (2000.) *Vanishing Voices: The Extinction of the World's Languages*. Oxford, UK: Oxford University Press.

Nkhata, A. B., and C. M. Breen. (2010). A Framework for Exploring Integrated Learning Systems for Governance and Management of Public Protected Areas. *Environmental Management* 45: 403–413.

Nkhata, A. B., C. M. Breen, and W. A. Freimund. (2008). Resilient Social Relationships and Collaboration in the Management of Social-Ecological Systems. *Ecology and Society* 13(1): 2. www.ecologyandsociety.org/vol13/iss1/art2/.

Noble, J. (2013). *The Dynamics of Emergence*. http://integralwithoutborders.org/sites/default/files/Integral%20Emergence.pdf.

Nyambe, N. (2005). Organizational Culture and Its Underlying Basic Assumptions as a Determinant of Response to Change: A Case Study of KwaZulu-Natal's Conservation Sector, South Africa. PhD dissertation. University of KwaZulu-Natal, Pietermaritzburg, Republic of South Africa.

Oates, J. (2002). West Africa: Tropical Forest Parks on the Brink. In *Making Parks Work: Strategies for Preserving Tropical Nature*, J. Terborgh, C. van Schaik, L. Davenport, and M. Rao. Washington, DC: Island Press, 57–75.

Onaran, K. S., and F. H. Sancar. (1998). Design Review in Small Communities. *Environment and Planning B: Planning and Design* 25(4): 539–557.

One Sky. (n. d.). Leading from Within Project Overview: For Guest Speakers and Facilitators. Project document. Smithers, British Columbia: One Sky.

Ormsby, A., and C. Edelman. (2010). Community-Based Ecotourism at Tafi Atome Monkey Sanctuary, a Sacred Natural Site in Ghana. In *Sacred Natural Sites: Conserving Nature and Culture*, ed. B. Verschuuren, R. Wild, J. McNeely, and G. Oviedo. London, UK: Earthscan and IUCN. 233–243.

Osburn, H. K., and M. D. Mumford. (2006). Creativity and Planning: Training Interventions to Develop Creative Problem-Solving Skills. *Creativity Research Journal* 18(2): 173–190.

Ostrom, E., and H. Nagenda. (2006). Insights on Linking Forests, Trees, and People from the Air, on the Ground, and in the Laboratory. *Proceedings of the National Academy of Sciences* 103(51): 19224–19231.

Owens, C., I. Wight, M. Hamilton, and C. Wieler. (2005). Integral Planning by Spiral design: At the Frontier of Sustainable Community Development. *PowerPoint* presented at the CIP/AACIP 2005 Conference Frontiers in Planning and Design, Calgary, Ontario, Canada. July.

Palahniuk, C. (2005). *Fight Club: A Novel.* New York: W. W. Norton.

Pande, P., and L. Holpp. (2001). *What Is Six Sigma?* New York: McGraw-Hill.

Parry, C., and M. J. Darling. (2001). Emergent Learning in Action: The After Action Review. *The Systems Thinker* 12(8):1–5.

Partidário, M. D. R. (2012). *Strategic Environmental Assessment Better Practice Guide—Methodological Guidance for Strategic Thinking in SEA*. Lisboa, Portugal: Agência Portuguesa do Ambiente e Redes Energéticas Nacionais. http://ec.europa.eu/environment/eia/pdf/2012%20SEA_Guidance_Portugal.pdf.

Partlow, J., and W. Booth. (2009). Swine Flu Devastates Mexico's Tourist Industry. *Washington Post.* April 30. www.washingtonpost.com/wp-dyn/content/article/2009/04/29/AR2009042904650.html.

Pascale, R., J. Sternin, and M. Sternin. (2010). *The Power of Positive Deviance: How Unlikely Innovators Solve the World's Toughest Problems*. Cambridge, MA: Harvard Business Press.

Peck, M. S. (1998). *The Different Drum: Community Making and Peace*. New York: Touchstone.

Pedersen, A. (2009). Personal communication. Director, Sustainable Tourism Programme, World Heritage Center, UNESCO, Paris, France.

Peters, T. (1988). The Mythology of Innovation, or a Skunkworks Tale, Part 2. In *Readings in the Management of Innovation*, 2nd ed., ed. M. L. Tushman and W. L. Moore. New York: Harper Business.

Pinto, J. K. (2013). Lies, Damn Lies, and Project Plans: Recurring Human Errors That Can Ruin the Project Planning Process. *Business Horizons* 56(5): 643–653.

Pinto, J. K., and D. P. Slevin. (1989). The Project Champion: Key to Implementation Success. *Project Management Journal* 20(4): 15–20.

Putnam, R., L. Feldstein, and D. Cohen. (2004). *Better Together: Restoring the American Community.* New York: Simon & Schuster.

Putney, A. (2007). La dimensión mágica de las áreas protegidas. Presentación magistral. El Segundo Congreso Latinoamericano de Parques Nacionales y otras Áreas Protegidas. Bariloche, Argentina. 30 septiembre a 6 de octubre.

Radachowsky, J., M. Hoben, D. Plumb, and R. McNab. (n. d.). Conflict, Complexity, and Conservation: Adaptive Co-management of the Mirador-Río Azul Zone of Guatemala. Unpublished.

Radin, D. I. (2006). *Entangled Minds: Extrasensory Experiences in a Quantum Reality.* New York: Paraview Pocket Books.

Rand, A. (1957). *Atlas Shrugged.* New York: Penguin Group.

Reed, M. S. (2008). Stakeholder Participation for environmental management: A literature review. *Biological Conservation* 141: 2417–2431.

Republic of Namibia and UNDP. (2010). Full Project— Strengthening the Protected Area Network (SPAN) Project. Project Document. Global Environment Facility.

Rifkin, J. (2003). *The Hydrogen Economy.* New York: Tarcher/Putnam.

Riley, B. (2011). A Garden in My Apartment. May. www.ted.com/talks/britta_riley_a_garden_in_my_apartment.

Rittel, H. W., and M. M. Webber. (1973). Dilemmas in a General Theory of Planning. Policy Sciences 4(2): 155–169.

Robertson, B. (2015). *Holacracy: The Management System for a Rapidly Changing World.* New York: Henry Holt and Company.

Robles, G., N. Vásquez, R. Morales, J. Kohl, and B. Herrera. (2007). Barreras para la implementación de los planes de manejo de las áreas silvestres protegidas en Costa Rica. Informe Final de Consultoría, Serie Técnica: Apoyando los Esfuerzos en el Manejo y Protección de la Biodiversidad Tropical. Volume 8. San José, Costa Rica: The Nature Conservancy.

Rogers, E. M. (2003). *Diffusion of Innovations,* 5th ed. New York: Free Press.

Roux, D. J., and L. C. Foxcroft. (2011). The Development and Application of Strategic Adaptive Management within South African National Parks. *Koedoe* 53(2). Art. #1049, 5 pages. doi:10.4102/koedoe. v53i2.1049.

Russell, J. (1994). Rethinking Conventional Zoning. *Planning Commissioners Journal* 15: 6–9.

Russell, P. (2008). *Global Brain: The Awakening Earth in a New Century,* 3rd ed. Edinburgh, UK: Floris Books.

Salafsky, N., R. A. Margoluis, K. H. Redford, and J. G. Robinson. (2002). Improving the Practice of Conservation: A Conceptual Framework and Research Agenda for Conservation Science. *Conservation Biology* 16(6): 1469–1479.

Sales, M., and A. Savage. (2010). Divergent Views, Shared Vision: The Scenario Game Board as a Tool for Building Robust Strategy. *Reflections* 10(3):34–38.

Sancar, F. H. (1994). Paradigms of postmodernity and implications for planning and design review processes. *Environment and Behavior* 26(3): 312–337.

Saposnik, K. (2005). Getting Better at Getting Better—How the After Action Review Really Works: An Interview with Marilyn Darling. *Leverage Points* 61. Pegasus Communications, Inc.

Sasidharan, C. K. (2002). Carrying Capacity Based Development Plan of Sabarimala—A Preliminary Approach. *Indian Cartographer* 22: 257–261.

Savill, R., and G. Mole. (2008). Horse Owners and Dog Walkers in Revolt against New Forest Plans. *The Telegraph.* October 17. www.telegraph.co.uk/news/uknews/3216596/Horse-owners-and-dog-walkers-in-revolt-against-New-Forest-plans.html.

Schein, E. H. (1996). Three Cultures of Management: The Key to Organizational Learning. *Sloan Management Review* 38(1): 9–20.

Schmidt-Soltau, K. (2004). The Costs of Rainforest Conservation: Local Responses to Integrated Conservation and Development Projects in Cameroon. *Journal of Contemporary African Studies* 22(1): 93–117.

Schön, D. (1983). *The Reflective Practitioner: How Professionals Think in Action.* New York: Basic Books.

Scott, J. C. (1992). *Domination and the Art of Resistance: Hidden Transcripts.* New Haven, CT: Yale University Press.

———. (1987). *Weapons of the Weak: Everyday Forms of Peasant Resistance.* New Haven, CT: Yale University Press.

Seligman, J. (2005). Building a Systems Thinking Culture at Ford Motor Company. *Reflections* 6(4/5): 1–9.

Senge, P. M. (1997). Leading Learning Organizations: The Bold, the Powerful, and the Invisible. In *The Leader of the Future: New Visions, Strategies, and Practices for the Next Era*, ed. F. Hesselbein, M. Goldsmith, and R. Beckhard, eds. San Francisco: Jossey-Bass, 41–58.

———. (1990). *The Fifth Discipline: The Art and Practice of the Learning Organization.* New York: Double Day Currency.

Senge, P. M., C. Roberts, R. Ross, B. Smith, and A. Kleiner. (1994). *The Fifth Discipline Fieldbook: Strategies and Tools for Building a Learning Organization.* New York: Doubleday.

Senge, P., C. O. Scharmer, J. Jaworski, and B. S. Flowers. (2008). *Presence: Human Purpose and the Field of the Future.* Cambridge, MA: Society for Organizational Learning.

Senge, P. M., B. Smith, N. Kruschwitz, J. Laur, and S. Schley. (2008). T*he Necessary Revolution: How Individuals and Organizations Are Working Together to Create a Sustainable World.* New York: Doubleday.

Silberman, N. A. (2013). The Tyranny of Narrative: History, Heritage, and Hatred in Modern Middle East. *Journal of Eastern Mediterranean Archaeology and Heritage Studies* 1(2): 175–184.

Simon, H. A. (1945) *Administrative Behavior.* New York: Free Press.

Simons, D. J., and C. F. Chabris. (1999). Gorillas in Our Midst: Sustained Inattentional Blindness for Dynamic Events. *Perception* 28(9): 1059–1074.

Simpson, M. (2010). *Under a Tarp in the Amazon*. Smithers, British Columbia: One Sky. https://www.youtube.com/watch?v=2wgrJjVfIUE.

Singapore National Parks Board. (2011). New Incentives to Promote Skyrise Greenery in Singapore. March 24.

Singer, S. L., and A. C. Edmondson. (2008). When Learning and Performance Are at Odds: Confronting the Tension. In *Learning and Performance Matters*, ed. P. Kumar and P. Ramsey. Singapore: World Scientific Publishing Company. Chapter as Harvard Business School Working Paper (2006): www.hbs.edu/faculty/Publication%20Files/07-032.pdf.

Smith, A. (1975). *Power of the Mind*. New York: Ballantine Books.

Sorenson, L. G. (2008). Participatory Planning Workshop for the Restoration of Ashton Lagoon: Workshop Proceedings and Final Report. The Society for the Conservation and Study of Caribbean Birds and Sustainable Grenadines Project. www.globalcoral.org/wp-content/uploads/2014/01/ashton_lagoon_workshop_report.pdf.

Spencer, L. J. (1989). *Winning Through Participation: Meeting the Challenge of Corporate Change with the Technology of Participation*. Dubuque, IA: Kendall Hunt Publishing Company.

Stankey, G. H., B. T. Bormann, C. Ryan, B. Shindler, V. Sturtevant, R. N. Clark, and C. Philpot. (2003). Adaptive Management and the Northwest Forest Plan: Rhetoric and Reality. *Journal of Forestry* 101(1): 40–46.

Stankey, G. H., R. N. Clark, and B. T. Bormann. (2005). *Adaptive Management of Natural Resources: Theory, Concepts, and Management Institutions*. Gen. Tech. Rep. PNW-GTR-654. Portland, OR: U.S. Department of Agriculture, Forest Service, Pacific Northwest Research Station.

Stankey, G. H., S. F. McCool, and R. N. Clark. (2003). Building Innovative Institutions for Ecosystem management: Integrating Analysis and Inspiration. In *Two Paths Toward Sustainable Forests*, ed. B. A. Shindler, T. M. Beckley, and M. C. Finley. Corvallis: Oregon State University Press, 271–295.

Stenseke, M., and A. S. Hansen. (2014). From rhetoric to Knowledge Based Actions—Challenges for Outdoor Recreation Management in Sweden. *Journal of Outdoor Recreation and Tourism* 7-8:26–34. http://dxdoi.org/10.1016/j.jort.2014.09.004.

Sterman, J. D. (2002). All Models Are Wrong: Reflections on Becoming a Systems Scientist. *System Dynamics Review* 18(4): 501–531.

———. (2000). *Business Dynamics: Systems Thinking and Modeling for a Complex World*. Boston: McGraw-Hill/Irwin.

Susskind, L., S. McKearnan, and J. Thomas-Larmer, eds. (1999). *The Consensus Building Handbook*. Thousand Oaks, CA: Sage Publications.

Susskind, L., and P. Field. (1996). *Dealing with an Angry Public: The Mutual Gains Approach to Resolving Disputes*. New York: Free Press.

Swemmer, L. K., and S. Taljaard. (2011). SANParks, People and Adaptive Management: Understanding a Diverse Field of Practice During Changing Times. *Koedoe* 53(2). Art. #1017. doi:10.4102/koe-doe.v53i2.1017.

Tackett, C. (2013). Sacred Albino Moose Killed by Hunters. Treehugger.com. October 14. www.treehugger.com/endangered-species/sacred-white-moose-killed-hunters.html.

Taleb, N. N. (2010). *The Black Swan: The Impact of the Highly Improbable*, 2nd ed. New York: Random House.

Talen, E. (1997). Success, Failure, and Conformance: An Alternative Approach to Planning Evaluation. *Environment and Planning B: Planning and Design* 24: 573–587.

———. (1996a). After the Plans: Methods to Evaluate the Implementation Success of Plans. *Journal of Planning Education and Research* 16(2): 79–91.

———. (1996b). Do Plans Get Implemented? A Review of Evaluation in Planning. *Journal of Planning Literature* 10(3): 248–259.

Teilhard de Chardin, P. (1959). *The Phenomenon of Man.* New York: Harper & Brothers.

Terborgh, J. (2004). *Requiem for Nature.* Washington, DC, USA: Island Press.

Thomas, L. (1974). *Lives of a Cell.* New York: Viking Press.

Thomas, L., and J. Middleton. (2003). *Guidelines for Management Planning of Protected Areas.* Cambridge, UK: IUCN.

Tilden, F. (1957). *Interpreting Our Heritage.* Chapel Hill: University of North Carolina Press.

Toffler, A. (1971). *Future Shock.* New York: Bantam.

Togridou, A., T. Hovardas, and J. D. Pantis. (2006). Factors Shaping the Implementation of Protected Area Management Decisions: A Case Study of Zakynthos National Marine Park. *Environmental Conservation* 33(3): 233–243.

Tupper, S. (2015). Dream of Tribal National Park Crumbling. *Rapid City Journal,* 3 May. http://rapidcityjournal.com/news/local/dream-of-tribal-national-park-crumbling/article_4c2954d2-580c-5ac9-93fa-fb7a88932f89.html.

Turner, J. R., and R. A. Cochrane. (1993). Goals and Methods Matrix: Coping with Ill Defined Goals and/or Methods of Achieving Them. *International Journal of Project Management* 11(2): 93–106.

UNESCO. (2013). Emergency Red List of Syrian Antiquities at Risk Is Launched in New York. Press release. September 26. www.unesco.org/new/en/media-services/single-view/news/emergency_red_list_of_syrian_antiquities_at_risk_is_launched_in_new_york/#.U8NYHrFZjt9.

———. (2012). *Operational Guidelines for the Implementation of the World Heritage Convention.* Intergovernmental Committee for the Protection of the World Cultural and Natural Heritage. http://whc.unesco.org/archive/opguide12-en.pdf.

———. (2010). *Atlas of World's Languages in Danger.* www.unesco.org/new/en/culture/themes/endangered-languages/atlas-of-languages-in-danger.

United States Forest Service. (2006). Little Venus Fire Shelter Deployment: Peer Review Report. July 24. Shoshone National Forest. www.wildlandfire.com/docs/2006/little-venus/Little_Venus_Deployment_Peer_Review.pdf.

Vucetich, J. A., and R. O. Peterson. (2012). The Population Biology of Isle Royale Wolves and Moose: An Overview. www.isleroyalewolf.org/data/data/home.html.

Vugdelic, M. (2010). Personal communication. Biodiversity conservation officer, Skadar Lake National Park, Montenegro.

Waldheim, C. (2005). *The Landscape Urbanism Reader*. New York: Princeton Architectural Press.

Weber, M. (1992). Bureaucracy. In *Classics of Organization Theory*, ed. J. M. Shafritz and J. S. Ott. Belmont, CA: Wadsworth Publishing Co.

Weber, R., D. W. Aha, H. Muñoz-Ávila, and L. A. Breslow. (2000). An Intelligent Lessons Learned Process. In *Foundations of Intelligent Systems: Lecture Notes in Computer Science/Lecture Notes in Artificial Intelligence (Book 1932)*, ed. Z. W. Ras and S. Ohsuga. Symposium, ISMIS 2000, Charlotte, NC, USA, October 11–14. Berlin, Germany: Springer-Verlag.

Wegener, M., K. Button, and P. Kijkamp, P., eds. (2007). *Planning History and Methodology*. Classics in Planning 5. Cheltenham, UK: Edward Elgar Publishing.

Weick, K. E. (2011). Putting HRO into Practice. Keynote address. April 20. Lansing, MI: University of Michigan.

———. (1976). Educational organizations as loosely coupled systems. *Administrative Science Quarterly* 21(1): 1–19.

Weick, K. E., and K. M. Sutcliffe. (2007). *Managing the Unexpected: Resilient Performance in an Age of Uncertainty*, 2nd ed. San Francisco: Jossey-Bass.

Wells, G. (2009). A Hard-Earned Lesson. *Fire Science Digest* 4: 2. January. www.firescience.gov/Digest/FSdigest4.pdf.

Wenger, E. (2000). *Communities of Practice: Learning, Meaning, and Identity.* New York: Cambridge University Press.

Wenger, E., R. McDermott, and W. Snyder. (2002). *Cultivating Communities of Practice: A Guide to Managing Knowledge*. Boston: Harvard Business School Press.

Wheatley, M., and D. Frieze. (2011). Leadership in the Age of Complexity: From Hero to Host. *Resurgence Magazine*, winter.

Wheatley, M., and M. Kellner-Rogers. (1998). *A Simpler Way*. San Francisco: Berrett-Koehler Publishers.

Wight, I., M. Hamilton, C. Owens, and C. Wieler. (2005). Integral Planning by Spiral Design: At the Frontier of Sustainable Community Development. CIP/AACIP Conference Slide 14.

Wilber, K. (2014). Talk at Integral Without Borders Retreat. Denver, CO. March 2.

———. (2007a). *Integral Spirituality: A Starting Role for Religion in the Modern and Postmodern World.* Boston: Shambhala.

———. (2007b). *The Integral Vision: A Very Short Introduction to the Revolutionary Integral Approach to Life, God, the Universe, and Everything.* Boston: Shambhala.

———. (2006). The Kosmos Trilogy, Vol. II, Excerpt A: An Integral Age at the Leading Age.

———. (2003). *Boomeritis: A Novel That Will Set You Free*. Boston: Shambhala.

———. (2001). *Sex, Ecology, Spirituality: The Spirit of Evolution*, 2nd ed. Boston: Shambhala.

———. (2000). *Integral Psychology: Consciousness, Spirit, Psychology, Therapy*. Boston: Shambhala.

———. (1997). An Integral Theory of Consciousness. *Journal of Consciousness Studies* 4(1): 71–92.

———. (1996). *A Brief History of Everything*. Boston: Shambhala.

Wilber, K., J. Engler, and D. Brown. (1986). *Transformations of Consciousness: Conventional and Contemplative Perspectives on New Development*. Boston: Shambhala.

Wildland Fire Lessons Learned Center. (2012). *Little Venus Fire Shelter Deployment*. Video in 2 parts: www.youtube.com/watch?v=zQN4KQ4t1_o and www.youtube.com/watch?v=RpXRtQliACI.

Wilpert, G. (2003). Toward and Integral Analysis of the Iraq Crisis. http://www.integralworld.net/wilpert3.html.

Wilson, E. O. (1986). *Biophilia*. Cambridge, MA: Harvard University Press.

Wilson, J. Q. (1989). *Bureaucracy: What Government Agencies Do and Why They Do It*. New York: Basic Books.

Wittenberg, J., and J. D. Sterman. (1999). Path Dependence, Competition, and Succession in the Dynamics of Scientific Revolution. *Organization Science* 10(3): 322–341.

Woodhouse, M. B. (1996). *Paradigm Wars: Worldviews for a New Age.* Berkeley: Frog, LTD.

Worboys, G. L., M. Lockwood, A. Kothari, S. Feary, and I. Pulsford, eds. (2015). *Protected Area Governance and Management*. Canberra: Australian National University Press.

World Heritage Center. (2011). Three Park Guards and Five Soldiers Killed in Attack at Virunga National Park (DRC). January 28. http://whc.unesco.org/en/news/705.

Wuerthner, G. (2006). *The Wildfire Reader: A Century of Failed Forest Policy*. Washington, DC: Foundation for Deep Ecology by arrangement with Island Press.

Wyss, J. (2000). Turmoil in Paradise: Galapagos Fishermen Revolt against Strict Quota on Lobster. *San Francisco Chronicle*. December 10. www.sfgate.com/news/article/Turmoil-in-Paradise-Galapagos-fishermen-revolt-3236289.php.

Yaffee, S. L. (1997). Why Environmental Policy Nightmares Recur. *Conservation Biology* 11(2): 328–337.

Yankelovich, D. (1991). *Coming to Public Judgment: Making Democracy Work in a Complex World.* Syracuse, NY: Syracuse University Press.

Young, C., A. Chadburn, and E. Bedu. (2009). *Stonehenge World Heritage Site Management Plan*. London, UK: English Heritage on Behalf of the Stonehenge World Heritage Site Committee.

Zimmer, C. (2007). From Ants to People, an Instinct to Swarm. *The New York Times*. November 13. www.nytimes.com/2007/11/13/science/13traff.html?pagewanted=all&_r=0.

Zimmerman, T., and T. Sexton. (2010). Organizational Learning Contributes to Guidance for Managing Wildland Fires for Multiple Objectives. *Fire Management Today* 70(1): 8–14.–181)

Subject Matter Index

About the Authors

Jonathan M. Kohl

Jon is the president and founder of the PUP Global Heritage Consortium (www.pupconsortium.net). The PUP Consortium is a nonprofit global network of people and organizations dedicated to introducing emerging paradigms into the heritage management and planning field as a way to stem the crisis of management plans that remain unimplemented and to promote a more holistic and Integral form  of management, with the ultimate goal of conserving natural and cultural diversity. He began to develop the Public Use Planning process when working at RARE Center for Tropical Conservation in Central America. He started this book project to create a forum to discuss the deeper theory that cannot always be articulated in field projects and intends this book to serve as the theoretical backbone for the consortium.

Aside from planning and visitor use management, his specialty is heritage interpretation and its relationship to protected area management, especially in the left-hand quadrants that are often left out of modern consideration. He has written extensively about interpretation and planning (www.jonkohl.com) and writes a bilingual blog (Spanish-English) on outside-the-box ideas about interpretation, especially relevant to developing countries (www.facebook.com/heritageinterpretation). He graduated from Dartmouth College (BS) and Yale University School of Forestry and Environmental Studies (MSc). He lives in Costa Rica—where he served as a Peace Corps volunteer in the 1990s at the National Zoo—with wife, Marisol Mayorga, and his two sons, Dion and Ian.

He credits his mentors for who he is today: Steve McCool (protected areas), Sam Ham (interpretation and environmental communications), Donella Meadows (systems and paradigm thinking and journalism), and Jay Heinrichs and Kimberly Comeau (nonfiction and fiction writing, respectively).

Stephen F. McCool

Steve is professor emeritus of Wildland Recreation Management in the Department of Society and Conservation of the College of Forestry and Conservation, the University of Montana, USA. Steve began his professional career by investigating biophysical impacts of wilderness use in the Boundary Waters Canoe Area in Minnesota during the mid-1960s and has continued working with wilderness and protected area managers his entire career, focusing principally on management of visitors and tourism, public engagement processes, and new paradigms of planning. His current approach to protected area stewardship is based on the premise that planning and management occur within the context of messy situations—conflicting goals and uncertain cause-effect relationships. These settings require substantially different approaches—in process, focus, public participation, and institutional design—compared to traditional tame problems. Thus, he focuses on "messy" issues associated with protected area planning, including the conflicts between recreation opportunities, integrated resource management, and application of frameworks to resolve competing demands. Recent publications include those dealing with governance and protected areas, frameworks for thinking about protected area management, an assessment of various visitor planning frameworks, and discussions about the relationships between tourism and protected areas. He has authored more than 200 publications dealing with protected area management and provided advice and service to a number of park and protected area agencies in the United States and abroad, including Canada, South Africa, Namibia, Mozambique, Belize, Brazil, Iceland, Croatia, and New Zealand.

He has held faculty positions at Utah State University and the University of Wisconsin–River Falls. He received a BS forestry degree from the University of Idaho, and holds MS and PhD degrees from the University of Minnesota. From September 1987 through August 1993, he served as the director for the Institute for Tourism and Recreation Research at the University of Montana. From January 1993 until August 1995 he worked as co-leader, social sciences staff, of the Interior Columbia Basin Ecosystem

Management Project, a large-scale ecosystem assessment process for the US Pacific Northwest. He is a member of the World Commission on Protected Areas and currently serves on its Tourism and Protected Areas Specialist Group.

Sam Ham, Series Editor

Sam H. Ham is professor emeritus of communication psychology and conservation social sciences at the University of Idaho, USA. Sam's work has taken him throughout the United States and Canada, and to nearly fifty other countries, where his approach to thematic communication is considered best practice in a wide variety of communication fields. Today, Sam's thematic communication principles are put into daily practice by tens of thousands of interpreters of cultural heritage and nature, as well as by museums, tour operators, zoos, botanical gardens, aquariums, national parks, and protected areas. Government bodies and private enterprises across the world have incorporated his theme-based principles into communication programs ranging from municipal sustainability and conservation education to tourism marketing, philanthropy, and interpretation of wine, beer, chocolate, and art. His nearly 400 publications include two best-selling books, *Environmental Interpretation—A Practical Guide for People with Big Ideas and Small Budgets* and *Interpretation—Making a Difference on Purpose*, both of which were published in four languages and in the same Applied Communication series as this book.

Sam and his wife, Barbara, live in Olympia, Washington, USA.

PUP Global Heritage Consortium

The PUP Global Heritage Consortium (www.pupconsortium.net) was founded in 2013 based on the Public Use Planning Process first launched in 1998. It unites people and organizations around the world dedicated to introducing emerging paradigms into the heritage management and planning field to reverse the global crisis of management plans not being implemented and to promote a more holistic and Integral form of management, ultimately to conserve natural and cultural diversity. The PUP Consortium is a non-profit, virtual network of members from around the world. The principal objective is to evolve the existing paradigm in heritage management from Technical Rationality to a Holistic Planning Integral approach.

During the first fifteen years, PUP worked with UNESCO's World Heritage Center in Guatemala, Mexico, Honduras, Indonesia, Montenegro, Macedonia, Vietnam, Belize, and Portugal. When PUP became the consortium, it began working in other countries such as the United States, Colombia, Costa Rica, and Panama. It builds a technical assistance, community development model that guides sites through an adaptive learning process that leads to a full and continuous planning and doing process without the need for outside assistance. Additionally, the consortium offers trainings, research, publications, and organizes events all directed toward a new paradigm in the field.